DISCLAIMER

This is a work of memoir. The events described in this book are based on the author's recollections. Some names, characters, businesses, places, events, and incidents have been changed, omitted, or fictionalised for privacy, legal, or creative purposes. Any resemblance to actual persons, living or dead, or events is coincidental.

Printed in the United Kingdom.

For more information or to book an event, contact:-
Email: hi@rogerwarner.net
http://www.rogerwarner.net

Visit the website for the *picture gallery* that accompanies this book.

Book design: Dave Buckley
Cover design: Roger Warner

ISDN – Paperback: 9798227545749

First Edition: October 2024
98,000 words

THE PROLOGUE

"A tiger chased a man; he escaped by leaping over a ledge,
He broke his fall by clinging to a tree root.
Hanging there, he saw two mice,
Together, they began to chew through the root,
Then he heard a second tiger, he looked down and below him,
there it was, looking up, waiting for him to fall.
Close by, he saw a big red strawberry,
he picked it up and ate it,
Umm, how delicious that strawberry was, he thought."

This Zen fable is an open-ended story,
and my interpretation is as follows:

'The tiger chasing us is our past; it will consume you if you fight it. The tiger waiting for us is our future; death awaits us all, and we can't avoid it. The root we cling to is our time on earth. The mice are the challenges we face in life that we can't avoid, accept them, don't be distracted by them.
The strawberry is our consciousness of living, our consumption of life itself.

CHAPTER 1
BANG

I heard a thunderous bang, like a gunshot, the explosion reverberating inside my skull. My body went limp and crashed to the ground, my face smashing into the freezing mud. Sharp needles of frozen grass scratched at my eye.

"I'm just playing rugby. Why would someone shoot me? Who brings a gun to a rugby match? That's insane; nothing makes sense."

As I lay there, I felt my feet begin to float, rising slowly from the ground, higher and higher, ascending into the frigid winter sky. My feet, legs, and body were all rising, but why was my face still pressed into the earth?

The other players were all around me, staring down like they were facing a plate of food they did not want to eat. They were frozen still, like statues, their eyes wide with panic as they looked at my contorted body.

"Don't touch him, don't move him."

How peculiar it all was – was I floating up to heaven? Panic set in, and I let out my first scream, "Hold me down, hold me down!" I needed the lads to reach up and grab my legs, to pull me back down to earth. Quickly, before it is too late. But there was no sound, and no one heard my screams. Over and over, "Hold me, please don't let me go."

I was suffocating, gasping open-mouthed, silently like a fish out of water, completely paralysed. My head pounded and flashed as my neck muscles worked frantically to suck in little puffs of oxygen.

Fat, muddy fingers touched my face, scratching a hole into the hard, frozen ground to clear the soil and grass out of my eye and mouth. It was Brian, our team captain. "You are OK, lad, you're OK. The doctor's here, and he will take care of you."

Shock is a bizarre thing, like drifting through another dimension. "Oh no, I'm dying, it's over." But where were the visions, the life flashing before me? No family memories, no kind faces – just dark, gloomy clouds getting closer and closer. Then it was dark.

I came round to the voice of an older gent. He was not one of the players. This man wore a uniform and a hat – he did not belong on a rugby pitch. He was kneeling next to me, speaking in a calm, assured voice. "We must put you on the stretcher, son. I need to move your shoulder; this might hurt."

Suddenly, pain, unlike anything I had ever felt before, erupted through my body. It was as if a bolt of lightning was burning through me, back and forth, like a red-hot knitting needle; it shot through my neck, shoulder, and head.

"What the fuck is going on?" I was trying to scream, but it was too weak to hear, though it echoed loudly inside my head. He kept his hand there, pressing down firmly, not letting up. It felt like he was flipping a switch of pain on and off, over and over. I cried out, "Stop, stop, please. Stop, take your fucking hands off me." But he did not stop.

Consciousness came and went. I knew I was in the ambulance; I had a blanket under my head, and the man was kneeling with my head in his lap, his knees heavy on each of my shoulders, holding my skull down into the blanket. He was keeping my neck, shoulders, and head static, steady in his grasp. I felt the ambulance slowly limp away, bumping along the field.

After what seemed like moments of darkness and confusion, I awoke again to the sensation of speed. We were travelling fast; the siren was screaming, and the driver was in a hurry. I realised where I was, and felt an odd sense of excitement. I imagined people standing in the street, watching the ambulance speeding past, thinking, "Who's in there? What happened to them? Thank goodness it's not me."

"It's me. I am the guy in the ambulance they are rushing to the hospital. How bizarre is this?" I thought.

My good friend and teammate, Alan Rogers, was clinging on, swaying from side to side. "Ah, good lad," I thought. "He's coming with me; I'm not alone." His face was red, and I could see Alan had been crying, but through his forced smile, he said, "Fuck me, mate, we've just gone through a red light, and now we're going the wrong way down a one-way street." Looking out the back window, he laughed, and added, "Gary's trying to keep up with us in his Spitfire."

Gary, our fullback, worked for the local newspaper and was thrilled. A big scoop coming in the next issue, no doubt.

I drifted back into unconsciousness, waking up again only when we reached the ECU at Redhill Hospital in Surrey. Alan was sitting reassuringly close to my side, watching over me. The cold, sterile atmosphere of the hospital was anything but comforting. Memories of my two eye operations as a small boy flashed through my mind – days spent in the hospital, terrified, and crying when mum and dad had to leave me alone.

"What have I done? What's wrong?" I thought.

My body felt like it was floating above me. The pain was gone, but I still could not breathe properly. I was struggling, working hard to suck in tiny breaths. I could only speak one word at a time. I knew I was in serious trouble.

I tried talking again, but it was just a whisper. "Alan–what's–going–on? I–can't–breathe."

"You've had a bad accident, mate; they're taking you in for an operation," Alan replied.

A nurse started cutting off my rugby shirt with giant scissors, slicing upward from my stomach to my collar. "No–don't–cut–my–shirt," I cried. That shirt had cost me a week's wages from my paper round.

"What–about–tonight?" I asked Alan. I was still struggling for air. I had a date lined up with a hot girl from my school at the football club dance that evening. She had finally agreed to meet me there on Saturday night. Alan was also supposed to meet up with a new date, and we had big plans. Two excited boys on a mission.

"I don't think we'll be going anywhere tonight, mate," Alan said. I had been looking forward to this evening for ages. Now, I was going to miss out. And for how long? How long would I be stuck in this bloody hospital – a week, two weeks, six weeks?

I know now that I was in shock. You cannot calibrate or fully process what is happening in that state. Ignorance truly is bliss, and at that moment, I was utterly ignorant of anything to do with spinal injuries or paralysis – fortunately.

Flat on my back, staring at the ceiling, doctors and nurses bustling all around me, suddenly my bed on wheels was being pushed at quite a pace down a corridor. A young male nurse looked down at me with a reassuring smile. All I could see above me were the fluorescent lights on the ceiling, flashing by one after another, faster and faster. Then they parked me, and a surgeon looked down at me. A huge bright light was directly behind him. This must be the operating theatre, I thought.

"Now, Roger, I want you to relax and count backwards from 10 to one, OK?" he said. I heard a machine start up; it sounded like a dentist's drill but louder. I think I counted to six.

I came around in the middle of the night, disoriented, and confused. Why was I lying here, frozen, motionless, flat on my back, staring at the ceiling? Gradually, the memory of the day returned, and a deep dread ran through me as I realised, I was alone in a hospital.

I could hear voices and people moving around close to me. Some poor soul in the bed to my right was coughing and spluttering violently. I could not see him, but I could tell he was close, which was horrible. You can tell when someone is in pain, and this guy is suffering immensely, fighting for his life. He was choking and gasping, the sound of it terrifying. Then suddenly, it went silent. He was gone. The fight must have been too much for him.

I felt sick, and scared. "Oh shit, people die here."

I awoke again in what must have been the morning. A young nurse was trying to feed me Rice Krispies from a bowl. She put some into my mouth, but I could not eat. I could not swallow, so I pushed them out with my tongue – the only part of my body I could move.

I heard footsteps, and a woman with an authoritative voice spoke. "Hello Roger, OK dear, we are moving you today. An ambulance will take you to a special spinal unit at Stoke Mandeville Hospital. They will be able to take much better care of you."

That was the first time I had heard the word 'spinal'.

I must have slept most of the way because it was hours later when we arrived at Stoke Mandeville. I was greeted by a group of enthusiastic nurses in pale blue uniforms. An older senior nurse in dark blue seemed to be in charge. A huge black man they called Angelo did most of the heavy lifting. He was a porter, wearing a brown robe, with a charming Caribbean accent and a big, reassuring smile. I felt safe in his hands. Together, as a team, they got me to Ward 1, the intensive care unit.

Dr Silver was a scruffy little chap with half-round gold spectacles balanced on the end of his nose. He did not say anything to me; he just efficiently gave instructions. They took me to the X-ray department, and I knew my treatment by a crack team of experts had begun.

I still could not move anything, and I could not feel anything either. I lay there in traction, like something out of a horror movie. They had shaved the sides of my head and drilled holes into my skull to fit this contraption on me. It was a pair of external callipers fixed by a couple of screws about an inch above each ear. The top of the calliper had a pulley wheel with a cable attached to a metal tray full of weights. This traction device was stretching my neck, pulling all the shattered pieces of bone back into place. It was excruciating, the weight so heavy it was dragging me up the mattress. Every 15 minutes, nurses had to pull me back down the bed.

I could not eat or drink, could not swallow anything. A nurse gave me an ice cube. "Roger, just let this melt in your mouth," she said. For the next five days, all I could consume were ice cubes.

I was laid flat, with no pillow under my head, just a tiny roll under my neck to keep it extended. The bed was electric, so it could be tilted left and right, with pillows along my sides to stop me slipping out. That allowed them to move my body weight around to avoid pressure points. They had fitted tubes to my body to put fluids in, and get fluids out.

My parents arrived that evening. Our home in Maidenhead was about 30 miles away, so not too far for them – about an hour's drive. They met with Dr Walsh, the hospital's director and an internationally renowned spinal injury specialist, and Dr Silver, my consulting doctor. Dr Walsh explained my neck had broken. I had been dump-tackled; some players had picked me up and dropped me on my head, with several of them falling on top of me. They had heard the snap, and everyone climbed off, knowing something was wrong. They could see it was severe as my head twisted at an abnormal angle to my body.

Dr Walsh showed my mum and dad the X-rays. My C5 and C6 vertebrae, the two discs, had fractured into multiple pieces and dislocated. He made it clear that I had suffered a severe injury and recommended that they prepare for the worst. He explained that recovery rates for my type of injury were only about 5%. My body had shut down; everything was paralysed, and only my diaphragm's spasm was keeping me alive. If my gut were full of food and waste, it could cause severe complications and infections. My athletic body had thick blood that might clot. He recommended that they make the most of the next few days. If I survived that, I could expect to spend the rest of my life in a wheelchair.

When my parents visited me for the first time, they tried to be cheerful. My mum told me I would be better soon and that I was to stay strong and brave. My dad, however, was white as a sheet, speechless.

Now in my late 60s, as a grandfather with two sons and five grandsons, I look back on those years with a sense of guilt that still lingers. Back then, I was the centre of attention, the poor young boy whose life had been shattered, with everyone focused on me. But it is only now, with time, that I realise the hell my mum and dad must have been going through. They must have been petrified. At the time, I did not see it – how could I? I was just a kid, and they were the grown-ups.

My dad was only 45, about the same age as my eldest son Sam. His heart must have broken, seeing his son lying there, helpless. My mum was the backbone of our family, the one who gave love, kept the peace, and held everything together. I was her pride and joy, and although she never showed it to me, she must have suffered terribly. I often wonder how they managed to get through it all. I wish I could hold her now, thank her again, hug her, kiss her, and tell her how much I love her.

Years later, mum told me that she and my father were dancing in the living room to Simon & Garfunkel's *Bridge Over Troubled Water* on the night of the accident. When the dreaded phone call came, she said she could never listen to that song again.

So, there I was, in the best hospital, being looked after by the best doctors, with my loving family. I was strong and young, a fighter. But even then, there was no denying that the odds were massively stacked against me. Yet, somehow, I survived. Was it God on my side? Or the gods, or just pure luck? It was karma or a combination of all those things. Whatever it was, something was on my side that day.

Looking back, I can see how a series of fortunate events and circumstances contributed to saving my life...

One: No time for lunch

As teenagers often do that day, I skipped breakfast, rushing to my morning job as a cleaner at Bisham Abbey Sports Centre near Marlow. After work, I hurried home. Mum had set my lunch on the kitchen table, happy to see me. "Sorry, mum, no time to eat," I said. "Don't be daft," she replied, "you didn't have any breakfast – you have to eat." But I could not. We were playing an away game in Surrey, and I had to get to Maidenhead Rugby Club to catch a lift – there was no time. At 15, I felt invincible. I could run all day and night, fuelled by endless energy reserves. Missing a meal was not a big deal – I would grab a Mars bar on the road. But now, I realise that if I had had breakfast and then that giant plate of lunch, my stomach would have been full of undigested food, causing dangerous complications after the accident.

Two: A doctor on my team

At Maidenhead Rugby Club, I played on the fourth team, a mix of young lads like me and older players in their 30s and 40s – some overweight but enthusiastic, some just not talented players, but all keen. Fortunately, one of the slightly older players on my team was a doctor. He was the one who stopped people from moving me, from carrying me off the pitch. Had they lifted me the way they wanted to, it could have killed me or irreversibly severed my spinal cord.

Three: Spinal injuries course

Just a week or so earlier, the ambulance driver had completed a training course on spinal injuries. Not all staff were trained in this, but luckily, because of that course, he knew how to move me safely. His careful handling of my spine prevented a complete break of my spinal cord, which could have been fatal or resulted in total and permanent paralysis.

Four: The intern doctor

Back then, senior doctors often took weekends off. Saturdays were typically for dealing with broken legs, cuts, and stitches from weekend sports activities, which made it an ideal time for trainee doctors to gain experience. That day, the young Canadian intern doctor in the Redhill Hospital casualty unit did not know how to operate on me. However, he was smart enough to call Dr Walsh, the Director of Stoke Mandeville Hospital, for instructions. My operation took place over the phone.

Five: Fitness training

In addition to rugby, I played football for Windsor Rovers on Sundays, and two nights a week I trained at Maidenhead Rowing Club, lifting weights and joining in the team's workouts. I was incredibly fit and had a very muscular neck. The doctor later explained that this fitness enabled me to drag air into my lungs while lying face down in the mud in shock.

Under the circumstances, I could have been in a much worse state. What followed was a fight for survival, a battle to get back on my feet, and a struggle to live a healthy, everyday life.

Maidenhead Advertiser: 9 February, 1973

Rugby boy, aged 15, breaks neck

The condition a 15-year-old Roger Warner of Alwyn Rd, who broke his neck in a rugby match on Saturday was yesterday [Thursday] described as satisfactory.

It will still be weeks before doctors at Stoke Mandeville Hospital near Aylesbury, where Roger is in the special spinal unit, can make a definitive statement about his future, said a hospital spokesman.

The tragedy happened 10 minutes into the second half of the game between Maidenhead rugby club B2 and the team from Reigate Surrey being played at Reigate.

Roger went down in a cluster of players after a tackle. He was taken by ambulance to nearby Redhill Hospital, where an emergency operation was performed, and he was then transferred to Stoke Mandeville.

His father, engineer Mr Charles Warner said Roger himself is in remarkably good spirits he has really taken it very well.

Roger is an all-round sportsman at Furze Platt secondary school.

As well as being the vice-captain of the school's rugger XV, he has played for the county under-15s and took part in the South of England trials. He is in the football first team and captain of the school basketball team. He also has a place in the school cricket team and is a keen athlete.

CHAPTER 2

WHO'S THAT BOY?

A 12-year-old boy stepped out of our house and saw the No 10 Marlow bus, a red single-decker, idling at the bus stop across the road. Without hesitation, he sprinted towards the shop 200 yards up the road, determined to beat the bus. He pulled ahead, putting distance between himself and the noisy machine. Then, the bus engine roared to life, accelerating and catching up. The boy pushed himself harder, running as if his life depended on it, legs stretching, lungs burning. It was a surge of power.

He made it! Barely beating the bus by a few seconds, he stood there, breathing deeply, watching it drive past. He jumped, punching the air in exhilaration. The rush was real; it was as significant a victory as scoring a goal or acing an exam. At that moment, the boy knew he could achieve anything if he tried hard enough.

I felt invincible, yet I was so innocent. Now, at 67, I am reflecting on my youth for the first time.

After leaving Stoke Mandeville Hospital and rejoining society, I spent my life looking outward, focusing on the obstacles ahead of me rather than inward. I was not aware of how I walked, how I looked, or how I made others feel. Years later, I learned that my sister often avoided me because seeing me in my broken state greatly upset her.

Was I insensitive? Perhaps. I did not care what people thought of me. I did not expect to be looked at differently or seek special treatment. I did not join 'disabled clubs' or groups, not out of disrespect; I admired those who overcame their challenges and pushed themselves in 'disabled' sports. Instead, I adapted to games I could play without a wheelchair, where my walking stick was a sufficient aide.

For instance, my parents were members of the local bowls club. My mother played for England and was President of the Berkshire Bowls Association. They suggested I join them one weekend. Though it felt odd, I learned the sport with young players in their 40s and me at 17, enjoying the strategy and competition, even against much older opponents. Similarly, I taught myself to throw darts with my left hand due to paralysis in my right and played pool, using the table for balance. My disability did not stop me competing in pub leagues. In 1976, I won the *Reading Evening Post*'s Sportsman of the Year trophy for participating in regular pool and bowls leagues.

Writing this has required me to examine myself in detail for the first time, talking to family, old friends, and even former patients from the hospital ward in 1973. Trying to piece together those events, emotions, and memories, I wonder: who was that boy? How did he cope with such a terrible situation? How did he find the courage to soldier on and get through those challenging times?

Some might call me a narcissist. I do not think I am. I can be pushy and dominant, a 'Sigma' personality type. I am strong-willed and independent, and I get grumpy from frustration and struggling with simple tasks like opening doors. Hearing non-disabled people complain about things I cannot dream of doing, like walking to the shops, can be maddening.

Admiring my achievements does not come naturally. Retrospectively, I see I was just doing what was needed. It was like a mission; something terrible happened, and 'young Roger' had to deal with it. He did not analyse it; he just faced it head-on. Ignorance was bliss, allowing me to work through those dark days. I doubt I could handle such a calamity now with the wisdom and pragmatism of age.

Before that fateful day, I was confident, competitive, active, a winner at sports, and successful. The world was my oyster. I went to Furze Platt Comprehensive School in Maidenhead, where I had a great social group, many friends, and a stream of girlfriends. I was in the top grade academically, excelling in some subjects and struggling in others. My parents encouraged work and independence, giving me several paying jobs. I grew up in a comfortable home with a loving family, surrounded by a close-knit extended family.

My father was my hero, capable of building walls, fixing cars, and solving mechanical problems. He encouraged me to focus on my strengths and advised me against following his engineering footsteps. On the other hand, my mother was the peacemaker, always ready to talk and listen, praising and encouraging. Their belief in me was a vital asset.

At the time of my accident, my life was whole and active. I was the school basketball team captain, playing rugby for Berkshire, and part of Windsor Rovers' football squad. I was deeply involved in sports, balancing these commitments with paper rounds, cleaning jobs, and my responsibilities as vice-captain and prefect at school. I had reached the under-16s England rugby schoolboy trials, and played for several southern counties.

Around this time, my sister and her husband lived in Sydney, Australia. My brother-in-law, who had played rugby union with me at Maidenhead, told me about the popularity of rugby league in Australia. He spoke about the excitement of the game and how it was a professional sport there, with star players earning substantial salaries. He also mentioned that the clubs often took on 16-year-old apprentices, which sparked my idea. I planned to leave school, move to Australia to stay with my sister, and try to break into one of the Australian rugby league teams. It was an ambitious goal, but I was determined to pursue it.

Looking back, I see a boy with a strong work ethic, pride, and resilience. Despite my injuries, I did not consider myself disabled. I was injured, and recovering, which gave me the drive to push myself. My family's support was crucial. My mother's constant encouragement, my father's strength, and the love from my sister and friends gave me the confidence to rebuild myself.

Reflecting on it all, I realised how important that foundation was. Without their support, the outcome could have been much sadder. Their visits, words, hugs, and smiles gave me the strength to believe in myself and my future.

CHAPTER 3
FIGHT

And so, it began – my battle to rebuild my life one week after the accident that shattered my world. I had broken my neck, fracturing and dislocating two vertebrae, C5 and C6, but I had survived. After one night in Redhill Hospital, they transferred me to Stoke Mandeville in Buckinghamshire, England, renowned as the world's leading spinal injuries hospital. They had planned to airlift me, but due to a significant accident that Sunday, the helicopter was not available. Instead, I was taken by ambulance – a special one with an advanced suspension system.

The doctors stabilised me. I had undergone several X-rays, and the traction was doing its job. My recovery was steady, better than expected – no deadly blood clots, no septic infections. My lungs were working again, and my breathing was improving.

After five days of surviving on nothing but ice cubes, I could finally sip soup through a straw, getting some much-needed nourishment into my body. I was on a cocktail of medications – blood thinners, vitamins, laxatives, antibiotics, sleeping pills, and muscle relaxants. I was taking 10 pills at a time, four times a day. I rattled like a jar of gobstoppers.

Flat on my back in that hospital bed, I had no feeling in my body. Occasionally, I felt pins and needles in my shoulders and arms as some sensation began to return, but it was far from ordinary – just partial sensitivity. I could not move a thing except for my eyeballs and my mouth. Sleep was elusive, and my head throbbed constantly because of the clunky contraption screwed into my skull. The weight of it was relentless, and the wound where it was anchored to the bone kept getting infected. The pain was excruciating, and the dressings had to be changed daily.

The angels

Changing my bedsheets was an ordeal. It required a team of six – two male orderlies and two female nurses to lift and turn me, while two more nurses, usually led by Sister Humphries, the formidable head of the intensive care ward, swiftly removed the old sheets, and replaced them with fresh ones. While they had me raised, they would wash and clean my body.

One day, during one of these routine turns, a nurse holding my head did not rotate it coordinated with the rest of my body. The metal pin in my skull jumped out of the hole, skidding about a quarter of an inch through my scalp and leaving a bloody wound. The pain was indescribable, and the noise vibrated in my skull. They had to put the pin back in the hole. A doctor was there to oversee the process. The young nurse was so upset and apologetic, but there was no point in letting her worry about it. With a grin, I reassured her, "It's all right, dear."

The staff were terrific. They were like family to me. I depended on them for everything. Beyond the routine tasks – bowel evacuations, catheter changes, bed baths, shaves, feeding, giving me my pills, and changing my dressings – they also had to turn me every 30 minutes to prevent bedsores. But there were other, more personal needs, like scratching my head. They had cut most of my hair but not all of it, and after a few days, it itched terribly. They could not wash it with water and conventional shampoo for fear of moving my neck. They tried using dry powder shampoo, but it did not help.

There is nothing more maddening than an itch you cannot scratch. I challenge anyone to resist scratching for 20 minutes the next time their head or face itches. Now imagine not being able to move your arms to relieve that irritation – it is torture.

"Nurse, nurse, please help me," I would call out across the ward, unable to see if anyone was there. I would hear a voice, "I'll be there in a minute; I'm just taking care of Douglas." Finally, after what felt like an eternity, the nurse would arrive. "Yes, Roger, what is it?" "Nurse, please, scratch my head for me," I would beg. She would understand my frustration, having done this hundreds of times.

"Where is it, dear?" she would ask. "Yes, there – left a bit, right a bit, harder – yes, that's it!' She would scratch and I would feel the pressure of her nails relieving irritation. It was ecstasy. "Thank you, thank you, nurse." "No problem, dear," she would say before moving on. And sure enough, it would start all over again five minutes later. Sometimes, nurses were unavailable, so I had to learn to cope with it.

Realising I was in trouble

Those first few weeks were surreal. Everything was so unfamiliar. My ignorance and naivety shielded me, in a way, from fully grasping the gravity of my situation.

I went through distinct stages. First, there was shock – the inability to reason or fully comprehend what had happened. Then denial – this cannot be real; it is not as bad as they say. And finally, terror – as the full realisation of my condition began to sink in.

It is incredible how quickly life can change. One minute, I was a busy teenager, preparing for exams, playing sports, juggling two part-time jobs, and trying to impress the pretty girls. The next, I was an invalid. My old life had ended, and a new one had begun. Now, my world was reduced to just my head, my eyeballs staring at a ceiling all day, every day. My interactions were limited to the nurses, doctors, physiotherapists, and occupational therapists who came to change my tubes, give me pills and stretch my limbs – the days seemed endless. I lived for the evenings when family and school friends would visit.

Mornings were the highlight of my day. After breakfast, changing my bedsheets, and a bed bath, around 9 o'clock, my physiotherapist would arrive to give me my workout. She was a tall, stunning Swedish woman named Emma, with bright blue eyes and jet-black hair. Her distinct Nordic accent filled the ward as she cheerfully greeted me, "Hello, my dear, how are you today?" Despite everything, I could not help but smile. She was a vision – pretty, always cheerful, and her sunny personality washed over me like a warm breeze. "I'm well, thank you – better now that you're here," I would say, winking, and flashing a smile. I had not lost my will to live; a pretty lady still made my heart race.

But it was not just about the charm; we had serious work to do. My muscles had not yet wasted away, so keeping the blood pumping and the legs moving was crucial.

"Just my bloody luck!" Emma would shout, playfully complaining to her fellow physiotherapists across the ward. "Trust me to get a 15-year-old rugby player with huge bloody muscles that weigh a ton! Why couldn't you be a skinny little boy?" she laughed.

It was a relief to have someone treat me like a person, not just a large, helpless body that needed moving. She explained what had happened to my body, what we had to do to fix it, and what required me to work hard and stay strong.

Spasms were becoming a problem. As my shattered nervous system began to recover and rewire itself, my body would erupt in involuntary movements. These spasms could toss me around the bed, which was dangerous if it jarred my neck. The doctors increased my dose of muscle relaxants, but because I had such powerful limbs, the spasms were still a challenge for the nurses and physiotherapists. They often had to hold me down, and it was common for them to take a knee to the face or a foot to the stomach. I would apologise, and they would grin and say, "No problem," but I knew I had hurt them.

Apart from when people came to my bed and looked down at me, I could only see that bloody ceiling. How far can you see with your eyeballs when you cannot move your head? Maybe 30 feet wide by 40 feet deep? The ceiling was creamy with tiny green, blue, brown, and grey flecks. It looked like a splatter paint effect. I could not see anything else – just that ceiling. I was so bored.

Friendship is a powerful energy

Some 10 days had passed since I arrived at Stoke Mandeville. It was Valentine's Day. I could hear them – voices in the distance – the gang had arrived. At last, someone to talk to, a couple of hours of cheerful faces, news, and gossip from school.

The school organised the visits. They came in two cars at a time – one teacher with three kids in one car, and another with three kids in the other. This way, about six of my school friends could visit each evening, taking turns so I could see as many of them as possible.

At first, the visits were daily, but naturally, they tapered off to two or three nights a week.

One month after Valentine's Day, I turned 16. Another group of friends showed up, determined to make it feel like a typical birthday. Despite the circumstances, they did their best to bring the usual cheer, laughter, and the spirit of celebration.

My best friend Glenn, a black boy from the USA who went to a different school from me, would often come with my parents. A couple of the older lads, Dave and Chris, were in the year above me. Dave had been in the hospital the year before with severe burns from a barbecue accident. He was lucky to survive, and I had visited him in hospital then. Now, he and Chris rode their 50cc mopeds from Maidenhead – a gruelling trip. They told me they nearly didn't make it and had to leave early to face the long journey home. Their visits meant the world to me. I can never thank them enough for their unwavering friendship.

As the days passed, my friends grew more relaxed around me. The initial shock of what had happened had subsided. They had had time to process it, to cry with each other, and to come to terms with seeing me in the prison of my broken body.

Those visits meant everything to me. Most of the time, they were a welcome distraction, a lifeline of normalcy that pulled me out of the abyss. Seeing my friends, and my mum and dad, brought a sense of relief, a temporary escape from the reality of my situation. We would laugh and share stories, and it felt like things were almost normal again for a few hours. But there were also moments when the laughter felt hollow, and the stories stung. Hearing about what was happening at school, the gossip, who was dating whom and how the rugby team was doing all reminded me of the life I was missing out on.

The darkest night

Those stories twisted my heart. It was hard to swallow the fact that life was carrying on without me, that the world had not stopped just because mine had. There were nights when staying positive felt like an impossible task. I tried to put on a brave face for them, not letting them see the darkness that sometimes took over after they left. But once I was alone, reality crashed over me, and the 'why me?' questions started swirling in my mind.

As they left each evening, they would call out, "Good night, Roger. It was great to see you." I would muster a weak response, "Thanks for coming, guys. I appreciate it. See you all soon, yes?" And then I would hear their voices fade away, "Yeah, bye, mate." And just like that, they were gone.

One night, after they had left, something inside me snapped. It started with a deep breath – a spasm in my chest that filled me with air, but it was more than that. It was as if all the emotions I had been holding back finally erupted. Suddenly, tears streamed down my face, my eyes burning hot, my breathing quickening as my heart raced. It felt like the end of something, though I could not quite put my finger on what.

This reaction took me by surprise. I did not expect it or even know where it was coming from, but it hit me like a wave, and I could not stop it. I did not want to stop it. I let myself sob, releasing all that pent-up pressure, not caring what came after. I needed to let it out, to let it all go. And when the sobs finally subsided, I ended it with a scream – a scream that felt like it had been building inside me for far too long.

Years later, my sister confided in me that my cheerful demeanour and positive attitude had made it easier for mum and dad to cope with everything. It must have been incredibly tough for them to see their son in such a state but knowing that I was mentally strong seemed to lighten their burden if only a little. It gave them something to hold onto, a reassurance that I was still fighting, still me, despite everything that had happened.

CHAPTER 4

FAITH

I cried for more than a few nights. Sometimes, the pressure just became too much to bear. It is difficult to put into words the sense of helplessness and hopelessness that enveloped me, lying there in the darkness, alone and afraid. The quiet was overwhelming, a vast, empty silence where I felt lost in space, with only my mind and thoughts to keep me company. My hopes felt strangled by fate; it was a metaphorical prison. I know what it is like to lose your freedom; I have been locked up and imprisoned in an actual jail cell. I understand what it means to lose your liberty, to be at the mercy of someone else's control, with your freedom denied until they decided you could go.

But paralysis is different – it is a prison with no door, a cell you can never leave. It is a heavy suit you cannot take off, stifling you, pressing you down into the bed as if hundreds of hands held you in place. The weight was unbearable, the feeling a kind of endlessness death.

One night, I lay there in the dark, my mind racing like a drowning boy, panicking, reaching out for something to hold onto, something that could save me. I was desperate for a path, a way out of my solitude. I searched for meaning, asking myself, "There must be a reason for this. Is this my calling? Is this my path to Jesus?" I prayed to God, asking Him to help me.

We were not a profoundly religious family. I had been baptised as a baby, but we did not attend church regularly or keep a Bible in the house. Yet in this, my most desperate moment, the loneliest time of my life, I turned to God for help. I prayed sincerely, diving into my soul, asking Him to save me from this hell. I believed, or rather, I hoped, that faith in God was the answer. I thought believing in God, in Jesus, would lift me out of this abyss and give me the strength to walk again. I was sure that this was the answer. What choice did I have? How could I dare to turn my back on God? Doing so might mean the end of me, the final judgment, the end of hope.

For a week, I struggled, searching for something to hold on to. The long, sleepless nights were a torment. I was at a crossroads, surrounded by darkness, caught in a storm of raging emotions. Which way should I go? Where would I find faith? Fear grew in me, panic and depression consuming me. I felt myself sinking further into a downward spiral. I called out to Jesus, but my questions echoed in empty space. My frustration at my predicament grew more intense. There were no answers, no signs, no inner strength to be found. I felt lost, stranded, abandoned by God.

I lay there, silent and motionless, for several minutes, thinking intently. A clarity settled over me. Turning to God and looking to Jesus for help was not working. I realised then that this path was not for me.

Many years later, a profound encounter with a Buddhist monk in a sacred temple changed my life forever. From him, I learned that faith is like the wind – it comes, and goes, sometimes blowing so strong it knocks you to your knees, or at other times, it might lift you like a feather into the blue sky. Sometimes, a cool, light breeze drifts over you, awakening and refreshing you. But faith blows within you, and you alone.

During those dreadful nights, the wind of faith blew so hard it tumbled me over and over like a piece of tumbleweed until finally, I settled. I understood then that I could not pray to God for a miracle to walk out of that place. I had to believe in goodness, in the power of love. I had to believe in myself – whether I walked or did not walk, I would be okay. I realised that I had faith – in myself, my doctors, my nurses, my family, and my friends. I knew then that I could smash through this challenge. It was a dawning enlightenment, a belief in myself. God could help me if He wanted to, but it was up to me and the power of my spirit to save myself.

Looking back, I can see that this was God's work. He did not ask for recognition, my belief, or even thanks. He empowered me with a fighting spirit. That was the beginning of a determined and positive mindset, the preliminary stages of my pragmatic and decisive personality forming. I adapted to the process of evaluating my options, understanding my predicament, making clear decisions, and getting on with what I needed to do to make the best of it.

CHAPTER 5
MOVING

After those first few agonising nights, the nurses gradually allowed me to have soup, which I sucked through a straw. A couple of weeks later, I moved on to mashed potatoes, then ice cream, and, eventually, minced beef and vegetables. They had to spoon-feed me, of course, which is not easy when you are flat on your back. My sister often volunteered to feed me, pretending I was a baby to annoy me.

I stayed in traction, flat on my back, for eight long weeks. When they finally removed the traction contraption, they fitted me with a foam collar to support my still fragile neck. I was allowed to sit up in bed at a slight angle for about 15 minutes every couple of hours. It was 10 weeks before I could sit up in bed properly with just the collar fitted. A week later, I could finally get out of bed and sit in a wheelchair. At first, it was only for 15 minutes, but by the third day, I could stay in the chair for an hour. Gradually, I was allowed to remain in the chair for three or four hours a day.

My body had been horizontal for so long that it took a while to adjust to being vertical again. My blood circulation was weak, and the elevation change made me dizzy. I experienced violent pins and needles, which can be dangerous.

One of the disadvantages of having no sensation is that you do not feel pain – a crucial safety mechanism. Pressure ulcers are a significant complication of spinal cord injuries, and they can have grave consequences. Constant attention to sores and pressure points was vital, and regular movement was essential.

You had to check everything. You might be sitting on a sharp object or the edge of a metal frame, not realising it is damaging your flesh.

After three or four weeks, I regained some sensation in my arms, but I still could not move my hands or fingers. I could raise my arm from my chest to my face, but I could not get it over my head, and once it was up, I could not bring it back down again.

As time passed, reality began to set in. I had battled with my faith and felt in control of my situation, but it was so hard to see little or no progress. My heart, my will, and my emotional strength were all weakening. I nearly lost my way; I almost gave up.

I still could not do basic things like washing my face. I accepted that I needed people. Those beautiful nurses cared for my every need, all those things I could no longer do for myself. I became accustomed to needing help for everything. But that realisation came with a deep sense of humiliation. I felt pathetic, overwhelmed by the hopelessness of my predicament. I longed to do all those simple things for myself, but could not.

Don't look for problems – find solutions

Eventually, I started looking for alternatives and inventive solutions that would enable me to function and do some simple things for myself. Gradually, I found comfort and security in knowing that people were there for me.

The staff in the occupational therapy department were geniuses. They created devices to help me regain some independence. One of their inventions was a regular music stand; the kind musicians used to hold sheet music.

They placed it over my bed at an angle so I could look up at it from my flat position. A book was attached to it, with the pages facing down, held in place by elastic bands.

The occupational therapy department made a wooden stick with a rubber thimble on one end, and the other end was sewn into a leather wristband fixed to my arm with Velcro. Using my wrist, and the rubber on the end of the stick, I could pull a page out from under the elastic band and continue reading the book.

This same device was later adapted, replacing the stick with a toothbrush, allowing me to brush my teeth. Fortunately, I found this a personal challenge and was motivated to make it work. It was messy, and the foamy results were funny to those watching. For me, it was just another step forward. What's next?

I remember a patient in the bed opposite me whose mother visited daily. He was a young lad, about 19. He refused to try this new device, not wanting to humiliate himself in that way. He found it all annoying and preferred waiting for a nurse or his mother to brush his teeth.

Looking back now, I can see the difference between him and me. My glass was half full, while his was half empty. This challenge was no different from racing that Marlow bus to the shop – a victory for me. He, on the other hand, was still angry. And rightfully so, a negligent car driver had knocked him off his motorbike, and he had crashed head first into the curb, breaking his neck badly. But in his head, he was still a victim, questioning his fate, asking, "Why me? It's not fair."

These are thoughts we all have when tragedy strikes. The music plays one minute, then it stops, and everything is different. He was not ready or able to deal with his situation. You've got past that. You must accept that the music has stopped; you cannot fight that. Constant denial will slowly eat away at your heart. Years later, I heard he had passed away soon after leaving the hospital from "complications".

The lesson I learned back then was this: if you are a teenage rugby player, strive to be the best teenage rugby player there is. But if you are a person with paraplegia, with hands and arms that do not work correctly, trying to brush your teeth – then just be the best at that.

It worked for me. I competed against myself, felt accomplished by achieving the most minor things, and slowly rose from the ashes of my doom, bit by bit. I realise now that it was the admiration of others that helped me. I gained a new kind of self-respect and faith in myself; having found an inner strength I did not know was there.

The physiotherapists and occupational therapists soon recognised my super competitive nature and desire to do more for myself, so they devised more solutions and challenges for me. I loved music, as most teenagers do, and I had some new albums on cassette tape. One was Pink Floyd's *Dark Side of the Moon,* which had recently been released. My mum and dad bought me a cassette tape player, and the occupational therapists helped set it up so I could hold it, load the tape, and play it myself.

With its stick and rubber, my wrist-controlled tool worked perfectly to press the buttons and open it. Using my wrists to grip the tape, I fumbled through the complicated process of loading the cassette. But I managed it. My success would earn me a round of applause from observing visitors. I felt like a performing seal, but I never found it demeaning.

Most people worried I would not be able to do it, so it was a massive relief for all of them when that music finally played. I was not going to be defeated. I was going to play my music myself, and I knew I would find a way, and win eventually.

The breakthrough

As the weeks, then months, passed, these challenges continued to come – being able to sit up, eat regular food, move my arms, scratch my face and head. Slowly, I started to do things for myself, giving me back a tremendous amount of dignity and self-worth.

And then, one day, it happened.

It was morning, about eight weeks after my accident. Emma, my physiotherapist, was working on my routine. I mentioned that I thought I had felt pins and needles in my left big toe, but the sensation was brief, and I could no longer feel it. She continued working on my legs, pushing my left knee up to my chest, then pulling my leg straight, extending my foot out. Then she pushed my knee back up to my chest, straight up the middle, bending it over to the left, turning it over to the right, and finally stretching it back down to straight again. She said, "Okay, Roger, try to move your toe again."

I had no feeling, and it wasn't easy because my leg did not feel like it was there. My foot did not feel like it was mine – it looked like someone else's body. I had to visualise my big toe moving. Suddenly, Emma leapt into the air, her arms raised, her fists clenched, turning, and screaming. She shouted to her colleague further down the ward, "Yes, yes, yes, he's moving his toe!"

She looked at me with tears in her eyes, so vibrant, so alive, and continued screaming, "Roger, Roger, you have done it, my love, you have movement! That was not a spasm – you moved your toe on command. This is fantastic; you have movement!"

I think Emma had been hoping rather than expecting me to move, so to her, this was a tremendous relief. Naturally, I was excited – my movement was coming back to me. But I had been expecting it. I knew it would happen; it was just a question of when. This was the progress I was working on for another win over the odds.

From that day onwards, we worked incredibly hard on my movement. I had to push and resist, push and resist. Emma would create resistance and coach me to use my power to move. Gradually, increased movement began to return to my arms and legs. I still had no sensation there or movement in my hands or feet, but I could feel the muscles in my legs, arms, and shoulders waking up.

The progress was fantastic.

CHAPTER 6

INCOMPLETE

To help you understand my story more fully, I'll explain what a spinal cord injury (SCI) is and what the terms "complete" and "incomplete" mean. When damage to the spinal cord is termed "complete," it usually means the nerve is entirely severed, separated into two. This is a catastrophic injury, often resulting in death or complete paralysis from the point of the injury downwards. To put it another way, the higher the damage to the spinal cord, the higher the paralysis begins.

Back in those days, most spinal injuries were "complete" due to a lack of knowledge and proper handling of injured patients from the moment of the accident to their arrival at the hospital. Often, more damage was done after the initial injury by well-meaning people who thought they were helping by moving or carrying the injured person.

By contrast, incomplete injuries were rare. "Incomplete" refers to cases where the spinal cord suffers considerable damage enough to cause total paralysis and complete loss of sensation, but the spinal cord is not entirely severed. This is what happened to me.

A recent study showed that only one-in-seven, or about 14%, of those who experience complete paralysis and loss of sensation immediately after injury, as I did, regain a significant amount of movement. 1973, that statistic was even lower – just one-in-20 or 5%.

The spinal cord is a tube-like structure filled with a bundle of nerves and cerebrospinal fluid. This fluid protects and nourishes the spinal cord, which is surrounded by cord linings, called meninges, and the vertebral bones. The spinal cord is about an inch across at its widest point and roughly 18 inches long.

Most people have seen a spine, perhaps a skeleton, in a school science lesson or at a hospital. You might have noticed how the bones are small where the head joins the neck and gradually get more extensive and thicker as you move down the back.

The spine consists of eight cervical vertebrae in your neck (C1 through C8), 12 thoracic vertebrae between your shoulder blades and the middle of your back (T1 through T12), and five lumbar vertebrae in the lower back (L1 through L5). The sacrum is found behind the pelvis and consists of five more bones (S1 through S5), which are fused into a triangular shape. The sacrum fits between the two hip bones, connecting the spine to the pelvis.

Your nerves exit the spinal column in pairs from under each vertebra and branch out throughout your body. Specific spinal nerves control each area of your body in a logical arrangement. The nerves in the cervical spine (neck area) branch out into your arms, which is why a neck issue can sometimes cause pain radiating down your arms. The thoracic nerves govern the middle of the body, the lumbar nerves extend into the outer legs, and the sacral nerves control the middle of the legs and the organ functions of the pelvis.

We have two major types of nerves: sensory and motor. Sensory nerves send information such as touch, temperature, and pain to the brain and spinal cord. Motor nerves send signals from the brain back into the muscles, causing them to contract either voluntarily or reflexively.

My injury involved the dislocation of two vertebrae in my neck, C5 and C6. Each vertebra is also fractured into multiple pieces. I remember being completely confused when the doctor showed me my X-ray; it did not look like a spine at all – more like a plate that had shattered into countless pieces after being dropped on the floor. At that early stage, it was not possible to know if I had a chance of recovery; most cases did not improve beyond complete paralysis.

My spinal cord injury left me totally paralysed and unable to move or feel anything from the neck down. But as my body healed, and recovered, my injury was eventually classified as "incomplete".

I began to experience the rehabilitation, the awakening of my sensorimotor functions. The bruised nerves in my spinal cord were slowly coming back to life because they were not completely severed – just bruised so severely that they had stopped working "completely".

The reason I remain partially paralysed today is that while some of my nerves recovered, many others did not. They were too damaged to heal.

This is why Emma, my physiotherapist, was so excited, and worked me so hard because, after about six weeks, I started to regain some reflexive movement.

My athletic and muscular build before the accident meant that muscle wastage was not as severe as it could have been. The sooner muscles start working again after a spinal cord injury, the better the chances of recovery, especially for walking.

Emma treated me both physically and psychologically to maximise my neurological recovery and support my bodily health. She often said, "Roger, you don't need to feel guilty for thinking about and missing what you've lost. Yes, your body has been significantly damaged, but you still have a chance to recover a lot of movement. You will be able to go back into the world, and have a good life. We will work together to rebuild this body and make you as strong as possible. We'll teach you new ways to do things."

She educated me about my body, my injury, and the care I would need as I prepared to resume my life, and told me, "You know, nearly all of the patients I treat who have been spinally injured for several years are happy people."

I understood that I had new challenges to overcome, and victories to win. I had to rebuild what remained of my body, find the muscles and movement that could still be recovered, and learn to maximise and use what little physical strength I had left. From then on, I also had to focus on building my cerebral strength – to sharpen my wits, increase my knowledge, and use my imagination.

One day, I woke up shaking, my body vibrating as if plugged into an electrical supply. The nurse came over to try to settle me, but I continued to rattle about, shaking, and bouncing. It was like shivering, but I was not cold. After a few minutes, it began to slow down, and gradually I became still. Strangely, I was left with a sensation all over my body. It felt like I was covered in little ants –

thousands of them, crawling over every square inch of my skin. It was horrible. I called the nurse back, and she tried rubbing my skin, but it made no difference. I could not move, could not touch myself, could not scratch the itching. It felt as if I were lying in a bath full of insects. It was torturous, and I began to feel extremely uncomfortable. I called out, "Nurse, please, nurse, do something! It is agony!"

The doctor came to see me. He was puzzled. He explained that it was a nervous reaction, part of the healing process. "The nerves are waking up, causing your nerve endings to create the sensation of ants crawling on your skin," he said.

The blood nurse took a sample from my right arm. She dropped it as she turned around to put it in her trolley, and the glass tube smashed. She looked at me apologetically, and said, "Sorry, Roger, I've got to do it again," and she took a sample from my left arm. I joked, "Steady on; I'll have no blood left at this rate. Leave me alone!"

They tried washing me with wet towels, but that did not work. They tried covering me with ice bags, but that did not help either. Eventually, they pulled the curtain around my bed, removed my covers, and surrounded my naked body with half a dozen fans blowing chilly air onto my skin at maximum power. Finally, some relief – the cool air numbed the irritation. Gradually, it became bearable, and the sensation had gone away by later in the day.

But this was a significant development. The reflexive movement was returning to my body. Spasms were beginning to occur in my muscles – these are the motor nerves reacting, causing muscles to contract involuntarily. Arms and legs moved on their own accord, spasming, like when you have slept on an arm, and it starts to tingle as the blood flow returns.

My body was going through changes. Could this be the beginning of my recovery?

CHAPTER 7
CELEBRITIES

Back then, Ward One was exclusively a men's spinal ward, and we would see about five new patients arrive each week. The injuries were usually the result of motorbike accidents, car crashes, horse riding mishaps, construction site falls, the occasional victim of violence, and, of course, sheer dumb stupidity.

One guy ended up in our ward after he and his girlfriend had gotten too adventurous in the back of his brother's car. His brother, driving at high speed down a country road, spent too long watching the show in his rear-view mirror, went off the road, and crashed into a tree.

Ward 1 had its share of interesting characters. Among them was Robert Wyatt, a well-known musician. His band, Soft Machine, was at the forefront of the underground music scene. Apparently, Robert had walked off a fourth-floor balcony at a Lady Jane's party in Maida Vale while intoxicated, resulting in paralysis from the waist down.

Robert was good friends with the guys from Pink Floyd and had several famous visitors, including his stepbrother, the actor Julian (Wyatt) Glover, who appeared in movies such as James Bond's *For Your Eyes Only, Star Wars, Raiders of the Lost Ark, Harry Potter,* and *Troy.*

Bob, as he was known, was also close to the celebrity DJ and music show host John Peel. Peel visited him regularly and even signed a personal autograph for me one time, writing, "Best wishes from the world's most boring man." He told me to tune into his radio show that evening because he was premiering a new album. I did, and it turned out to be Pink Floyd's *Dark Side of the Moon.*

Later that year, Pink Floyd performed two benefit concerts at

London's Rainbow Theatre. Robert's band, Soft Machine, supported them, and John Peel was the MC of the shows. The concerts raised £10,000 for Robert.

A year later, Robert Wyatt appeared on *Top of the Pops,* singing a cover of *I'm a Believer.* It caused quite a stir because the BBC did not want him to appear in his wheelchair. They insisted he sit in a regular chair, but Robert refused, insisting on using his wheelchair.

For a while, the bed next to mine was occupied by a young man named Vincent Davey Jr. He was a couple of years older than me and had been a motorcycle racer, competing in Super-bike racing for the Gus Kuhn team, which had won the British 500cc Championship in 1969. Vincent Jr had his accident while racing his Norton 750 Commando Super-Bike at Cadwell in 1973, leaving him with a badly broken back and paralysis from the chest down.

Vincent had some notable visitors, including motorcycle racing legends Mick Grant and Barry Sheene and many of the top racers of that era. His father, Vincent Davey Sr, was the son-in-law of Gus Kuhn, the British TT and Speedway Champion. At one point, Kuhn's motorcycle dealership on Clapham Road in London was the second-largest BMW dealership in the world, also selling MV Augusta and Nortons.

Vince Sr gave me a book, *the Castrol Motorcycle Racing Manual.* He had taken it with him from race to race throughout the season and had all the great motorcycle racers featured in the book sign their photos for me. It was a priceless treasure, one that I cherished deeply. Unfortunately, a couple of years later, I took it to school to show my friends, left it in a desk, and someone stole it.

One night, the ward's usual quiet was interrupted. The noise of machinery and bright lights outside the windows illuminated the ward in a ghostly dance of shadows. We were all confused – why would construction workers suddenly be working around the ward so late at night? The following day, I woke to find that chain-link fencing and barbed wire, about 20 feet high, had been erected around the ward, along with spotlights.

The staff were now wearing identity badges. It was all extraordinary.

Later that morning, there was some commotion as a new patient arrived. He was put in a private room with closed doors and armed guards stationed outside. For the first couple of days, it was a big mystery. Gossip spread around the ward, but nobody, not even the nurses, seemed to know anything. Eventually, the truth came out. The new patient was a British Army sergeant who had been shot through the spine in Northern Ireland.

On 23 March, 1973, there was a gruesome murder by the IRA in Belfast, known as the "Honey Pot Murders." The killings were part of an elaborate plot. The IRA ambushed four soldiers, three of whom died, while only one survived.

The soldiers were off duty, in civilian clothing, and had met two girls a week earlier. They arranged to meet the girls again that night at a hotel in Lisburn. The girls told them there was a party and drove with the soldiers to a first-floor apartment in Antrim Road, a quiet, mixed residential area of north Belfast. The apartment was set up for a party, with food and drinks on the tables and a blazing coal fire, which allayed any suspicions the soldiers might have had.

One of the girls left, saying she would return with more friends. When she came back, it was not with more girls but with two gunmen – one armed with a machine gun, the other with a pistol. The IRA ordered the soldiers to lie face down on a bed and shot them each in the head. The gunmen and the girls fled, but one soldier, severely injured, managed to crawl out of the apartment. The apartment occupant on the next floor found him in the hallway.

Our new guest, surrounded by security, was the sole survivor of that honey trap. A bullet had fractured his spine, and part of his jaw and tongue were also shot away. The Army named the dead soldiers as Staff Sgt Barrington Foster, 28 years old, Sgt Michael Muldoon, 26, and Sgt Thomas Penrose, 28, the only married man of those slain, who had a child. Our survivor was known only as David. We never learned his real name.

A few weeks later, when we were both able to leave our beds, we ended up in the hydrotherapy pool together. Patients went down two at a time. I remember the shock when his door opened, and a security guard wheeled him out. Another smartly dressed guard took the handles of my wheelchair from the nurse who was pushing me. "Hello, son," he said, "let's go." He then went ahead to push me to the pool. I could see his gun in its holster inside his jacket – he did not try to hide it. "Christ," I thought, "I hope there are no fucking IRA bastards around – I could be collateral damage." Dave was a nice guy, paralysed from the shoulders down, but he was managing his recovery quite well.

Then, one day, he and his entourage left as suddenly as they had arrived, and we never saw him again.

CHAPTER 8
SAVILE

During my time at Stoke Mandeville in 1973, Jimmy Savile was one of the most famous people who regularly visited the ward. His name has since become infamous, with shocking allegations emerging after he died in 2011. I do not take a position on his character or behaviour – I can only share what I experienced personally back then.

To understand the significance of his presence, it is essential to grasp just how famous Savile was at that time. He was a massive star in the UK, known for his eccentricity and flamboyance. Savile hosted BBC's hit show, *Top of the Pops,* and had a Sunday BBC radio show and a Saturday night TV variety show. He was on everyone's TV screens every day.

He was also featured in the Clunk Click public safety TV adverts, promoting the importance of wearing seatbelts. This campaign eventually led to compulsory seatbelt use in the front seats of vehicles in the UK by 1983 and doubly led to saving lives.

Savile was also widely recognised for his extensive charity work. One newspaper described him as a "prodigious philanthropist," and he was awarded an OBE in 1971 for his contributions. He was known for his catchphrases like "Goodness gracious," "As it 'appens" and "Guys and gals." His long bleached blond hair, loud dress sense – usually bright-coloured tracksuits or shell suits – and oversized gold jewellery made him instantly recognisable. And, of course, there was always a big cigar in his hand.

This was the man I met during my first week at Stoke Mandeville. Initially, I only heard him – his unmistakable voice and signature "Now then, now then" echoed through the ward.

Mine was the first bed on the right as you entered, closest to the sisters' office. The newest patients were positioned near the entrance, while those who had been there the longest were further down the ward. My sister, mother, father and grandmother sat around my bed. I could not see Savile, but I could hear the excitement in their voices as he greeted them.

My grandmother could not believe the great Jimmy Savile was standing right before her. He eventually leaned over my bed, and I saw his pointy face and white-yellow hair for the first time. He wore a bright purple tracksuit and signature gold chains swinging around his neck. "Now then, young man, what's all this I've been hearing about you?" he said.

I looked up at him from my horizontal position, my skull gripped by clawing steel traction equipment, grinning but completely confused about what he was talking about. By this point, he had his arm around my mother and said, "Your son has really messed it up for me in here!" My mum, clearly starstruck, smiled and said, "Oh, Jimmy…"

He continued, "You see that pretty nurse over there – the one with the ...," he gestured with his hands a pair of breasts, "well, I call her Nitroglycerin. She was my girl until this handsome young man arrived in the ward." Looking down at me, he jokingly added, "I'm not happy with you, not happy at all."

Everyone was giggling, and my grandmother, who had been crying earlier, stood up. Savile took her by both hands and kissed her on the cheek. He saw the tears in her eyes, and with genuine warmth, he said, "Now then, Roger's grandmother, don't you get upset, my love. This young man will be up and out of here in no time."

Despite all the tales of him working as a porter, I never saw Jimmy Savile in a brown uniform nor witnessed him doing any work at Stoke Mandeville. I saw the ward sister scolding him, saying, "Mr Savile, please, this is not visiting time – we're trying to do our work here." He would look sideways and say, "Who cares? I've got some patients I need to talk to," and then laugh it off, continuing as if she was not there.

There is no denying that his presence was a massive boost to many patients who were suffering not just from physical injuries but also from the mental toll of their situations. His goal was clearly to meet as many patients as possible during his visits and create as many smiles as possible. He enjoyed being the big star, the focus of attention, but that made him such a force. While he did take liberties with the staff, they all seemed to join in the fun – it was all part of his act, and an act it was.

Helping my father

The second time I saw him, it was about 7:00pm. My mum and dad were sitting quietly on my bed about three weeks after my injury. The initial shock had subsided, but the reality of my situation was starting to set in, especially for my dad, who was extremely depressed. He was so quiet that I could not even hear him.

Jimmy Savile walked into the ward, came over to my bed, leaned over, and said, "Hello, young man, how's it going?" He continued, "Promise me you haven't tried anything on with Nitroglycerin (a nickname he'd given to a buxom nurse); give me a chance; I'm older than you; it's not fair competition." I grinned and replied, "It's each man for himself, Jim." He laughed and then turned to my dad, "Hey Mick, do you fancy a ride to the pub in my Rolls-Royce?"

My dad was taken aback. "The pub, Jim?" he asked.

"Yes, let's go and have a pint. Come on, we won't be gone long – let's you and I have a chat."

I could not see what was happening beyond my bed, but I heard my dad leaving with Jimmy, and they were gone for a couple of hours. When my dad returned to the ward, he seemed in much better spirits. He sat beside me and started telling me what had happened.

My dad used to own a car repair business and was a car enthusiast. He had restored cars for wealthy classic car owners and was familiar with Rolls-Royce, so he enjoyed the ride to the pub and back.

He told me Jimmy was a fantastic man, unlike the public persona. They had a deep and meaningful conversation about life, trials, challenges, and dreams. My dad learned that Savile had worked in the coal mines as an 18-year-old and that he had been injured in an explosion that broke his spine.

He said this was why Savile was interested in Stoke Mandeville's spinal injuries unit. Jimmy told my dad how much he hated going down into the pits and how one day; while walking home, a Rolls-Royce drove past him, splashing him with water from a puddle. At that moment, Jimmy said he had decided to leave the pit and get his own Rolls-Royce.

I do not doubt that Jimmy Savile helped my dad that evening. He saw how depressed my father was and took him out to give him some space from the hospital to relax and enjoy a beer and a chat. We did not see Savile for a couple of months after that.

It was early summer, a lovely sunny day. I was in my wheelchair inside the ward, looking through the double doors to the garden outside, where three other patients were sitting in their wheelchairs on the lawn. To get to them, you could walk through the doors and down the steps, but for me, it would have required a considerable effort to push myself about 200 yards through the hospital, then outside and across the car park. In my condition, I did not have the strength to get much further than the end of the ward on my own.

Jimmy Savile arrived in a bright red tracksuit and sat on the grass, chatting with the lads outside. Angelo, the gigantic Caribbean hospital porter, noticed that I wanted to be out on the lawn with the others. He called over his fellow porter, a muscular Moroccan man with a mop of fuzzy hair, to help him.

With the ward's boss, the fearsome Welsh sister Sister Humphries, overseeing the task, the two of them picked up my wheelchair with me in it and carefully carried me down the steps to the garden. Finally, I was able to join the conversation with Jimmy and the others. Savile stood up and said he would be back in 10 minutes. When he returned, he had four ice creams, handing one to each of us. After about 20 minutes, he said, "Goodbye, guys, I've got to go."

The E-Type Jaguar

A couple of weeks later, three of us lads were sitting in the car park by the hospital entrance, soaking up some sun and watching the comings and goings, when Savile arrived in his E-Type Jaguar. He walked over from the parked car and joined us for a chat, sitting on a bench beside us.

After a while, he said, “Wow, it’s a scorching day. Who fancies coming down the pub for a pint?”

There was a wheelchair-accessible pub five minutes down the road. I explained that I could not go – I was not allowed to leave the hospital grounds because my neck injury was still very delicate, and I was still wearing a collar. Sister Humphries would kill me if she caught me leaving in Jimmy’s car.

The other two lads were further along in their recovery than I was, with lower spinal injuries stronger with full use of their arms and more able to take on a journey in the car. Savile got the first chap into the Jag, folded his wheelchair, and off they went. He dropped him at the pub and returned for the second guy, but this lad could not get into the Jaguar.

Jimmy then ran across the car park to where a yellow Triumph Herald was parking. A young nurse got out of the car, just arriving for work. Savile did his customary yodel, put his arm around her, turned her around, and whispered in her ear. When he let her go, she walked into the hospital, smiling and laughing over her shoulder at him. He came back to us, stopped, and raised his hand triumphantly, saying, “How’s about that then, guys and gals?” In his hand were the keys to the Triumph Herald. With its wider door and higher roof, he was able to get the other lad in and took him off to the pub.

The burnt boy

I met Jimmy Savile again later that summer. It was a Sunday, and a group of us were sitting outside in our wheelchairs by the hospital entrance, soaking up some sun. Savile was coming out of the hospital and saw us sitting there. He came over and sat on a bench beside us. After a few minutes, he explained that he could not stay long – he was officially on his way to open a garden fête nearby. As he began to walk away, an elderly couple entering the hospital noticed him. The lady, who must have been in her 70s, shouted, “Oh, oh, Mr Savile!”

He must have been used to this because at once he turned and smiled at her. She grabbed her husband’s arm and dragged him over to Savile. “Oh, Jimmy, I’m so pleased to see you. I wonder if you would be so kind – my grandson is in Ward 9. He was severely burned in a fire. It would make his day if you could come and say hello to him," she said excitedly. Without hesitation, he stopped, turned, and gave us a knowing wink – he knew this would make him late for the fête. He put his arms around the couple's shoulders and hustled them back into the hospital, saying, "Let's go and see your boy."

That was the last time I ever saw Jimmy Savile.

Military hospital

Stoke Mandeville Hospital Spinal Injuries Centre had been a military hospital during WWII and was converted to a spinal unit in 1944. When I arrived on 4 February, 1973, it was little more than a rundown wooden barracks-style building, barely holding itself together.

Over the following years, I learned that Savile raised £40m for Stoke Mandeville. His efforts helped build the new ultramodern Spinal Unit, the National Spinal Injuries Centre (NSIC), and the St Francis Ward, a dedicated space for children and teens with spinal cord injuries. NSIC is renowned internationally for pioneering work treating spinal injuries in adults and children worldwide.

CHAPTER 9
EMMA

I saw Emma walking into the ward, her tall frame moving with long, confident strides. She was close to six feet tall, dressed in dark blue trousers and a crisp white physio shirt. She was not what you would call beautiful, but undeniably pretty. Her shoulder-length black hair, bright blue eyes, and pale skin were shiny and healthy. She was slim, with large, firm breasts that made her shirt stretch tight across her chest – no bra, and it was an impressive sight. Always bubbly and cheerful, her broken English spoken with a charming Scandinavian accent, she was enchanting to a young lad like me.

I was waiting beside my bed when Emma took the handles of my wheelchair and began pushing me down the corridor to an exercise room. For some reason, I was in a down mood that day, feeling sorry for myself. It did not happen often, but when it did, I lost all my motivation. I did not want to train or do anything. Emma noticed my mood and tried to cheer me up.

"Hey, young man," she said.

"What?" I replied, not interested. I was not feeling good that day.

"I met a nice young girl," she said, her tone playful. "Her name is Susan; she is 16 – the same age as you. She's just been admitted to Ward 6. I told her about the handsome rugby player I'm looking after in Ward 1, and she asked if she could meet you. Do you want to go and meet her?"

Suddenly, she had my attention. The thought of meeting a lovely young girl was an easy decision after weeks of being confined in a men's ward. "Yes, okay, let's see her," I said, perking up.

Emma pushed my wheelchair down the long corridor and eventually reached Ward 6. As we entered, I noticed the signs saying it was a burns unit. She pushed me up to a bedside, and at once, I was horrified.

"Roger, say hello to Susan. Susan, meet Roger, the handsome rugby player I've been telling you about," Emma chirped.

I caught a glimpse of Susan's red lips through the bandages that covered her head. One of her eyes was visible, surrounded by raw, red skin, while the other was covered. Her left arm, shoulder and chest were wrapped in bandages, and her right hand was heavily dressed. This poor girl, I thought. It was shocking – nothing like what I had expected. I felt terrible, even sick. My mate Dave was recovering from severe burns at the time, so I knew how much pain and torture that involved. I felt sure Susan must be enduring the same excruciating experience.

I forced a smile and said, "Hello, Susan. It's lovely to meet you. My goodness, what happened to you?"

She could not speak very well, so Emma answered for her. "Susan was in a house fire. She was very severely burned, but we're going to help her get better, aren't we, Susan?"

Susan smiled with her one visible eye.

On the way back to the ward, I could not help but ask Emma, "I cannot believe it… that poor girl. Will she be okay?"

Emma replied, "She's got a steep path ahead of her. Her burns are severe. She'll be scarred for the rest of her life. She might lose eyesight in one eye, and we're hoping we can help her regain the use of her left arm."

I sighed and looked at her. "Emma, you did that on purpose, didn't you? Was it shock therapy?"

Emma did not deny it. "Roger, I just wanted to remind you that there's always someone worse off than you, okay?"

"Yeah," I replied quietly.

Standing tall

One evening, Emma came to my bedside. She was not in uniform – she was wearing regular clothes, and she was with a man who must have been in his early 40s. My mum and dad sat beside me when Emma introduced him as Bernard.

He was standing, though I could tell he could not walk correctly. He was not entirely "normal", but he stood there for several minutes, talking to us quite well. He explained that he had broken his neck in a car accident two years earlier and that, at one point, he was in the same situation as me – paralysed.

But he got better, and now he was up and able to walk unaided. I was impressed. In my new reality, he was a superhero.

By then, I had come to terms with the fact that I would not be running around again. But to be able to walk and stand as he did – that would be a big win for me from where I was at that moment.

Hard goodbyes

Towards the end of my stay at Stoke Mandeville, I was allowed to go home for weekends. Some of those weekends I spent at my girlfriend's house. Leaving my wheelchair at the front door, her father would pick me up and carry me inside, placing me on the sofa and later carrying me up the stairs to put me in Victoria's bed. She or her dad would take care of my urine bottles, wash me and help me dress and undress. Her mum would feed me and bring me cups of coffee. It was a warm and safe place, and I enjoyed it so much – what was there to complain about?

Gradually, one by one, each patient went home. Departures were emotional. We had spent such sensitive time together, building relationships based on a collective understanding of each other's bad fortunes. Watching them being wheeled out of the ward for the last time, with their attentive family pushing their new wheelchair, sitting awkwardly, trying to wave goodbye, forcing a smile… it was poignant. We all knew they were leaving this safe, comfortable place to face the toughest journey of their lives out in the world, wondering how they would cope. And we knew we probably wouldn't meet again.

Mended, not recovered

I am not sure you ever really recover from something like this. Your bones mend, and your body heals as far as it can. I had accepted my fate and what had happened to me. I acknowledged it, adjusted, and adapted to the consequences, but I do not think you can call that recovery.

To recover something means to get it back, right?

What I had was more of an exchange. I got something different back; I became a new version of myself. I had lost so much. My strength, my physical ability, my education, my dreams of being a professional sportsman – dreams of anything that involved my physical power – all gone. Even the chance of becoming a father one day – you can never feel good about that. It's a trade-off for not dying. I simply had to carry on.

I called it surviving. My life had been knocked off its tracks, and I had to get it back on track. But I would never be the same again – I just had to learn to live with my new, weaker body.

CHAPTER 10
HOME

I finally left Stoke Mandeville Hospital for good after about 10 months of full-time treatment. My neck had mended as much as it could, and I had gone as far as I could go there. I was able to stand and take a few steps on crutches, but I still needed my wheelchair to get around.

Returning home to Maidenhead to live with my parents was a new chapter. What I needed now was intensive rehabilitation to work on my movement and strength and to get back on track with my education.

Life after the hospital and attending the rehabilitation centre turned out to be a surprisingly enjoyable time for me. I was recovering quickly, making new and interesting friends, and reconnecting with my old social circle. They had all evolved to accept the latest version of me, and it was a relief to realise that many of the things I feared losing were still there.

I could still have girlfriends, my mates still took me to the pub, to parties, even to rugby matches. Most of the obstacles I feared would stand in the way of my old life were managed, one way or another, and together, we always found solutions.

It was March 1974, my 17th birthday, and I was having a small party with a few close friends. Christine, an ex-girlfriend, brought along a lumbering hulk of a lad named Marty. He was Irish, 16, tall and muscular, with a thick wad of reddish-blond hair that all the girls loved.

He looked awkward, sitting alone in the corner, not knowing anyone. The rest of us were old friends, tight-knit, and he did not fit in. Without asking, he changed the record on the player, which was a bit bold for someone no one really knew. Then he placed his drink on my brand-new Pink Floyd LP cover and spilt beer all over it. I went nuts. "What are you doing? Take your pint off that!" I snapped.

"Calm down, little fella, there's no harm done," he replied dismissively.

"Who are you, anyway?" I shot back.

My rugby mates stood up and surrounded me, and Marty quickly realised he was not welcome. Deciding that leaving was his best choice, he made a swift exit.

A few months later, I ran into him again at my local pub, the New Inn. With a sarcastic grin, he recognised me and said, "It's good for you that you can't walk; otherwise, I would've thumped you," and he laughed.

I could not help but fire back, "It's lucky for you, you mean, that I can't walk because I would've kicked your arse." We both laughed, and he bought me a drink. That night, a great friendship began.

A few months later, Marty and I decided to go to a concert by the famous African band Osibisa at Skindles, a riverside hotel in Maidenhead. Initially, I was hesitant, worried about the long night, the crowds, and my ability to stand for extended periods. I was still getting around on one walking stick and did not have the strength to stand for too long.

But Marty would not take no for an answer. "Come on, little fella, don't worry. I'll take care of you. We're going, OK?"

True to his word, he dragged a bar stool to the edge of the dance floor so I could sit when I got tired. I leaned my stick against it and tried to enjoy the show. The band was ripping, and the place was electric. Marty's girlfriend, Anne, was sitting on his shoulders, and they were both having the time of their lives, dancing and jumping around. Then Marty tripped and fell, and Anne landed on my wooden walking stick, snapping it in two. It was a catastrophe for me; I could not move without that stick. But we did not let it ruin the night. We carried on for the next two hours, with Marty eventually carrying me out to the car on his shoulders. From up there, I had a magnificent view of the band, and we were all soaked with sweat by the end of it. But hell, it was a great evening.

That night gave me an appetite for life, and my confidence was rushing back. One night, out with friends, I drank a bit too much. I was still learning my limits, but I went too far. I could not stand, let alone walk on my crutches. So, my friends did what any drunk mates would do – they found a supermarket trolley, sat me in it, and, laughing all the way, took turns pushing me the three miles home. My dad, always understanding, would carry me to bed, undress me, and take care of me in those wild, excessive days.

Around this time, my parents applied for a grant from the council to build an extension on our bungalow – a purpose-built accessible space just for me. It was meant to give me independence, with a wheelchair-accessible entrance, a private bathroom and a shower.

But it was a disaster. The builder was utterly incompetent. There was a 10-inch step from the footpath to the front door – a big problem for someone in a wheelchair. A light bulb dangled dangerously beside the shower head, and the work dragged on forever. The builder ran off, having already been paid, and my poor dad ended up doing most of the work himself.

1974 was a tough year. The country was in turmoil. Prime Minister Ted Heath's battle with the unions had led to a three-day working week, inflation soared to 16%, and power cuts were frequent. The price of petrol shot up, and there was rationing due to the OPEC oil embargo, a result of the Arab-Israeli war. Northern Ireland's troubles were flaring up, with the Provisional IRA bombing the British mainland.

I was back at school a couple of days a week, but trying to catch up after a year away was incredibly challenging. The teachers were good, but I had little hope of sitting my exams.

Despite the grim political and economic situation, culturally and personally, things were looking up. My friends were frequent visitors, taking me out to the pub for a beer on weekends. I was enjoying life in my new private space, my original purpose-built flat. I had a new National Panasonic hi-fi to play my latest albums – my room was filled with the sounds of *Crime of the Century* by Supertramp, *Stranded* by Roxy Music, *Tubular Bells* by Mike Oldfield – and I was reading great books such as *Chariots of the Gods?* by Erich von Däniken, *The Godfather* by Mario Puzo,

Caravan to Vaccares by Alistair MacLean. I had adapted to my new life on crutches, finding comfort and independence in the safety of our family home.

When I turned 17, I got my provisional driver's licence, and Social Services provided me with an Invacar. At the time, these little light-blue cars were the solution for disabled people who wanted to drive themselves around. It was a small, fibreglass three-wheeler powered by a 500cc motorbike engine. I could drive it with 'L' plates, load my wheelchair and crutches, and go off on my own. It was independence at last.

The Invacar was delivered brand new, shining on the back of a trailer. It was adapted with handlebars instead of a steering wheel and a unique accelerator and brake system that allowed me to drive it without needing much grip in my hands. To brake, all I had to do was press down on the handlebars. I spent that first day zooming around town quite happily.

That evening, I took the Invacar to the Horse & Groom pub in Cookham. I had a few beers with mates and proudly showed off my new toy. Come closing time, Steve asked for a lift home. Steve, a rugby back row forward, was 6'4" and a big, heavy lad. The Invacar only had one seat, so he sat on the floor. I sped out of the car park at about 11:15pm when the village was quiet, going to sleep.

Speeding down a narrow country lane, I took a right-hand bend a bit too fast. With Steve's weight to the left, the little car rolled onto its side, sliding through someone's front hedge and onto their lawn.

The two of us crumpled in a heap on the floor, laughing our heads off, until the panic set in. Steve climbed out the door facing the stars and quickly pulled the car back onto its three wheels. He jumped back in, and I reversed out of the driveway just as all the lights in the house came on. We escaped without being spotted and laughed all the way home. My father walked into my bedroom the following day, scratching his chin.

"What has happened to your Invacar? All the fibreglass is smashed at the front and down the left side."

I had to tell him the truth. He raised his eyebrows, shook his head and blew out a breath, grateful that I was still alive.

CHAPTER 11
REHAB

My sensation was very patchy. I had some feeling in parts of my body and none in others. I remember having to be incredibly careful when I put my foot in the bath because my right foot and leg still had no feeling at all. The water could be red-hot, and I would not know it.

I had some numb sensation in parts of my arms, and my hands and the rest were like dead meat. I could impress my friends by stubbing out cigarettes on parts of my arm or my elbows or hands. My hands were not working, and I could not straighten my fingers; I had a very light grip; I could hold a beer can, fortunately, but I could not hold anything small; I still could not grip a pen. I had my leather wristband, which I could use to keep my toothbrush, and I also used it to hold a pen, but my writing was terrible, like a drunken spider had crawled across the page.

In the summer of 1974, my sister wanted me to be Godfather to my niece Katie; this meant spending a long time in the church; my nurse suggested fitting a catheter with a urine bag attached to my leg, but I refused, I didn't want to be dependent on this, and now I had some feeling there, fitting one was very painful, inserting the tube up into my bladder through my penis.

My bladder was working; I had some sensation but not much control; it would only allow me seconds of holding it before the pee would arrive.

For the months after I left the hospital, I always carried a urine bottle with me to avoid wetting myself; I got to the point where I did not care who saw it. So, I took it to the church with me, and sure enough, I had to go. I got my dad to push me to the rear of the church, and while the congregation were singing, I took a satisfying pee into my bottle, took it outside and emptied it down a drain. Another milestone was reached: an entire day out far from a toilet, my independence was absolute.

On leaving the hospital, the education authority wanted me to return to school a couple of days a week to try to catch up with my lost fifth-year education. That was an 'O' level year, and I had missed all my exams. I was to be in the sixth form but, effectively, retake my 'O' levels. However, due to the topography at my school (it was not very flat), Furze Platt thought I would be better off going to Cox Green School because it had better wheelchair access. I did not want to attend that school; we used to thrash them at rugby, football, and basketball, and to me, it was a step down, not to mention that all my mates were still at Furze Platt.

Fortunately, my good friend Dave Gray offered to be my caregiver. We would be in the same class, and he would push my wheelchair and make sure that I could get to all my lessons. The school obliged by moving some of the classes to ground floor classrooms so I could attend.

I found the experience of returning to school a bit difficult, for just two days a week. I was not a good student anyway and had missed a year of studies. It was challenging to catch up. I hated being there. I was uncomfortable being 'the boy in the wheelchair'. With all those students and teachers watching me in my new fragile state, it was a reminder of everything I had lost, everything I was not.

In early 1974, I was fortunate to have been admitted to Farnham Park Sports Rehabilitation Center, a converted manor house that was considered one of the top sports injury rehabilitation centres in the world. It was run by Dr John Williams, who was internationally recognised as a pioneer in sports injury medicine and rehabilitation treatments.

While most people there were inpatients, I could be an outpatient because I lived nearby. An ambulance would pick me up in the morning and take me the eight miles to Burnham Beeches and Farnham Park Rehabilitation Center, and then later, it would take me home to my mum's cooking by dinner time.

I longed for those alternate three days a week where I could go to join other injured patients at the rehabilitation centre, patients who came from various backgrounds and situations, different ages, where we were all new to each other, all facing challenges, at various levels, from twisted ankles to terrible burns. Severely damaged by accidents, even recovering from strokes and cancer, some were amputees who had prosthetic limbs fitted and needed to learn how to walk or use their new artificial limbs.

One guy there had had his index finger surgically removed and relocated to where his lost thumb had once been. This was pioneering stuff in 1974. It was fascinating to meet so many people who had such a variety of catastrophic accidents and learn their stories, some tragically sad, some hilarious.

Fred lived in Cookham, a village quite close to my home. The ambulance would pick me up each morning, and then we would pick up Fred next. He would ride back home with me in the ambulance each evening. One evening, the ambulance was parked in the car park. We patients were all onboard and ready to leave, but there was no sign of Fred. The ambulance driver was eager to go, leaving us all waiting on the bus while he returned to the centre to look for him.

Fred was a triple amputee. He had been run over by a drunken driver late one evening. The driver quit the scene, leaving Fred in a ditch by the side of the road, broken and bleeding. The driver went home and went to bed. A guilty conscience got the better of him, and he reported the accident to the police at 9 o'clock the next day, by which time, he was sure that he would have sobered up enough to avoid a drunk-driving charge.

By the time they found Fred, he had haemorrhaged much blood. They had no choice but to remove both of his legs and his right arm. Fred was only 32 and was a father of three young kids.

He had progressed to walking with two prosthetic legs and one prosthetic arm. The prosthetic arm had a crutch permanently fixed to it, and he could hold another crutch in his good left hand. It was painful to watch him walk, seeing the strength and determination it took for him to take each step. It was excruciating, but he was such a determined man.

I looked out of the ambulance's window and saw Fred about 50 yards away, gainfully trying to stride his way to the waiting ambulance. I looked around, and the driver was nowhere to be seen. The Ford transit ambulance (minibus style) was parked with the engine running.

It had an automatic gearbox. I was seated in the front seat and could not resist the opportunity to slide into the driver's seat and reverse the Transit ambulance back about 30 yards to collect Fred. I could see a big grin on his face.

As I drew close to Fred, I saw the ambulance driver running towards me, shouting, "Stop!" All the passengers were cheering me on, and you would think I had just scored a goal in an FA Cup final. It was hilarious; even the ambulance driver smiled at me while helping Fred enter the ambulance.

One of the 'inmates' was Dave Bedford, English 10,000-metre world record holder and British record holder at 3,000 and 5,000 metres. He was famous then; we all recognised him on our TVs. He had run in the 1972 Munich Olympics, although he did not win anything. He was not amiable, as I remember; he had a high opinion of himself.

By contrast, another famous patient was much more friendly and amenable. One day, we were asked if we could all present a gift for a raffle to raise much-needed funds for a local charity. My mum had prepared a shopping bag full of groceries for me, which I took with me that morning.

We all gathered in the library. I presented my gift alongside my friend Mike; he was the guy I partnered with at the gym, and we helped each other with stress exercises and training. Occasionally playing snooker in the library, I would insult him for being such a terrible player, and he would insult me for being such a bad loser. He would sometimes join a gang of us for lunch at the local pub, the Green Man.

Later in the year, I could drive myself to Farnham Park with my Invacar (the blue three-wheeler). Often, I would see Mike's Citroën SM (Maserati) with him sitting in the passenger seat because his left ankle was smashed into bits, and he could not drive. I would get as close as possible and have a 'burn up'. I remember, on arriving, getting out of my three-wheeler in the car park and him admonishing me, telling me not to drive so stupidly that I would kill myself.

I looked at Mike's gift and was astounded. It was a gorgeous gold-framed oil painting of a motorbike racing around the Isle of Man TT track.

I said, 'Wow, Mike, I love your painting. Who is it?'

Surprised, he looked at me and said, "It's me, on my six-cylinder Honda, notching up the lap record around the Isle of Man." And he laughed.

I looked again at the painting, and I looked at him and said, "You are not 'that' Mike Halewood, are you?"

He laughed, "Yes, that's me."

I felt like an idiot. This was Mike from Holyport. He told me he had had a car crash.

I said, "Mike, you told me you had a car crash. You left out a bit of detail there, mate?"

He crashed his Yardley McLaren Formula One car at the German Grand Prix at Nurburgring in August.

I laughingly said, "I am sorry. I did not recognise you without your helmet and goggles."

He bought his new Lamborghini Miura in one day, to show us all, he was a true gentleman, a lovely man.

Known simply as 'Mike the Bike', I was so sad to learn of his death on 21 March, 1981.

Mike, along with his two children, left the family home in Tanworth-in-Arden in the Midlands to go to the local fish and chip shop for the evening meal. But on the way they collided with a lorry which made an illegal U-turn, his Rover hit it broadside. His young daughter Michelle was killed instantly; Mike sustained terrible injuries and died in hospital two days later, but his young son, David, received minor injuries and survived.

The man who conquered the terrifying Isle of Man so many times, who raced in Formula One through its most dangerous era, was killed in a stupid road accident.

This day began with occupational therapy. Even here, Dr Williams had devised ingenious ways to exercise. He had designed peddle lathes. We would propel the lathes using our injured limbs while turning wooden fruit bowls and candlestick holders. The 'hydrotherapy' pool was next. It was always fun because the fit young lady instructors would get in the pool in their swimsuits to help work my legs.

After lunch, I walked into the gymnasium with my two crutches. My physiotherapist was a young blonde Canadian girl, hard as nails, but very pretty. She had been training me, helping me restore strength and mobility, and eventually walking and balancing on one walking stick.

That day, she asked me if I would like to go outside for a walk. It was a lovely sunny day, so we set off for the nearby golf course. At first, I found it relatively easy, but I was pretty exhausted after making it to the first hole. I lost my balance and fell into one of the bunkers, the sand traps.

I woke up in the back of an ambulance with my very worried Canadian physio attending to me. I was taken back to the rehabilitation centre. I had pushed myself so hard. I passed out from exhaustion. They treated me with an IV drip and took me home early.

From that day onwards, I only ever used a single walking stick. Now, there was not much more they could do for me. I was still young and growing, and my body naturally became stronger each day. My lifestyle would ensure I pushed myself continuously from thereon.

I attended Farnham Park for eight months. I made some great friends and was proud of the progress I achieved there. I went there in a wheelchair, managed to walk on two crutches, and left needing only a single walking stick.

From now on, though, I had no more institutional safety, cosseting, or caring, no more professional help or guidance. I was back out into the world, my turn to compete in the race of life.

CHAPTER 12
18P A DAY

Our school rugby team was outstanding; we beat all the others in our district. The only one that ever beat us was Maidenhead Grammar School, and that was only when we played them at their place and their sports master was the referee. He interpreted the rules of the game differently than we did. It was difficult for him to accept that a bunch of lads in the comprehensive school could be better than his chosen boys, but we were.

I came across the same grammar schoolmaster at the England schoolboy trials. Two of us lads playing in the position of blind-side flanker, me and Michael Bennet, who attended Maidenhead Grammar. Michael was a talented player, but I knew he was not as good as me, you know these things when you're lads; no disrespect, he was a powerful and an excellent player, but he was one-dimensional, I believed I was better.

The selection process worked thus – one of us would play in the first half; the other in the second. I played in the first half. I had a great game and in a loose maul, about 10 yards out on the opponent's touchline, I managed to pick up the ball, break my way through about six players and score a touchdown under the posts.

In the second half, Michael took my position. He had a good game, too, but he did not score. So, I was disappointed, but not surprised, when he was selected ahead of me. It was his sports master who was one of the five members of the selection committee.

I give full credit to Michael; he played a good game.

I will never forget the guilt on that master's face that day when I looked at him dead in the eye, and again when I saw him several times in the future.

I was invited to join Maidenhead Rugby Club by my sports

master at Furze Platt school, along with four boys on my team. We all joined Maidenhead RFC. The club had an excellent reputation and produced five teams weekly, occasionally a sixth. We were in the fourth team, considered a good team; each player was either a former excellent and experienced player on the older side or a younger, up-and-coming player. The fifth and sixth teams usually consisted of the guys who just wanted an excuse to enter the bar after the game.

We played home matches at Braywick Sports Ground and travelled for away games. The club operated very well, providing training sessions, a full kit, excellent changing room facilities and good support for staff, ground and referees.

Compensation

As explained in earlier pages, I had great dreams and ambitions. I genuinely believed I would go to Australia and play professional rugby league. I loved the game and planned to make it my lifetime's work.

Through no fault of my own, my dreams were smashed when the accident happened. I am entirely at peace with the events that occurred that day; we were all boisterous lads playing a hard game; some people may have got too aggressive, some people may have got over-enthusiastic, it could have been me, but whatever happened. I accepted it, and I have lived with it.

But it is obvious that these situations are made easier with compensation. Insurance usually covers the catastrophic damage, injuries and losses that unfortunate accident victims endure.

I realised I was now facing a lifetime of disability, not knowing if I would ever walk again, if I would be able to have children, or even how long I would live. For sure, I was going to need a wheelchair, at the very least, walking sticks and crutches; my hands were paralysed, and my education derailed. I had endured a lot of pain and suffering in the process.

So, my parents were quite confident that a large insurance payout was just around the corner and that all this anguish, anxiety and fear about my future would soon be extinguished by a financial payout from the rugby club's insurance company. Our solicitor was a member of our club; in fact, he was in my team and played in the game when I had my accident; he was there and saw what happened to me, so we were confident that he would soon come back to us with a very worthwhile settlement.

After a few years, I finally received a payout from Maidenhead Rugby Club's insurance company. The amount I was given to carry me through the rest of my life, well from age 15 to 65, was 18 pence a day.

They had concluded that all my pain and suffering and the damage to my young body, my destroyed prospects were worth just £3,250. That was my nest egg to help me tackle the rest of my life.

According to our solicitor, I was not covered by the policy, which he claimed only covered loss of limb. The small amount was representative of my inability to use my right hand.

My parents were shocked and broken by this. They had thought I would receive a substantial amount, enough to buy myself a house at least, to invest and support me for the future. But no, I had just enough to buy a new Ford Cortina.

I told them angrily, "Do not worry about me. I will make my own money and look after myself."

I had no contact with the rugby world after 1975; Maidenhead Rugby Club did not follow up to see how I was doing.

Many years later a charity for injured rugby players was launched, SPIRE (Support Paraplegics in Rugby Enterprise). It was set up by Ian Beer, who was the president of the RFU at the time.

The purpose was to support catastrophically injured rugby players in any way possible. They contacted every player who had suffered a rugby injury, which had resulted in some form of paralysis to offer support. This was the first time I received any tangible help; they offered financial support in the form of small grants and gifts.

In 2008, RFU and SPIRE got together and formed a new charity called the RFU Injured Players Foundation (IPF). A board of trustees included former SPIRE trustees and new individuals appointed by the RFU, who had expertise in spinal rehabilitation. This innovative approach enabled the charity to respond much more quickly to reports of serious injuries and provide assistance from the moment the RFU was notified of an injury. The RFU committed to supporting the charity with the use of its offices, and a substantial donation each year.

In recent years, I have received financial support from the IPF, that has enabled me to buy expensive wheelchairs and other support equipment. They also provided me with tickets to England games free of charge, reigniting my faith in and love of rugby, after so many years away from the game.

CHAPTER 13
WORK

It was early 1975, and I was 17. I woke up with a knot in my stomach, a mix of excitement and nerves. Today was one of the scariest days of my life, my first job interview. If things went well, I would soon start my first real job, a significant step toward the independence I was striving for. After years of dependence on my parents and social security, the prospect of earning money and carving out my path was exhilarating. But, as I thought about what lay ahead, I felt the cold grip of fear.

I had no decent qualifications. Most of my friends from school were going for similar jobs, but they had at least three or four 'O'-levels, some with five or six, and 'A'-levels, including essential subjects like Math, English and the sciences. But I had spent my exam year in the hospital, missing out on what should have been the most critical year of my education.

By the time I returned to Furze Platt School, I had only six weeks of part-time studies, and even then, I was still in a wheelchair.

The school had "assessed" me, but not in the way that really mattered. They couldn't assess me for 'O'-levels, only for CSEs (Certificates of Secondary Education). I ended up with a paltry English CSE and a Technical Drawing CSE, which felt like consolation prizes for kids who hadn't quite made the cut. CSEs were seen as second-rate by employers; it was the 'O'-levels and 'A'-levels that truly carried weight.

After leaving Furze Platt School, I wasn't ready to let that be the final word on my education. I enrolled in evening classes at Windsor and Maidenhead College, determined to prove to myself and the world that I could do better.

Over the course of a year, I earned my English 'O'-level and an

Art 'A'-level. It wasn't easy, but it was worth it, a step closer to reclaiming my future on my own terms.

I was nervous, I felt completely unprepared. I hadn't learned anything of real value, and to make matters worse, my hands were still partially paralyzed. I couldn't hold a pencil properly, my handwriting was atrocious, and I couldn't even walk without crutches. How was I supposed to be of any help in an office? I couldn't carry things, move furniture, or even fetch the boss a cup of tea. I felt utterly useless.

My mum could see the nerves written all over my face. She made me coffee and toast, straightened my tie, and offered words of encouragement to boost my confidence.

"Roger, you're an extraordinary person," she said, her voice full of belief. "Any business would be lucky to have you. You are clever and strong; your willpower, good looks and charisma will carry you through this. You will be fine."

She continued, "You will achieve remarkable things in your lifetime. Today is just the beginning. Think of it as another small bean bag – throw it out there and go pick it up."

She hugged and kissed me as I stepped out the door.

I tripped

I drove my Invacar 12 miles to Reading and parked on double yellow lines outside the railway station. I carefully exited the car, took out my crutches, and straightened my new suit. I had to be sure not to fall over, especially not here in the city centre. Slowly, carefully, I made my way from the station across the main road to Foster Wheeler's forecourt in front of their towering office building in the heart of Reading.

My long, shoulder-length hair clashed with the sharp lines of my black pinstripe suit, but that was not what people were staring at. They were watching this young man, plodding along on crutches, wearing high platform shoes, dragging his heavy feet across the paving stones, as he made his way into the glassy tower of commerce that was Foster Wheeler's head office, one of the world's leading engineering firms in the oil industry.

I was not particularly interested in oil or engineering. What mattered to me was the job I was applying for, an apprentice model maker. I envisioned learning the craft, the trade and the art of making models, even if they were of oil refineries. The thought of being paid to acquire a new skill was all I needed to keep going.

Inside the reception area, my heart was pounding, and I was breathless from the walk. The nerves were overwhelming. I introduced myself at the desk, and a lady acknowledged my appointment, instructing me to take the lift to the fourth floor.

I made my way to the lift, standing there nervously, trying to catch my breath as a small crowd gathered. When the lift doors opened, people began filing in. Some offered to let me go first, but I declined, preferring to wait until everyone else was in. I did not want to risk someone bumping into me and knocking me over.

Eventually, everyone was inside, facing out toward me, waiting for me to enter. I took one step, then another, but the toe of my right platform shoe caught the lip of the lift floor, which was not quite flush with the level of the foyer. I tripped and fell forward, my face plunging into a gentleman's groin. He caught me under the arm before I hit the ground and, using all his strength, lifted me upright. I could not help but notice his gold watch, expensive wool suit, and shiny leather shoes. This was a well-turned-out chap, I thought.

Finally upright, we stood face to face. Embarrassed and breathless, I said, "Thanks, mate."

He was pretty old, with suntanned, wrinkled skin and wavy silver hair. In an American accent, he replied, "Are you okay, son?"

Still reeling from my embarrassment and surprised by his accent, I replied, "Yes, no harm done. Thanks again for saving me – that was a good catch."

He laughed, "So, do you work here at Foster Wheeler?" he asked.

"No, not yet, but I hope to by next week. I am here for an interview today," I said.

"What's your name, and what job are you interviewing for?" he asked.

I told him, and he said, "Good choice, Roger."

The lift doors opened on the fourth floor, and the human resources manager was there to meet me. As I stepped out carefully, the suntanned gentleman in the expensive suit put his foot forward to stop the lift doors from closing. He shook my hand and said, "Roger, it was great to meet you, son. I have no doubt you will get this job today, and I hope we will meet again."

"Thanks very much. Goodbye," I replied, still a bit in shock.

He stepped back into the lift, and the doors closed. The HR manager, a man in a light grey suit that was too tight on him, looked at me with surprise and curiosity.

"Ah, do you know Mr Delgado?" he asked.

"Sorry, who?" I replied, confused.

"The gentleman who was just talking to you as you got out of the lift," he clarified.

I laughed as I explained, "No, he just caught me when I fell over a couple of minutes ago."

"Well, he just happens to be our worldwide Group CEO. He is visiting from the USA, so that was a fortuitous meeting for you," he said.

New wheels

Mum was right again – I got the job. It was my first full-time employment, and I was now an apprentice model maker, earning £25 a week.

I got my provisional driver's licence as soon as possible, and dad took me to look at some second-hand cars. With £300 in hand, I bought a used Vauxhall Viva SL90. It was automatic, and I still remember the registration: TOO 333E.

Dad, ever the expert in everything, took on the role of a driving instructor. He believed there was no need to waste money on a professional when he could teach me. I had already gained some experience driving the Invacar, but this did not require a full car licence, only a motorbike licence with 'L' plates. Driving the Viva was different, I had to pass the test like anyone else.

I failed my first test for overtaking an ambulance on a bridge, but I passed at my second attempt.

Finally, I could return that embarrassing, ugly, light-blue fibreglass three-wheeler, the Invacar, with a note of thanks. Driving a real car was a massive step forward; another bean bag reached.

My girlfriend Victoria's cousin, Martin, who also worked in Reading, took the train daily. We decided to carpool, I would drive, and Martin would chip in for petrol, £3 a week. Now 18 and with my first proper car, I drove it like any other 18-year-old, fast and carefree. But the daily 25-mile commute to Reading soon took its toll. The engine exploded one evening when racing a Morris 1100 down the A4. We drifted to the side of the road and parked up in a lay-by.

Dad decided it was time for me to invest in a newer, more reliable car. He did not want me to deal with old bangers breaking down on me. We went to look at his friend's garage, where I found a one-year-old Austin 1300 automatic. Dad got me a great deal, and now I had a reliable, presentable car. The freedom that came with it was exhilarating, driving down to the coast and exploring far and wide with my mates. It was a taste of the adventure I craved.

But, after three months at Foster Wheeler, I decided to quit. As an office junior, I spent most of my time in the filing office, searching for microfilms for the draftsmen in the technical drawing department.

When I questioned my role, I was told I needed to complete six months in all departments before settling into the model-making department. I was not prepared to wait. The cost of driving back and forth daily ate up half my salary, and I had learned nothing of interest – least of all model making or design. I was bored stiff.

Mentor

Then I saw an ad for a Design Studio Junior in the *Maidenhead Advertiser.* It piqued my interest, a chance to do something involving art. Infotech was a publishing company that produced brochures, manuals and direct marketing materials for the then fledgling computer industry. Their office was in Maidenhead town centre, just a few minutes from home.

I had just earned my Art 'A'-level from attending night classes at Windsor College, and I hoped it might be enough to land the job. The man who interviewed me was Adam, one of the directors, a young Canadian aged about 27.

"Roger, do you mind me asking about your disability and why

you need walking sticks?" he asked, surprising me with his directness.

I smiled, appreciating his forthrightness. I explained how my accident had left me needing crutches to walk and how my hands were still partially paralysed, making it difficult to hold a pencil. I told him how my time in the hospital and rehab had affected my education and how I had once hoped to go to college to study fashion and shop window design, but could not due to my lack of qualifications.

Adam nodded thoughtfully. "OK, Roger, I will offer you this job, but I want to train you as a mentor. I do not work in your department, but I will spend a few hours a week with you after work in the studio to teach you typography and graphic design. Do you agree to that?"

"Hell yes, that is fantastic! Thank you, Adam. Thank you so much," I replied, thrilled.

He smiled and said, "I'll teach you more in six months than you'd learn in three years at college."

As I drove home, a grin spread across my face. I could not wait to tell mum and dad about my success. They had been dismayed when I walked out of my job at Foster Wheeler, but now I could say I was earning the same salary while getting a free education, and it was just around the corner, not 12 miles away.

I felt very satisfied with myself. I had made a bold move by resigning from my first job, but it paid off in several ways. During the day, I worked in the print shop and helped in the studio as a junior, producing overhead slides and primary artwork. Then, after 5:30pm, Adam would come in, spend 15-20 minutes at my desk with his books, and set me tasks to complete. He would leave, and I would stay as long as it took to finish the work, which he would check the following morning.

Adam taught me so much about graphic design. For the first time, I was genuinely enjoying my work. I liked the job and the people I worked with.

I went on holiday with Martin Bedwell, Victoria's cousin, that summer. We drove to Devon in my Austin 1300, now fitted with Minilite wheels and racing seats. We stayed with my aunt Doreen and my two younger cousins Julian and Nigel in Ilfracombe, just a short walk from the beach. It was my first long road trip in my car, and the sense of freedom was intoxicating. Driving more than 200 miles to the other end of the country with one of my best mates was the adventure I had always dreamed of.

Working at Infotech was great, but there was one thing I could not stand, everyone smoked. The studio manager, Ed, often had two or three cigarettes lit simultaneously in different ashtrays around the office. In the small room where I spent most of my time, a woman chain-smoked untipped Senior Service cigarettes, 40-60 a day. The air was thick with smoke, like a permanent fog, making me ill.

I had been with the company for about a year and had learned a lot, but the money was not much compared with what some of my friends were earning. I was restless. It was time to move on.

George Bishop was my inspiration

I saw a job in the *Maidenhead Advertiser* for a graphic designer, offering more money. It was at White Waltham, near home. I jumped at it, had the interview and started the following week.

I thought it would be a fun workplace – an aviation company had to be exciting, right? It was on the same airbase where my father had been stationed at the end of World War II. It was here that he and my mother met at an RAF dance in 1944.

ML Aviation Company specialises in designing and making aircraft handling equipment for the Ministry of Defence. But working with a bunch of retired RAF guys was, to put it politely, boring. My dream of being a graphic artist designing album covers and T-shirts was fading fast as I spent my days putting together catalogues on how to push a heavy trolley under an aircraft wheel.

Fortunately, my desk was next to an old gentleman named George Bishop. He was a hugely talented artist who painted in oils and watercolours but only used acrylics for his commercial work at ML Aviation.

He had previously worked on Jaguar car brochures and Airfix model box covers. I loved watching him paint and learning by observing his technique. He showed me how to mix and apply paints, use retardants and learn other tricks I had not learned in college.

George's paintings of Tornado fighters in combat, Harrier Jump Jets and Lynx helicopters landing on aircraft carriers in stormy seas were thrilling. These action-packed images, displaying ML Aviation's manufactured equipment, were used as corporate gifts for senior executives and hung in boardrooms worldwide.

But the work itself was far from thrilling. One day, my boss, an ex-RAF squadron leader with zero experience in publishing or design, asked me to make 350 name badges for delegates at an exhibition to be held the next day. I began stamping the names using our Dymo Label maker, the standard method in the '70s for making sticky plastic name labels.

I had done about 200 badges when the boss approached my desk. He checked them and said, "No, these will not do. I want you to make them on the bromide stencil machine."

This process was painstakingly slow, each letter had to be selected one at a time, exposed onto photographic paper, and then the name had to be cut out with a scalpel and stuck onto a pin badge. It would take ages to do even one name this way, let alone 150.

I said, "We cannot do that. It will take forever and cost a fortune in photo paper. These are name badges. We usually use the Dymo machine for these."

He angrily said, "Just do what I asked you to do!"

I looked at him, perplexed, and said, "Surely you're not serious?"

"Oh, I am deadly serious, boy. Do what I tell you to, or face the consequences," he said with a hard stare.

I never felt comfortable around him, and I didn't particularly appreciate how he treated George, a true gentleman who was exceptionally skilled and at the top of his craft. The disrespect he showed toward George was something I couldn't overlook.

I put the Dymo machine down, looked him in the eye, and said, "Tell you what, boss, you can do it yourself."

Everyone in the office stopped and stared, listening to the exchange. I picked up my things, looked around the room, and smiled at them as I said, "Goodbye, lads. Sorry, I cannot work for this man. Wish you all the best."

George smiled and clapped as I walked past him to the HR office to hand in my resignation.

I had no intention of wasting my life letting a little man push me around because he could. That day, I realised I already knew more than him. He was treading water in a job which he did not like, just to earn a salary. I was not going to do the same.

I knew my life was too precious to waste. I was desperate for adventure and excitement. So, when Marty, my Irish friend, invited me to go to Ireland with him, I could not wait to pack my bags and set off on the next journey.

CHAPTER 14
IRELAND

It was 1976, September had rolled in, and I found myself on a three-week holiday, wandering through Ireland with Marty. The Northern part of the island was entrenched in bloody conflict, with the IRA on one side, the Protestant Unionists on the other, and the British Army wedged in between, trying to keep the peace. But peace was elusive, and the bloodshed was at its peak – a bleak time.

I, an Englishman with a disability and his towering Irish mate Marty were an odd couple exploring the South – the Emerald Isle, as they call it. Marty was eager to show me his homeland, a place far removed from the violence of the North. Ireland, even then, was a deeply devout Catholic country where religion was the cornerstone of daily life. I was an outsider, an Englishman, yet I felt welcomed. The Irish people were warm and friendly, save for a few pubs in Dublin where Marty warned me to keep my mouth shut lest they discover my nationality.

Marty, who worked for his brother Bobby in the road construction business back in England, had borrowed one of Bobby's many cars – a 1959 Mercedes 180, a beautiful classic. This would be our chariot for the journey.

Ireland was everything I had imagined and more. The countryside was breathtaking, with ancient castles around every corner and many farmhouses still without electricity. Pubs dotted the landscape, each one a haven of music and laughter. I recall one town where five pubs stood in a row. The people were amazing – funny, generous, and endlessly cheerful. And, my God, could the men drink?

Our first week was spent at the farm of Marty's eldest brother, Patrick, in County Wicklow. Patrick was a farmer with about 60 cows and several fields of crops. It was harvesting time, and the local farmers worked like a cooperative, helping each other bring in the harvest. That day, it was Pat's turn. By 6:00am, several tractors had gathered in the yard, and the farmers were in Pat's kitchen being served a hearty breakfast by his wife – boiled cabbage, potatoes and thick slices of ham.

Pat had come into our room earlier, trying to wake us, but Marty and I had no intention of working in the fields. Pat was not having it. He stormed in and, with no warning, pulled out his dick and started pissing on Marty's bed.

"Jesus fucking Christ, are you mad?" Marty shouted, leaping out of bed and chasing Pat, who ran out into the yard, laughing.

Marty turned to me, "Come on, fella, we've got to help him."

I protested, "I'm not going to be much help, am I? What can I do on a walking stick? I'll stay here and read my book."

Marty, still in the spirit of Pat's prank, pointed his dick at me. I jumped out of bed, "Alright, I'm coming! You fucking Irish are all mad!"

We washed, dressed, and headed out to the yard, where the tractors were already leaving. Pat pointed to a huge blue tractor and said, "Alright, Roger, you're in this one. It is Flannery's. You'll drive down to the bottom field."

I looked at him, then at Marty, and laughed, "Yeah, right."

The step into the cab was chest height. "How the hell am I supposed to get in there?" I asked.

Pat and Marty grabbed an arm each and lifted me into the cab. Pat explained the pedals – right for go, left for stop. "It can't be easier than that, now, can it?"

I was terrified. The tractor was a monstrous machine, and I had no idea what I was doing. But I followed the tractor in front of me, bouncing around on the seat, shaking with fear. We left the yard, turned down a lane, and into a large field where a gang of lads began loading hay bales onto the trailer behind me.

By the end of the day, I had gotten the hang of it, driving slowly up and down the fields. The sun was shining, and it turned out to be a fun day after all. The day ended in a pub, Guinness all around.

Marty raised his glass, smiling at me, "Did you enjoy that? You did well there, Roger."

I felt exhilarated, even proud. I had taken part in this massive effort to bring in the hay. The camaraderie and friendliness were unique.

Off to church

The following week, we visited Marty's mother in Kilkenny. Mary had a small farm where she bred and trained eventing horses. She was a stout woman with a strong face and a kind demeanour. Devoutly Catholic, she insisted that Marty and I attend church with her on Sunday. Marty made it clear; this was no joke. It was essential to his mum that we would be seen at the service.

Reluctantly, I went. The quaint stone church stood at the edge of a rural village, and the experience felt entirely foreign to me. Locals arrived in cars, vans, Land Rovers, and even tractors, parking near the churchyard. Slowly, they filed inside, and the priest began his sermon. The collection plate made its way around, and when it reached me, I hesitated, unsure. Marty dropped in some coins and nudged me to do the same. It all felt so contrived, like a performance.

Where was God in all of this? Finally, the service ended, and I thought it was over, but no – now came the socialising, the congregation gathering outside, catching up, parading in their Sunday best. I understood it was a social network of sorts, binding the community together, but I still could not see God anywhere.

Thankfully, someone mentioned the pub, and one by one, the cars started to drive away.

The horse

The next morning, Marty took me to the stables. The vet was there, examining a pregnant mare that was gravely ill. He told Mary the horse was nearly ready for the knacker's yard.

Marty suggested taking her to the factory now, at least to get some money, but Mary disapproved.

The vet said, "Just don't let her lay down. If she's still standing tomorrow, she might have a chance." Marty handed me the reins and asked me to walk her down the lane. I raised my walking stick and laughed, "How am I supposed to walk a bloody horse?"

"She can't outrun you," Marty said, laughing. "Just pull on the rein, and she'll follow."

The mare was clearly unwell, but I did not want her or her foal to die. So, I took the reins and began to walk, the horse slowly following. But after about 80 yards, she stopped, refusing to move further. I tried everything – encouraging her, shouting, even pleading. Nothing worked. I stood in the middle of the lane, utterly stranded, when a voice startled me.

"Are you having trouble with your horse?"

I could not believe it; he appeared like a little leprechaun out of nowhere.

I said, "Yes I am, she won't move."

He came through a small gap in the hedge, and he took the horse by the rein. He said, "Here, lad, let me take her for you." He went to move the horse. "Come on now," but still she would not move even for him. The old gentleman was wearing wellingtons and a tweed jacket; he looked at me and said reassuringly, "If there is one thing a horse cannot resist, it is fresh grass."

He reached down, grabbed a thick handful of long green grass, and put it in front of the horse's nose. Sure enough. It got the horse's attention, and she turned her head, but only as far as she could without moving her legs.

He smiled at me as he tempted her again with the grass. But all she would do was reach out her neck. She did not move her legs. He sighed, looked at me, and said firmly, "okay, well, if there's one thing that a horse loves, it's the sight of the open field".

At this point, he dropped his handful of grass on the ground. He bent down and started to undo some old rotten ropes tying a large five-bar gate to the fence post. The gate had not been opened for many years because it was now well buried in the turf.

He struggled for several minutes as he tried to drag the heavy gate open wide enough that the horse could see through to the field beyond. He took the horse's head, pointed her to the open field, slapped her hindquarters, and shouted, "Go on, nag."

She did not move an inch. He looked back at me, smiled, and said, “I’ll give her a slap.” He swung a firm arm. And he smacked her hard on the arse; she did not move. He looked at me again, smiled, and said, “Would you like a cup of tea? My house is just around the corner.”

Leaving the horse, we walked a short distance to a quaint little cottage that looked like something out of a storybook. His wife, a plump woman in an apron, greeted us with a warm smile and offered me apple pie. We sat in their kitchen, chatting about Ireland, the horse, and my limp while chickens wandered in and out of the room. An hour passed before I remembered the mare.

“Oh my God, the poor horse!” I exclaimed, and we hurried back to the lane. But the horse was gone.

Back at the farm, I found the mare standing outside the stable.

Marty laughed, “What happened to you? The horse returned alone, and we thought you had vanished!”

I laughed, relieved. “Thank goodness for that. I thought I had lost her! I’ve been having tea and apple pie with your neighbours, the Fitzpatricks,” I said.

In 1976, we travelled all around that country. I met many interesting people, experienced incredible generosity, and enjoyed countless great pubs.

The Irish love to sing, dance and play music. That trip taught me a new kind of freedom, less about material things and more about community and sharing what you have with others.

CHAPTER 15
LOVE

Anne towered over me, both in height and intellect. She was 19, with golden hair that cascaded down her back like a river of sunlight and hazel eyes that sparkled like caramel in the summer sun. She could sing and play the piano and the guitar, but somehow, she did not know she was beautiful.

At 20, I was hopelessly in love with her. What set Anne apart from my other friends was that she did not know the boy I was before the accident, the strong, fast and cocky version of me. She only knew the wobbly, faint shadow that remained.

"Boy, are you coming to my house today?" she asked one day, with the same casualness that someone might use to invite a friend over for tea.

Anne treated me like I was normal. There was no trace of the pity or delicate concern I had grown so accustomed to from others who knew the path I had been forced to walk. To her, I was not the guy who had broken his neck playing rugby – I was just her boyfriend. I called her "Toad," partly to tease her but also because I did not want her to realise just how stunning she was. I feared that if she did, she might leave me.

Her kindness and innocence drew me in, and she became the centre of my universe for the next two years. We were inseparable, spending nights at each other's homes and sharing our lives.

Bedtime

Anne's best friend, Ingrid, was another blonde beauty, though she had blue eyes and a slightly shorter, more buxom frame. Anne often remarked that Ingrid was the prettier of the two, though I could not imagine anyone more beautiful than Anne. One weekend, when

Anne's parents were away, Ingrid came over for a visit. She wanted to go out on Saturday night, but Anne and I decided to stay in. Ingrid said she would see us the next day.

That night, Anne and I were fooling around on the sofa, but a petty argument led me to storm off upstairs, leaving her alone to watch TV. I was too stubborn to sleep in her mother's double bed, so I crawled into Anne's narrow single bed, still fuming. I fell asleep quickly, only to wake around 3:00am, needing the bathroom. My anger had subsided by then, and I decided to join Anne in her mother's room. It was pitch dark, and I did not want to wake her, so I quietly slipped into the warm bed beside her. Her body was naked and hot, and I snuggled up close, seeking comfort.

Then Ingrid turned over to face me. I froze, shocked to realise I was in bed with her, not Anne. Ingrid, clearly drunk, just laughed, urging me to continue my accidental caresses. My eyes adjusted to the darkness, and I saw her grin. Anne woke up and, upon turning on the light, saw the situation and leapt out of bed in a rage.

"Oh my God, what are you doing?" she screamed.

I stammered, "I thought it was you! When I got into bed, it was dark. I did not know Ingrid was here!"

Ingrid, still laughing, explained that she had shown up around midnight after a fight with her boyfriend and asked to stay. As the situation became more apparent, Anne started laughing too. Eventually, she invited me to stay in bed, but she made it clear that I was to behave myself. She climbed back into bed, positioning herself between us, and we fell asleep talking, the tension of the moment dissolving in shared laughter.

Go to work

It was 1977. In those days, life felt surreal. I had recently walked out of my tedious dead-end job at ML Aviation, spent a glorious time in Ireland with Marty, and now I was dating beautiful Anne, feeling an incredible sense of happiness. My lazy days were financed with unemployment checks, my time filled with drawing, painting, playing music and losing myself in art and dreams. One morning, my father interrupted my solitude.

"Are you going to get up or stay in bed all day?" he asked, irritation tinged with concern.

"Bed sounds good, don't you like the music, dad ?" I replied lazily, letting Pink Floyd's *Dark Side of the Moon* wash over me.

His response was stern. "You must get a job, son; you can't stay like this."

That conversation led to an unexpected job offer from my father's good friend, Burt Farr, a well-known local character, in his 70s with a red nose and a big belly. Burt owned a betting shop, among many other businesses, and despite my protests that I knew nothing about horse racing, he assured me that I could learn. The job was challenging, and the world of horse racing was exciting and that appealed to me. The salary was way better than anything I had earned before, so I took it. Soon, I was a turf accountant, managing bets and interacting with the colourful characters who frequented the shop.

Bookmakers often keep accounts with other bookmakers to lay off bets and manage risk. Burt had an account with William Hill, placing bets on races daily. He often gave me a list of horses and potential odds, instructing me to place bets on his behalf if those odds were available. Burt also taught me an important lesson: if strangers entered the shop and placed large bets, dependent on the odds, I was to lay the bet off with William Hill.

One day, the door opened, and I spotted a shiny black Porsche parked outside. A man in a suit – someone I had never seen before, which was unusual – entered the shop. He sat on one of the benches, reading the *Racing Post.* As the starter called the horses to the gate, the man approached the counter and quickly placed a £500 bet on a horse with 7/1 odds. That was a considerable bet in those days.

I took his bet and called William Hill using Burt's account just as the starting gun went off. I asked to place £600 plus tax on the same horse. With a professional account like Burt's, at William Hill, I was often allowed to place a bet a few seconds after the race started. I was thrilled when the horse won; my quick thinking gave Burt a £4,200 payout which covered the punters bet and earned him a £700 profit.

When Burt came in later that afternoon, I eagerly shared the story of my successful bet. He looked at me with his usual stern expression and said, "Well, that is your job." But as I left the office, he stopped me and said, "Well done today, boy," handing me £50, a massive tip for me back then.

Working for Burt was more rewarding than I could have imagined. I quickly became proficient at the job, and Burt, recognising my efforts, increased my responsibilities and salary.

I bought my uncle's 1972 Ford Capri 2000 GTXLR; it was Vista orange with a black vinyl roof and Rostyle wheels. I was living 'large', as we used to jest.

Burt even offered me the flat above the shop, a significant reward. Anne was thrilled at the idea of us moving in together, already planning our future with curtains and saucepans. But I was startled by my hesitation. Though I loved her, I was not ready to settle down, not yet. I had so much more I wanted to do. It was a realisation that hit me hard and explaining it to Anne was even more challenging. She took it as a sign that I did not love her, and it marked the beginning of a rocky period in our relationship.

CHAPTER 16
GERMANY

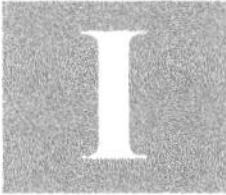n the autumn of 1978, a new chapter in my life opened when I received a brand new black Mini 1000 through the Motability Scheme.

It was one of the first cars provided under the scheme, and I could not wait to customise it with wide wheels.

That car symbolised freedom and adventure, and soon, adventure was calling in the form of a trip to Germany to visit Marty.

Martin Smith and I drove 600 miles non-stop to Heidelberg via Belgium and Luxembourg in the Mini, braving icy roads and freezing temperatures.

We had no plan, just the name of Marty's construction company and the hope that we would find him. After a futile search, we spent a freezing November night sleeping in the car, parked behind a luxury apartment building. Early the next morning, we were startled awake by a knock on the window.

A beautiful woman, wrapped in a heavy coat, stood outside. Through the frosty glass, I could see her concerned expression. She spoke to us in German, and when I explained in English that we were lost, she could see we were frozen, so she invited us into her warm apartment for coffee.

Martin and I looked at each other. We could not believe our eyes. What a fantastic place! It was modern, luxurious, friendly and warm, and this gorgeous lady cared for us. I looked at him and said, 'Talk about landing on your feet?'

He grinned and winking said, "It was my idea to park here."

Her name was Claudia, and she could not have been more kind. She fed us breakfast, offered us a place to shower, and even tried to help us locate Marty.

Eventually, we found Marty's VW camper van parked by a building site. He was stunned to see us and laughed at our foolishness for making such a trip in the dead of winter. We spent two days exploring Germany, sleeping in his van. For our last evening, we went to Heidelberg Marktplatz. Marty wanted to show us the beautiful market square with the massive, illuminated Heidelberg Castle dominating above. We sat in a beer house, drinking German lager and remembering past times, laughing and telling tales.

Martin had this wild mop of long, red, curly hair and I had just gotten my long black hair permed. It was the era when Liverpool and England footballer Kevin Keegan's hairstyle was all the rage, and we were right on trend.

We both wore these tight-fitting Italian Army shirts that we'd scored for next to nothing at an Army surplus store in Cologne. Feeling pretty pleased with ourselves, we cruised through the cobbled streets until we found a pub that caught our eye. It had this massive bay window with dimpled glass, coloured lights flashing, and music thumping from inside – it looked like a fun spot.

We parked the car, and with the help of my walking stick, I managed the short walk up the steps and into the pub. The place was packed and deafeningly loud. As two English lads, we felt out of place, but made a beeline for the bar to order a couple of lagers.

It didn't take long for things to feel a little off. The bartender was bare-chested, his black hair slicked back with grease, and he wore a big chain around his neck. Behind him, on the wall, was a calendar featuring a photograph of a naked man lounging on a sofa. I caught Martin's eye and nodded toward the calendar. He glanced over, then looked at the bare-chested barman, and a grin spread across his face.

We turned around to scan the room, and it hit us – there were no girls in the bar, not a single one. The penny dropped. No one bothered us, though; Martin and I probably looked like a couple. Martin grinned at me and said, "Okay, time to drink up and get out of here."

I nodded in agreement, and we made a quick exit, laughing as we hopped back into the Mini and continued on our way.

The Red Army Faction, that notorious left-wing terrorist group, was causing havoc in West Germany in 1977. Known more commonly as the Baader-Meinhof group, they were led by Andreas Baader and Ulrike Meinhof. Their mission was clear – they opposed the capitalist structure of West German society and the presence of US armed forces. They made their point through a brutal campaign of murders, bombings and kidnappings.

The next morning, with our quest completed, we set off on the long drive home. Martin and I were slowly driving down a city street, minding our own business, when out of nowhere, a black BMW and a black Mercedes-Benz came speeding up beside us. The Mercedes suddenly cut in front of us, forcing me to brake hard. Before I knew it, two men jumped out of the car. One had a pistol, the other a machine gun. The guy with the machine gun looked particularly menacing, draped in a long black coat that made him seem even more threatening.

They were shouting in German, barking orders for us to get out of the Mini. We were terrified, what the hell was happening? The man with the pistol reached in, snatched the keys from the ignition, and started rifling through the car. Then, he opened the boot to the rear, clearly looking for something. All he found were two rucksacks with our belongings. After a quick exchange of words with the other guy, he threw the keys back at me, and just as quickly as they had appeared, they were gone.

Later, we found out there had been a murder, and the police were looking for a car with foreign plates. With our UK registration, it was no wonder they pulled us over. It was terrifying to have guns pointed at us, but as we pulled away, the fear gave way to nervous laughter. It was one hell of a story to tell the lads at the pub when we got home.

Back in England, things with Anne became more strained. She was frustrated with my apparent lack of commitment while I was busy living in the moment, bowling, playing darts and hanging out with friends. The tension between us came to a head when I suggested we take a break. Hurt, Anne left for the south coast to start a new job. I missed her, but I figured we would eventually get back together. Life had a way of circling back, or so I thought at the time.

CHAPTER 17
BAKER STREET

It was a cold, wet Saturday morning in December 1978, and I was lying on my bed, feeling bored and missing Anne. I was playing my new Gerry Rafferty album, *City to City,* loud enough to fill the room. The song *Baker Street* was particularly captivating, taking me on an imaginative journey to a better place. I found myself singing along:

"Winding your way down to Baker Street,
Light in your head and dead on your feet.
Well, another crazy day,
You'll drink the night away,
And forget about everything."

The music inspired me to consider leaving my mundane life behind and starting anew. I felt an urgent need to move on.

Martin and I had such a fun trip to Germany in my Mini, and he felt the same boredom. He worked as a fitter at a local engineering company and had recently separated from his long-time girlfriend, Carol. We spent many nights at the Crooked Billet pub, drinking pints of bitter, playing pool, and feeding the jukebox with 50p pieces, all in an effort to forget our troubles.

That road trip through France, Belgium, Luxembourg and Germany inspired us. We often talked about sunny places and grand adventures.

One night, I told Martin, "I have got to get out of here. I want to see the world, and I will do it this time. Do you want to come with me?"

"Yeah, absolutely. Where are we going?" Martin asked.

"I fancy Greece; I want blue skies, sunny beaches, wine, women and song. I want to sit on the beach and draw portraits of tourists for money. We could find jobs in bars or something," I replied.

Martin suggested, "We could buy an old van, kit it out with beds, a cooker, a toilet, the works, and drive it down there. We could live in it."

"That sounds like a plan," I agreed. "Let's get a van and get started."

Martin soon found an old Commer BF, an ex-RAF bus that needed some work on the engine, but had a sound body. He drove it back from London to my house and parked it on the lawn. He started servicing the engine, checking the brakes and tyres.

My father thought we were mad, but understood our dream. He helped us by building a tube steel framework inside the bus, creating bunk beds, and installing a portable toilet, a cupboard, a sink, a small gas stove and storage racks.

Everything was coming together nicely.

However, that winter was harsh. The extreme cold caused the engine block to freeze and crack, making the bus beyond repair. We had resigned from our jobs weeks earlier to work on the bus and were living off dole money. We ended up selling our equipment at a loss and eventually sold the non-running bus to some gipsies for £10. It was heartbreaking.

We were jobless, broke and stuck in England for another freezing winter. Martin's father reminded him that he had an uncle in the USA. After some phone calls, Martin's uncle Frank, who lived in sunny Pensacola, Florida, invited us to stay with him. Our dream was reignited. America, what could be better? We were thrilled. I had some savings, about £800, and Martin sold his car and motorbike, amassing about the same amount. We figured this would last us a month, and we would have a momentous time.

My dad was pleased with our alternate plan. He understood our need to escape. However, my mother was apprehensive about my physical disabilities. "How are you going to manage on buses and hitchhiking with your bag and that walking stick?" she asked.

I smiled and reassured her, "Do not worry, mum. We are going to the USA, not the jungles of Africa. We'll be fine."

Martin added, "Don't worry, Betty. I'll look after him. We'll stick together, no matter what."

Following the launch of Skytrain by Freddie Laker in 1977, British Airways introduced heavily discounted standby tickets – perfect for Martin and me. We were flexible with our schedule and waited at Heathrow Airport for two available seats.

Luckily, we secured tickets on the first day, 9 February. We boarded a brand-new Boeing 747, the Jumbo Jet, heading to Miami. It was our first time on an aeroplane, and in 1979, this colossal plane was the epitome of modern aviation. We were flying in it, embarking on an epic journey around the world.

CHAPTER 18
USA

ith my walking stick firmly in my right hand, my rucksack securely on my back, and proudly sporting my new blue leather loafers, we made our way to immigration.

A stern black woman in uniform approached me, her tone brisk as she asked, "What's your reason for coming to the United States?"

"Holiday," I replied without hesitation.

She continued, "Do you have sufficient funds to sustain yourself?" I assured her I did, explaining that I was staying with relatives. With a large thump on the desk, I was granted a three-month visa.

Back in those days, we carried traveller's checks, and before leaving Heathrow on 9 February, 1979, we exchanged some pounds for US dollars at the bank's currency exchange.

During the flight, we struck up a conversation with a couple of girls who were curious about our destination.

"Pensacola," we told them. As we left the terminal in Miami, their friend picked them up in a minivan, and they kindly offered us a lift to the Greyhound bus station. My first impression of Miami was that it resembled Bracknell, but with sunshine.

I am not sure what I expected, but the biggest impression was the enormous American cars, the distinctive accents and the lovely, warm weather.

They dropped us off at the bus station, where we navigated our way to the ticket desk. We were a bit taken aback to learn that Pensacola was 700 miles away and would take at least 12 hours by bus. We quickly decided to break the journey in Fort Lauderdale, just 40 miles away, and continue the next day.

After being dropped off, we found a motel just a short walk

from the bus station. It was cheap – only $12 a night – and even came with a vibrating bed. Insert a quarter into the slot, and the bed will shake you to sleep.

As we settled down in our room, we heard the roar of a noisy V8 engine and squealing tyres. We stepped outside the door and saw a red Camaro doing a burnout in the parking lot. A couple of lads, probably the same age as Martin and me, were having a momentous time; we looked at each other and smiled. This was, indeed, another world.

The next day, we returned to the Greyhound station and bought tickets to Tallahassee. Martin had spoken to his uncle, who suggested meeting us there and driving us the rest of the way to his home in Pensacola. The entire journey would take nearly 15 hours, but we did not mind; we could sleep on the bus.

Greyhound buses were the most affordable way to travel long distances in the US. You could get pretty much anywhere on one, but because they were so cheap, they attracted a wide variety of characters. To the casual observer, Martin and I might have looked American, but as soon as we opened our mouths, people quickly realised we were English. Tourists were not common in 1979, especially in the southern states, where black people were much more noticeable than in the UK.

One of our closest friends, Glenn, was a black man from the US, so we were not unfamiliar with this, but what shocked me was the stark racism. Blacks seemed to hate whites, and whites seemed to hate blacks. So, when it came time to choose a seat on the bus, people were surprised when I happily sat next to a black person.

On one occasion, a group of black lads tried to intimidate me into moving. Perhaps due to my naivety and sheer exhaustion, I simply said "no". They were taken aback, but eventually relented when I told them I would move if they found me another double seat. They were surprised by my boldness, but I was too tired to care what happened to me. Others on the bus warned me not to be stupid, while Martin just laughed. As it turned out, once they realised we were English, we all started chatting and sharing jokes and stories. They were curious about life in England and we were equally intrigued by their lives in Florida and Alabama.

Several weeks later, when I got off the bus to be collected by a friend, I gave a kiss on the cheek to a black girl who had been sitting next to me. As I did, a white guy exclaimed, "What the hell are you doing? Are you some kind of goddamn n***** lover boy?" I was shocked. I could not believe my ears, but we were his guests, so we had no choice but to get into his car.

Martin's uncle Frank and his wife picked us up from the bus station in Tallahassee and drove us to his home in Pensacola. I was struck by how different he seemed from the other folks we had met in the States. He was born in England and migrated to the US after World War II. Frank was married to a lovely 'southern belle' lady named Joanne, and between them, they had five kids – Jane, Stephanie, and Wes were Joanne's. And Dale and Blaine were Frank's boys; they no longer lived with their parents, they had all moved out.

From the moment we arrived, they were all so excited to see us. As soon as we got to their house, they threw a party, inviting many neighbours to meet the two English lads who had just landed in their quiet Southern town.

It was quite a novelty for them to meet some real English boys, and they could not get enough of our accents. They kept asking us to tell jokes and stories, hanging on every word. Everyone was so friendly and incredibly generous, making us feel right at home. Martin and I shared a bedroom with views of palm trees and blue skies – we could hardly believe our luck.

During the day, Joanne and Frank would go off to work, leaving us to our own devices. Frank had given us the keys to his Ford LTD coupé, a massive seven-litre, two-door beast of a car, and we were like pigs in shit. We drove that car all over town, revelling in its freedom and sheer thrill.

On the weekends, the family would gather for a barbecue, and those were some of the best times. One afternoon, I was reading a book and, with my walking stick in hand, decided to find a quiet spot. I took myself across the garden and settled at the base of a towering pine tree, leaning my back against the rough bark. The ground was carpeted with several inches of pine needles, soft and cushiony under me. As I put my hand down into the needles to steady myself, I suddenly felt a sharp, stabbing pain in my finger. I yelled out in surprise and pain, yanking my hand back to see blood trickling from the wound.

Frank came over, a shovel in his hand, and took one look at my finger. "Show me your finger boy," he said, his tone calm, but firm. As he examined it, he nodded. "Yep, that's a snake bite."

"A what?" I stammered, the shock setting in.

He pointed to a small yellow and black snake slithering away through the pine needles. "There it is. I see it."

"Is it poisonous?" I asked, my voice probably higher than usual.

Frank looked me straight in the eye and said, "Well, it depends. If it is a corn snake, you're okay. If it's a coral snake, you'd be dead by now." Then he let out a deep laugh, the kind that made you feel a little more at ease, even if just for a moment. With a practised hand, Frank began beating the pine needles with his shovel, eventually chasing the snake away. I watched as he calmly dealt with the situation as if it were all part of a day's work.

As I sat there, nursing my bleeding finger, I could not help but think how different life was here, how every day brought a new adventure, a new story to tell. The snake bite turned out to be harmless, just another tale to add to the growing list of experiences that made those days in Pensacola so unforgettable.

CHAPTER 19
PENSACOLA

Martin and I were taking Frank's car into Pensacola town, and I was behind the wheel, feeling remarkably good about the day ahead. As we were driving, I signalled left to pull into a gas station, and just as I was making the turn, a pickup truck came out of nowhere and crashed into us. The impact shook the car. Both vehicles were immediately pulled over and we got out to assess the damage.

Martin walked to the front of the car to check out the situation, and before we could even fully grasp what had happened, an American guy with long shoulder-length blond hair got out of the truck, his girlfriend by his side. He was apologetic from the start, admitting fault and offering to pay for the damage.

While we were standing there talking, a patrol car parked across the street suddenly pulled over and stopped right next to us in the middle of the highway, lights flashing. Just as the cop arrived, the American guy handed me a bag of candy. He said, "Look, this is a bag of candy I got at Mardi Gras. Please take it. I'm sorry for damaging your car."

I did not think much of it and tossed the bag onto the back seat. That is when what looked like a sheriff, complete with a cowboy hat, came over and asked, "What happened here?"

As soon as I started speaking in my English accent, he realised I was not American. He turned to the guy from the truck and asked him what happened. The American admitted that it was his fault and even asked if he could just leave after offering to pay for the damage.

But the sheriff was not having any of it. "No, I have got to give a ticket, and we have to do the paperwork," he said, taking all our details down.

The American guy tried to reassure me, saying, "Don't worry, I'm sure the insurance will cover the damage."

Now, understanding I was English, the policeman asked me where I came from. It was easier just to tell Americans that I was from London. He said, oh, my grandmother lives in Manchester. Have you ever been there? I said, "Yes, of course," and he said, "Oh, maybe you passed in the street sometime."

He laughed, and we all laughed and said, "Yeah, maybe." We wrapped things up, and I drove the car back home; my nerves rattled more from the encounter with the sheriff than the actual accident.

When we returned, we went into the kitchen and sat at the dining table, nervously preparing to tell Frank what had happened. I explained how the front light of his car had been damaged in the accident. Frank listened calmly and then went outside to take a look. When he came back, he just shrugged and said, "No problem. It's easy to fix, and I'm sure the insurance will take care of it."

Feeling relieved, I remembered the bag of candy the pick-up driver had given me and handed it to Frank.

He smiled and poured all the small bright-coloured candies into a bowl on the table, and that is when we saw it – a plastic bag full of marijuana hidden beneath all the candy. We all erupted in laughter, the tension from the accident melting away at that moment. I could not believe our luck that the policeman had not seen it. The situation was absurd, but it made for one hell of a story.

Dave and my Gyro

We had been in Florida for about a month when I got an unexpected phone call from my friend Dave, who worked for an international airline. He said, "I went to visit your mum, and did you know you've got two Gyro cheques sitting at home that you need to cash?"

I had completely forgotten about them. I had not signed off on the unemployment benefits before leaving, not because I was trying to cheat the system, but because I genuinely did not think I would receive any money.

I could claim about £150 in benefits; all I needed to do was sign the back of the cheques.

Dave, being the spontaneous guy he was, said, "I'll come out there and see you. I've got three days off. I'll bring the cheques. You can sign them, and I'll bring them back and cash them for you. I can get free flights from London to Paris, then Paris to Atlanta, and then I can hop into Pensacola."

I asked him if he was sure, and he replied, "Yeah, it'll be a laugh."

A few days later, I got a phone call – Dave had arrived at Pensacola airport, but there was a catch.

He said, "Mate, you need to come and get me. The United States Air Force has arrested me."

I was utterly baffled. "What are you talking about?" I asked.

"It's complicated, but just come and get me," he said, holding back laughter.

So, Martin and I borrowed Frank's car and drove to the Air Force Base. Shortly after we arrived, a military Jeep pulled up and parked next to us. Two MPs got out and escorted Dave to our car, handed him his bag, and said, "Goodbye." Dave climbed into the car, laughing like a madman.

We were all laughing, roaring, trying to get the story out of him. "Dave, what the hell is going on? What have you been doing?"

"Well," Dave started, still chuckling, "while I was waiting to call you guys, I couldn't help but notice some really interesting aircraft. So, I was wandering around, taking photographs of fighter jets. Apparently, these chaps did not like that one bit. They promptly took my camera, removed the film, and told me to get the hell out of there."

We could not stop laughing. The absurdity of it all was too much. Without missing a beat, we decided to head straight to a strip club close to the airbase.

While we were there, one of the dancing girls, clearly looking for a tip from Dave, noticed his aluminium camera case. She asked him, "Are you a photographer?"

Dave, with his mischievous grin, replied, "Yes, I am."

She was naked; she leaned in closer and said, "Would you like to take some photos of me?"

"Sure thing," Dave said, unpacking his camera, following her around the club, and snapping away. When he finally returned to the table, we could not help but tease him.

"I thought they took your film!" I spoke.

"They did," Dave admitted.

Martin said, "So, is there any film in your camera now?"

Dave burst out laughing, "Nope! But come on, I really enjoyed that. So did she. She asked me to send her the photos. I've even got her address!"

We all cracked up, realising how typical this was of Dave – always in some sort of adventure, even when it did not make the slightest bit of sense. The night was one for the books, a perfect mix of chaos and hilarity that I would not have missed for the world.

A beautiful family

We spent five unforgettable weeks in Pensacola at Martin's uncle's house. It was a beautiful, detached bungalow tucked away in a gated community where each home sat on a full acre of land, surrounded by tall, whispering pine trees.

The place had a serene, almost idyllic feel, especially when we arrived. We had not come to America with much money and did not expect to stay long, but we quickly learned just how generous Americans could be. They would not let us pay for a thing, so there we were, living for free, eating for free, and spending what little cash we had on beer and cigarettes.

However, not just the free living made those weeks in Pensacola special. We would head out to Pensacola Beach every day, a stretch of pure white sand that seemed to go on forever. The Gulf waters were warm and clear, a shade of turquoise that looked like something out of a postcard.

Sometimes, we would explore further down the coast, finding quieter spots where we could have the beach almost to ourselves. Those were the best days when the only sounds were the sea birds calling overhead and the waves lapping at the shore. We would bring a cooler filled with cold beers and sandwiches, making a day of it.

Sometimes, we would be in downtown Pensacola. Palafox Pier had many lovely eateries, water views and some of the most wonderful sunsets I have ever seen, painting the sky with shades of orange and pink. We would sit there in silence, taking it all in.

It felt like we were two incredibly lucky guys.

Evenings were often spent at the bungalow, where Martin's uncle and his family would host casual barbecues on the back patio. The scent of grilled meat would mix with the fresh pine air, and we would eat until we were stuffed. There was always laughter and storytelling, a warmth that made us feel like we were part of something larger, part of a family, even though we were thousands of miles from home.

The Camaro

It was a Saturday night, and Martin and I walked into the kitchen, feeling sharp in our best shirts and shoes, ready for a night out. Joanne was standing by the counter, looking as elegant as ever. She had this effortless grace about her, with her short red hair perfectly styled. Joanne was the beauty department manager at the big department store in town, and she always carried herself with that kind of poised confidence.

"Wow, you boys look dressed up for some fun. Where are you headed tonight?" she asked with a smile, speaking in her deep Southern accent.

"We're going to check out a club that was recommended to us," we replied, trying to play it cool.

Without missing a beat, Joanne reached into her pocket and pulled out a set of keys. She dangled them in front of us and said, "Well, if you want to impress the ladies, you better take my car, not that nasty old Ford Frank drives."

We could not believe it – Joanne drove a brand-new Camaro V8. It was gorgeous, in a stunning pale yellow with a rich red interior and shiny alloy wheels. The car looked like it had just rolled off the showroom floor, sleek and powerful. Martin and I stared at those keys like they were made of gold.

We could not believe our luck. We practically jumped out of our skins with excitement, immediately arguing over who would drive. In the end, I cannot even remember who won the argument, but I do remember the thrill of cruising down the road in that beautiful machine. The engine purred like a big cat, and heads turned as we rolled up to the club.

It was a fantastic night, one of those evenings where everything just seemed to go right. But what stuck with me was not just the car or the fun we had – it was Joanne's generosity. She did not have to lend us that car, but she did it with a smile to make our night a little more special. It is the type of kindness that stays with you, a reminder of the lovely people who make life's adventures all the more memorable.

Stoned

Martin and I used to indulge in a bit of marijuana back in the UK, mostly at weekends and parties. We got our gear mainly from Afghanistan or Pakistan. We had to be careful, of course – it was against the law. One thing that surprised us both was how liberal the marijuana scene was in Florida.

One night, Wes, Stephanie, Jane, Martin, and I decided to go to a club in town. We all piled into the back of Wes's custom Ford van. As we drove, Stephanie lit up some joints of Mexican weed, Acapulco Gold marijuana. By the time we got to the club, I was absolutely stoned. We all were. The van was filled with uncontrollable giggles, and I literally could not get out of the van. I had no control over my body, and for the next hour, I just lay there on the mattress in the back of the van, laughing hysterically. It was the most potent weed we had ever smoked.

As I lay there, I remember the sensation of being utterly weightless, like I was floating on a cloud. The music from the club outside mixed with our laughter, creating a surreal soundtrack to the night. Wes's van was like a mobile party den, with its custom interior and cosy mattress in the back. He had decked it out with blankets and pillows, making it the perfect place to crash when the high got too intense.

Stephanie and Jane were in fits of laughter, stumbling over each other as they tried to help me sit up. Martin was no better, leaning against the side of the van, his eyes barely open as he chuckled at our predicament. It felt like time had stopped as if we were caught in this endless loop of laughter and haze.

Eventually, we all managed to pull ourselves together and make our way into the club. The lights, the music, the people – it all hit me like a tidal wave. Everything was amplified, every sensation heightened. We danced, laughed, and enjoyed the night in a way only youthful exuberance and a good high can bring. It was one of those nights that became a legend among friends, a story retold with fondness and laughter.

Looking back, it was one of the wildest nights in Florida, a night that perfectly captured the freedom and recklessness of 1979. We were young, carefree and living in the moment, making memories that would last a lifetime. The liberal attitude towards marijuana was just another part of the adventure, a surprising and welcome contrast to the caution we had to exercise back home.

Jane

I had gotten involved in a romantic fling with Martin's cousin Jane. She was eight years older than me – attractive, funny, and full of life. She had a condominium in the town. We would sneak off, and I would stay at her place overnight, drinking beers under the moonlight on her balcony.

There was something magical about those nights: the music, the marijuana, her mystical free spirit, and life seemed to stretch out into infinity. But after a few weeks, I could feel the pull to move on. I was not ready to settle down when there was so much of America left to explore. After five weeks, to our surprise, we still had most of our money left, and that is when we started thinking about hitting the road and seeing more of the US.

Martin's cousin Dale, Frank's son, lived in Huntington Beach, California – about 40 miles south of Los Angeles. Huntington Beach was the mecca of severe surfers, especially guys our age. Martin's cousin had moved out there to ride the massive waves and had landed a job in an auto body custom shop.

The idea of heading out to California, of seeing those legendary beaches and that iconic surf culture, was too tempting to resist. So, we made our decision. We headed down to the bus station and bought tickets to cross the USA; we planned our trip to cover epic cities and states, a trip that would take us over 2,200 miles and would be four days on the bus; we were so excited, to see what the next chapter of our adventure would bring.

As we boarded the bus, we waved goodbye to Jane and Pensacola, the place that had given us so much more than we ever expected. The beach, the sun, the laughter, and the fleeting romance were all part of a chapter that would forever be etched in my memory, a time when life was simple, free, and full of endless possibilities.

CHAPTER 20

GO WEST

nd so our cross-continental bus ride began, from Pensacola west to Mobile – a fascinating coastal port town with a rich and complex history.

Mobile is known as the "City of Six Flags," a unique title that reflects its past under the rule of six different flags: English, French, Spanish, the Alabama state flag, the Confederate flag, and, of course, the United States flag.

As we rolled into the city, I could not help but think about all the layers of history embedded in the streets as we passed by some beautiful old buildings.

The buses, typically, drove for three-to-six hours between stations. During that time, you would either stay on the bus and continue your journey or disembark to connect to another bus headed in a different direction. These stops offered a chance to stretch your legs, explore the area, grab food, and freshen up at the station's facilities.

From Mobile, we moved on to Biloxi and then to New Orleans, about 150 miles. New Orleans was something else – entirely vibrant, chaotic and alive in a way few places are.

But when we arrived, the city was in the midst of an unbelievable police strike. The entire force had stopped working, and we saw officers driving around the city with their lights flashing and sirens blaring, not in service, but in protest.

The city buzzed with wild energy, and the streets were filled with people and noise as if the very absence of order had become its own kind of order.

Next, a 975-mile stage as we journeyed to Baton Rouge, then Houston, and finally to San Antonio, where we had a stopover with enough time to take in the sights.

The Alamo

We visited the famous Alamo, the Spanish mission and fort that was the site of the legendary battle in which the Mexican forces defeated the Texan defenders, including the famous Davy Crockett. Standing there in that place steeped in history, I felt a deep connection to the past – a reminder of the battles fought and the lives lived long before my own journey began.

The Battle of the Alamo commenced at dawn on 6 March, 1836, the 13th day of the siege. The fighting lasted roughly 90 minutes, and by daybreak, all the Texan defenders had perished, including Crockett, a former congressman from Tennessee.

El Paso

The next leg of our journey was a long 550 miles to El Paso, Texas. El Paso is striking. The city sprawls out at the base of the mountains, with the Rio Grande marking the border between the US and Mexico just to the south.

In 1979, it had a ferocious reputation for trouble – crime and drugs were said to be rampant. But Martin and I were blissfully unaware of all that. When our bus pulled up at the covered station, we casually told the two black guys we had been travelling with that we planned to walk into town and grab something to eat.

One of the passengers grabbed Martin's arm, his voice serious. "Wait, we will come with you. You do not want to be walking around here alone – this is a dangerous place."

Sure enough, about five of us wandered slowly down the street together, heading toward what looked like a lively bar with coloured lights and loud music spilling into the night. But as we got closer, a huge fight broke out inside, and police cars started arriving from every direction.

What surprised me most was the sheer number of different law enforcement vehicles that appeared – the city police, the border patrol, the highway patrol, the county sheriff's office – all in different coloured cars. It was almost amusing, but the situation was serious.

We wisely decided to avoid the trouble and turned down a side street, eventually finding a small, cheap-looking restaurant serving

Mexican food. It looked affordable and inviting, so we all settled in. As I looked at the menu, I realised I did not recognise most of the Mexican dishes, except for chilli con carne – a dish my mum used to make regularly. Confidently, I ordered, "Chilli con carne, please."

When it arrived, the dish came with a side of what looked like some kind of paste and a plate of tortilla chips. It looked delicious, so I dug in immediately. Big mistake. The chilli started burning through the roof of my mouth, and my eyes began to water uncontrollably. The guys burst out laughing and pointed to the bean paste, suggesting I shovel some of it up with the tortilla chips and eat it to cool down the burning sensation.

It worked, and suddenly, the meal became delightful again. We had a fun time, laughing and enjoying the food. We slowly walked back to the bus station when we finished our beers, feeling a bit more familiar with this intimidating town. Soon enough, we were back on the bus, heading 320 miles to Tucson, Arizona, ready for the next chapter of our adventure.

American Beauty

As the bus rolled westward, I found myself seated next to a young Native American girl. She had joined the bus after me and took the vacant seat beside me. Dressed in denim, she wore a few pieces of jewellery that hinted at her heritage – beautiful, handcrafted items that added a touch of elegance to her casual attire. She was strikingly pretty, with a quiet presence that immediately drew my attention.

Feeling a sudden urge to capture this moment, I asked if drawing her portrait would be all right. To my surprise, she agreed. For the next several hours, I lost myself in the familiar rhythm of pencil against paper, capturing the delicate lines of her face, the soft curve of her lips, and the way the light gently played off her features. We exchanged a few words, but mostly, I worked in silence, absorbed in the details.

As I sketched, the world outside the bus was transforming. The night began to give way to dawn, and I was treated to one of the most epic sunrises I have ever witnessed. The sky shifted through a breathtaking palette of colours – first a deep, inky black, then a rich purple, which slowly lightened into shades of pink. The pinks deepened into a dusty yellow, casting a warm glow over the desert before finally giving way to day's clear, bright blue. It was an awe-inspiring sight that I have never seen replicated anywhere else in the world.

When I finally finished the portrait, I handed it to her, and the smile that spread across her face was worth every minute I had spent on it. She was genuinely pleased and, as she left the bus, I felt a sense of connection – a brief but meaningful encounter in the vast emptiness of the desert. That stunning sunrise, the girl, the endless desert – it all combined to create a memory that has stayed with me ever since, a moment of unexpected beauty and peace amid our long journeys.

The Wild West

The journey westward from Texas through New Mexico and into Arizona was a passage through vast, endless open expanses. The sky felt impossibly wide, a dome of infinite blue that met the earth at the distant horizon. The terrain was rugged and arid, dominated by the Chihuahuan Desert. The soil was dry and reddish-brown, dotted with hardy shrubs, mesquite trees, and, of course, cacti – tall, spindly ocotillos and stout prickly pears stood like silent sentinels in the desert.

The further west we travelled, the more desolate the landscape became. Small towns were few and far between, often comprising little more than a handful of buildings clustered around a single road.

A lone phone box, a petrol pump, and a small store for travellers were the only signs of life. The highway stretched out before us, a ribbon of asphalt cutting through the desert, with long stretches where you could see nothing but the road, the sky, and the unyielding desert. This place was harsh, yet beautiful. The sun was relentless, casting long shadows and bringing out the deep reds and browns of the earth.

The light changed throughout the day, painting the landscape in different hues – golden in the morning, stark white at midday, and a warm, almost mystical red as the sun began to set.

The journey from Tucson to San Diego

Our stop in Tucson was brief, just long enough to stretch our legs and take in the dry heat of the desert town. Then we continued to San Diego. As we left Tucson, the towering saguaro cacti stood tall against the deep blue sky, their arms reaching up to the sun in the vast Sonoran Desert. The road began to rise gently, leading us through southern Arizona's arid, rocky terrain. The sharp peaks of the mountains loomed on the horizon, their jagged silhouettes softened by the hazy distance.

Crossing into California, the terrain began to change subtly. The barren expanses of sand gave way to rolling hills covered in scrubby vegetation, and soon, we found ourselves in the vast emptiness of the Imperial Valley. This stretch of the journey felt almost other-worldly, with its stark, flat landscape and the occasional glimpse of agricultural fields. The arid desert gradually yielded to the rocky, mountainous terrain of the Peninsular Ranges. The road began to wind and climb, and the air cooled as we gained elevation. The mountains were rugged and imposing, their slopes covered with chaparral and dotted with boulders. The landscape was dramatic and wild, with steep cliffs and deep canyons that seemed to stretch forever.

Finally, as we crested the last range of mountains, the landscape opened up, revealing the coastal plain that led to San Diego. The vegetation became lusher and greener as we descended, with groves of eucalyptus and fields of wild flowers painting the hillsides in bursts of colour. The air was fresher, carrying with it the faint scent of the ocean as we approached the coast.

The last leg of our journey brought us into the vibrant, bustling city of San Diego. The Pacific Ocean finally came into view, its deep blue waters stretching out to the horizon, a beautiful contrast to the arid landscapes we had just passed through. When we arrived at the bus station and stepped out of the air-conditioned bus, it was a shock – 80 degrees and humid.

That journey from Tucson to San Diego in California was a breathtaking exploration of the diverse and stunning natural beauty of the American Southwest, a journey that left a lasting impression on me.

CHAPTER 21
CALIFORNIA

We spent a couple of days in a cheap hotel in San Diego, gathering our energy and planning the next leg of our journey. Huntington Beach was 100 miles north along California Highway 5, and we could do this stretch non-stop.

We had an address for Martin's cousin, Dale, but had not been able to make contact with him. So, he had no idea we were on our way. With that in mind, we hopped on a bus that took us to the Greyhound depot in Huntington Beach and, from there, we started walking.

We had some directions, but, as it turned out, they were not as reliable as we had hoped. The distance was much further than we expected, and the hot California sun was not making things any easier. I was using my stick to get by, and even though Martin was carrying my bag, the heat and the effort soon wore me down.

At one point, we heard the roar of motorcycles approaching. A gang of Hells Angels came rumbling down the road on their Harley-Davidsons. I mustered up the courage and waved them down. They slowed, looking at me with stern, puzzled expressions – probably not used to a random English kid flagging them down.

I asked them politely for directions. Their tough exteriors softened just a bit, and one of them smiled slightly before pointing us in the right direction. With that, they revved their engines and roared off into the distance.

Not long after, a sleek green Triumph TR7 convertible appeared on the road. I stuck my thumb out, and it pulled up beside us, to our surprise. Behind the wheel was a gorgeous young woman with a mane of wavy hair. We told her where we were headed and asked if she could give us a lift. The car was just a two-seater, so she offered to take me and the bags first while Martin said, "Sure, you go ahead. I will follow on behind. I'll meet you there."

She dropped me off at the house, and I found a spot on a low wall beneath a lemon tree, taking in the shade as I waited for Martin. When he finally arrived, we knocked on the door, but there was no answer. By now, we were both exhausted. We noticed a Ford Capri parked outside the garage, and to our luck, it was unlocked. We tossed our bags in the back seat, climbed into the front seats, and promptly fell asleep.

It was not long before we were jolted awake by a loud bang on the window. A tall guy with long blond hair stood there, angry and confused. Martin quickly jumped out of the car and explained, "Dale, it's me – Martin, your cousin from England!"

Dale's face transformed from suspicion to laughter in an instant. He pulled Martin into a bear hug, just as a customised Chevy panel van, painted in wild colours, pulled into the driveway. Three more long-haired surfer types jumped out, and introductions were made all around.

Dale took us inside, and it was immediately clear this was not your typical home. The place was devoid of furniture, except for about 200 LPs, a hi-fi system, some sleeping bags strewn on the floor, and an electric ping-pong game machine in the kitchen. In the middle of it all, there was a massive bowl of marijuana sitting on the kitchen worktop, like it was the most normal thing in the world.

Before we knew it, the lads had started rolling joints and cracking open beers. We settled down on the living room floor, playing music, smoking, drinking, and sharing stories. Laughter filled the room as we got stoned and soaked up the laid-back vibe. That was just the beginning of our few weeks in Huntington Beach, where time seemed to slow down, and life was all about sun, surf, and soaking in the good times.

Men at work

All the lads had their daily routines down to a science. The alarm clock would blare around 5:00am, and almost in unison, the radio would be tuned to the local surf report. The broadcaster would rattle off the height of the waves at various beaches along the coast, and the boys would huddle up, choosing their spot for the morning surf. With boards in tow, they would pile into their van, hit the waves for an hour, and then head off to work as if it were just another part of their day.

In the evenings, they would roll back home, grab some Mexican takeaway, and get stoned, unwinding from the day in the most Californian way possible.

I have to admit I quickly developed a taste for Mexican food. It was all new to me, but I found it delicious. Tacos, burritos, enchiladas – it was a whole new world of flavour I had not experienced before.

CHAPTER 22
MEXICO

It was late on a Friday afternoon when the guys started trickling back home from work. Dale walked in with a grin and tossed his keys onto the table. "Grab your bags, English boys," he said, a glint of mischief in his eyes. "We're going to Mexico."

Martin and I exchanged surprised glances. "Are we even allowed to go to Mexico?" Martin asked, half-joking, half-serious.

Dale chuckled. "Of course you are! We drive across the border and head down to La Bocana for the weekend. We're going to hit the surf."

In 1979, La Bocana, Mexico, was not on any tourist map. It was one of those hidden gems only known to the most adventurous surfers, the kind of place that needed more than just a surfboard – it demanded grit and a thirst for the untamed. Nestled on the Baja Peninsula, La Bocana was a wild stretch of coastlinc just south of the border, where the desert meets the Pacific in a clash of raw, untamed beauty.

The drive down was part of the adventure. Two Chevy vans packed with gear left the familiar sights of California behind and plunged into the dusty, rugged terrain of Baja. The further we drove, the more desolate it became – endless stretches of desert dotted with scrubby bushes, with the occasional jagged mountain range breaking the monotony.

You could feel the anticipation building as we got closer, the excitement of what awaited us at the end of that road.

Dale, Dean, Chris, and Mike were seasoned surfers, the kind of guys who had mastered the waves of California and were constantly on the lookout for bigger challenges. La Bocana was their kind of place – a spot that could humble even the best with its powerful, unpredictable waves. As Dale explained, "La Bocana isn't for beginners. The waves here are fierce, with swells that can rise to 10 feet or more. You've got to know what you're doing out there."

When we arrived at the border, it was the usual chaos – long queues, border guards with bored expressions, occasionally pulling cars aside for thorough checks with dogs sniffing for guns and drugs. Luck was on our side, though, and we sailed through with no trouble. As we crossed into Mexico, Martin, still wide-eyed with the novelty of it all, asked, "So, I'm guessing you didn't bring your marijuana to go surfing?"

The lads erupted in laughter. Once we reached our destination, they pulled out a shovel and dug up a plastic bag full of weed they had buried on an earlier trip. Chris grinned and said, "You don't bring ice to the North Pole, mate. We buy our gear here and stash it before we leave."

La Bocana was everything you would expect from a hidden surf spot – isolated, rugged, and beautiful. The beach was a stretch of stony sand with nothing but the sound of the waves crashing against the shore and the vast, open sky above. There were no amenities, lifeguards, or shops – just you, your board and the ocean.

The lads suited up in their wetsuits, strapping their boards to their backs as they carefully scaled down the rocky cliffs to reach the beach. It was a precarious descent, and at one point, Chris lost his footing and tumbled down a fair distance.

My heart was in my throat, but luckily, he landed on his surfboard, strapped to his back, and walked away with nothing more than a wrecked board. Without missing a beat, he climbed back up, grabbed his back-up board from the van, and headed back down to the surf.

Martin and I just looked at each other wide-eyed. "They're mad dogs," Martin muttered. "Are you going down there?" I asked. He shook his head, already rolling another joint. "Nope, I'm just going to sit here and watch the show." And what a show it was; we watched two majestic whales swim past and off into the distance.

What made La Bocana special was not just the waves – it was

the entire experience. There was a sense of freedom and connection to nature that was hard to find anywhere else. Surfing there was not just about catching the perfect wave; it was about understanding the sea, the tides, the wind, and letting the ocean set the pace. It was a pure, unfiltered experience where you were completely at the mercy of the elements.

The locals, few as they were, lived simple lives as fishermen and ranchers. They would watch the surfers with a mix of curiosity and amusement, always quick with a warm smile or a wave. Our two nights sleeping in the two vans were something else entirely. With no city lights for miles, the sky was a vast, star-studded dome, and the sound of the waves was a constant, rhythmic backdrop, lulling us to sleep under the stars, it felt like we were on the edge of the world, far removed from the noise and chaos of everyday life.

That weekend in 1979 left an indelible mark on me. Surfing in La Bocana was not just about the waves; it was about the solitude, the adventure, and the sense of being part of something much bigger than yourself. It was a reminder that the world was still vast and full of places waiting to be discovered by those willing to venture off the beaten path.

Pen pal

One evening, back in Huntington Beach, in the middle of our usual laid-back conversations, I casually mentioned that I had a pen pal in California. They perked up and asked where. “Vallejo,” I said, not knowing much about the place. They nodded knowingly and said, “Yeah, you can drive there from here. It is a beautiful drive north of San Francisco. You’ll love it up there.”

That got us thinking. We started planning our bus route, and before long, one of the lads said, “You know, you can take the Mazda station wagon. Nobody is using it right now.”

Martin and I looked at each other and then back at him. “Are you sure?” we asked.

He shrugged and said, “Well, there’s one slight problem. It doesn’t have any licence plates yet. It’s been re-registered from Florida to California, but the plates haven’t arrived. But hey, you’re

English. If the cops pull you over, just explain it to them. You'll probably get away with it."

We all laughed, knowing it was a bit of a risk but also recognising the adventure in it. How could we resist? The idea of driving up to Vallejo, cruising along the California coast, and seeing more of this incredible state was too tempting to pass up. So, we decided to go for it, figuring we'd just deal with any issues as they came. It was all part of the experience, after all.

CHAPTER 23
SAN FRANCISCO

The lads in Huntington Beach told us that if we were going to make the trip to San Francisco, we absolutely had to take California Highway 1. They promised it would be a scenic and memorable journey, spanning around 450 miles, and after spending so much time on Greyhound buses, the idea of a leisurely drive up the coast sounded perfect.

Martin and I set off for San Francisco on California Highway number 1 the next morning, as advised. We started from Huntington Beach, with our first leg taking us 45 miles up to Santa Monica and then another 30 miles to Malibu.

The stretch to Zuma Beach was particularly breathtaking. Zuma Beach, with its expansive sands and crashing waves, was one of the largest and most popular beaches in the area.

We spent some time there, just soaking in the atmosphere, watching surfers carve through the waves, their silhouettes sharp against the afternoon sun.

From Malibu, we pressed on to Oxnard, another 40 miles up the coast, where the beaches were just as beautiful, though perhaps a bit quieter. Then it was on to Santa Barbara, another 40 miles, with its Mediterranean-style buildings and palm-lined streets. By the time we reached Pismo Beach, 80 miles further up, we were beginning to understand why everyone had raved about this drive.

Unexpected breakdown

We had completely miscalculated the distance between towns, and before we knew it, the little Mazda sputtered to a stop, out of petrol. We found ourselves stranded in a lay-by on a lonely stretch of the highway near some cliffs. It was the last place you would want to run out of fuel. The sun was starting to dip, and with each passing minute, our concern grew. We had no choice but to hitchhike, hoping someone might pick us up and take us to the next town, where we could buy some gasoline in a can and hitch a ride back to the car.

Just as the last light was fading and we were starting to wonder if we would end up spending the night there, a big yellow school bus turned motorhome pulled up. The bus had seen better days, but it was still chugging along.

We stuck out our thumbs, and to our relief, the driver pulled over. He was a young American guy travelling with his girlfriend. The bus was their home – surfboards strapped to the roof, bicycles hanging off the back, the whole thing converted into a camper. They offered us a lift, which we gratefully accepted, but as night fell, they decided to pull up on the beach to smoke and drink. They told us we could not sleep in the van, but they had some spare sleeping bags and said we were welcome to crash on the beach. We were in no position to say "no", so we thanked them and accepted their offer.

We did not realise that, while the California coast might be blistering hot during the day, it is freezing at night, especially out in the wild like this.

All I had on was a T-shirt and jeans, and I spent the night shivering, trying to curl up and conserve some body heat.

At one point during the night, I was startled awake by the sound of footsteps. A stranger was standing right next to us. He looked down at us with a friendly smile and said, "Mind if I sleep near you guys? I do not want to be out there on my own." We were too cold and tired to care, so we told him to go ahead.

Early the next morning, the stranger got up just as the first light started to creep over the horizon. He said he had a long way to go and needed to hit the road early. We wished him well as he left. We tucked up in our sleeping bags to get some more sleep.

Martin and I woke up a bit later, still cold but grateful to be alive and in one piece. The two hippies who had given us a lift the night before brewed some herbal tea and shared it with us.

It was a small gesture, but it warmed us up and gave us the energy to face the day. They also gave us two oranges. We thanked them and said our goodbyes as we got a lift from a passing pick-up truck to the nearest gas station, which was still far away.

We sat in the sun in the truck bed; as we drove down the road, we spotted the guy from the beach standing there with his thumb out, trying to hitch a ride. We drove past him and could not help but laugh, giving him a wave as we went by. Eventually, we got our gas, found another ride back to the car, filled it up, and continued on our journey. It was just another day on the road, another adventure in the book, but one we would not soon forget.

Cambria was our next stop, just 50 miles beyond Pismo Beach; from there, we headed to Big Sur, 70 miles away, where the rugged cliffs and towering redwoods made us feel like we were driving through a postcard. The Bixby Creek Bridge, just 45 miles from Monterey, was one of those iconic landmarks that took our breath away, its graceful arch spanning the deep gorge below.

We continued to Santa Cruz, another 50 miles up the coast, where the vibe was more laid-back and beachier. The final stretch took us through Half Moon Bay, just 30 miles from San Francisco, where the landscape began to shift from rugged coastlines to the more urban scenery leading into the city. Crossing the Golden Gate Bridge felt like the perfect way to end the journey – a sweeping view of the bay, the city rising in the distance, the iconic red towers framing the sky.

We spent the night in a cheap hotel in San Francisco, resting up after the long drive. The next day, we headed out to Vallejo to visit Sharon, taking in the rolling hills of wine country as we drove.

With our detour for petrol and the countless stops to take in the sights, the drive took us three days in total. But it was worth every minute. The experience gave us a real sense of the epic scale of North America, and it was one of those journeys that stays with you – etched in your memory as a series of stunning landscapes and shared moments with good friends.

CHAPTER 24
VALLEJO

When I was about 14, in 1971, part of our English studies involved getting pen pals from other parts of the world. Our teacher contacted schools internationally, and I was paired with Sharon MacCallum, also 14, from Vallejo, California.

We wrote to each other about once a month, sharing details about our schools, families and daily lives. Our correspondence was easy and natural, a window into each other's worlds. I remember sending her cassette tapes of English bands, including Queen, as soon as their music came out.

Sharon was stunned and amazed by the sounds that had not yet hit the States. We both vowed to keep in touch, and even as life moved on and we left school, we still exchanged letters, though less often. She knew about my accident, and we stayed connected for a couple of years afterwards.

So, when I arrived in San Francisco, I did not hesitate to call her. I told her we were just a few miles away, and her reaction was one of pure excitement. "Oh my God, oh my God, you must come and see us! Please do come!" she screamed over the phone. "Of course we will," I replied, smiling because that had been my plan all along.

With directions in hand, Martin and I continued our journey up to Vallejo. We pulled into a modest suburban area where Sharon's family bungalow sat neatly on a street of similar homes.

The driveway was full of cars, and a motorhome was parked off to the side.

Once again, I was struck by the overwhelming generosity of Americans. We were welcomed inside and introduced to a crowd of aunts, uncles, and friends. There was food, laughter and a warmth that made us feel instantly at home.

Staying with the MacCallums

Sharon's dad, a big man of Irish descent who worked as an engineer on the Golden Gate Bridge, apologised that there was no space for us to sleep in the house. But he offered us the Winnebago motorhome. Martin and I were amazed by its luxury – carpeted floors, central heating, air conditioning, a TV, a toilet and an oven. It was as comfortable as any home.

Over the next few days, the family took us on a whirlwind tour of San Francisco. We rode the cable cars up and down the steep hills, explored Pier 39, and enjoyed fresh seafood with views of Alcatraz in the distance. One evening, they took us to the new Hyatt Hotel, where tubular glass elevators ascended outside the building to a rotating restaurant. We enjoyed a lovely meal there, watching the city's lights come alive as the sun set.

Sharon's brother lent us his Chevrolet Caprice one day, and Martin and I ventured the 32 miles into the city on our own to drive around and soak it all in. We took the Caprice down the famous Lombard Street, the twisting, snaky road, a San Francisco icon. It was hilarious navigating that massive car through the hairpin turns.

One day, Sharon suggested we take a trip up to Napa Valley to visit the wine country, and we could not have been more excited. We made our way to the prestigious Beringer Vineyards, a place steeped in history. Founded in 1876 by two German brothers, Beringer is the oldest continuously operating winery in California. The brothers had meticulously transported their entire house from Germany – brick by brick, tile by tile, and beam by beam – to rebuild it on the vineyard grounds in California.

The tour was nothing short of fascinating. We ventured into the caves and cellars, which had been hand-dug by Chinese labourers. These underground passages were cool and dark, supporting a stable temperature between 55°F and 60°F year-round – ideal conditions for ageing wine. As we walked through the dimly lit caves, we could feel the history all around us, the walls seemingly whispering stories of the past. Of course, no visit to a vineyard would be complete without sampling the wines, and we thoroughly enjoyed every sip, appreciating the flavours born from such a rich tradition.

Nevada

Our adventures did not stop there. Sharon had another surprise up her sleeve. She suggested we take the Winnebago and drive up to Reno, Nevada. It was a fantastic drive, about 188 miles via Sacramento, with the promise of seeing the city and the snow-covered mountains. In 1979, Reno was a bustling gambling city full of famous hotels, casinos and spas.

After a hearty lunch, Martin and Sharon decided to try snowboarding down the hills, while I opted to stay back and watch, content just to be in the crisp mountain air. Watching them navigate the snowy slopes, I felt a deep sense of peace – a moment of tranquillity in the middle of our whirlwind journey.

Leggett redwood Chandelier Tree

As we returned to Sharon's home from Reno, her father suggested we take a trip to the legendary Redwood Forest. Intrigued by the idea, we eagerly set off on our journey north the next day, covering the 260 miles toward Eureka. We were ready for the next chapter of our adventure.

The Redwood Forest was like nothing I had ever seen before – a place where nature's grandeur is on full display. Walking among those ancient trees, some of which had been standing for more than 2,000 years, was a humbling experience. Their massive trunks, so vast you could not even begin to wrap your arms around them, seemed to reach endlessly toward the sky. The tops of the trees disappeared into a misty canopy far above, creating an almost other-worldly atmosphere.

The air was cool and damp, filled with the earthy scent of leaves and soil. Sunlight filtered through the branches in narrow beams, casting an ethereal glow on the forest floor. It was serene, the kind of silence that made you feel like you had stepped into another world, far removed from the noise of everyday life.

One of the highlights of our visit was the Chandelier Tree in Leggett, a massive redwood with a drive-through tunnel carved into its trunk. This tree, 2,000-plus years old and still very much alive, was an icon of the Redwood Forest. Driving our little Mazda through that tree was surreal. I felt a mix of awe and disbelief – here we were, inside a living piece of history. The trunk was so wide it felt like entering a tunnel, and as I looked up, I could only imagine the massive branches far above, spreading out like a chandelier, each one thick enough to be a tree on its own. We took some photographs, trying to capture the moment, though I knew no picture could truly do it justice.

The Redwood Forest was not just a sightseeing trip; it was a profound reminder of nature's power and beauty, a stark contrast to the fleeting concerns of human life. Decades later, the memory of those towering giants remains vivid in my mind – a testament to the magnificence of our world.

After our time in the Redwood Forest, we headed back to Sharon's place for one last night. It was time to say our thanks and goodbyes.

CHAPTER 25
LOS ANGELES

Martin and I were grateful for the kindness and hospitality Sharon and her family had shown us. As we were leaving, Sharon's older brother followed us to the car. He handed us some pills and said, "Listen, this is a long drive you're about to take, and it can be dangerous if you get sleepy. You might want to pop one of these pills – they'll keep you going for a couple of days." He laughed, patted the car's roof and waved us off.

He was not wrong. We took the pills, and suddenly, I felt like I was on 10,000 volts. I felt invincible as if I could run through walls. We drove all the way back to Los Angeles, wide awake the entire time. But when we finally got back to Huntington Beach, I crashed hard and slept for a couple of days, waking up with the worst hangover of my life. To this day, I have no idea what was in those pills, but they sure did the trick.

The drive to Los Angeles was about 400 miles, a long haul by any standard, but with the aid of those mysterious substances Sharon's brother had given us, we managed to do it in one go. The energy they gave us was like nothing I had ever experienced. I felt like I could drive straight through a mountain if I had to. When we finally rolled into LA, the adrenaline was still pumping, and we decided to find a cheap hotel and stay over for a few days before making the 40-mile trip back to the house in Huntington Beach.

This stopover gave us the perfect opportunity to soak in the sights of the famous City of Angels. We were both keen to explore as much as we could in the time we had. In 1979, Los Angeles was a sprawling metropolis and it felt like the centre of the world to us. Everything we had seen in movies and on TV was suddenly right in front of us, larger than life. We wandered through the bustling streets, marvelling at the palm trees lining the boulevards and the iconic Hollywood sign perched on the hills. It was everything we had imagined and more. The city's energy was infectious, a mix of unique glamour and grit.

We spent a couple of days exploring, doing our best to take in as much of LA as possible, people-watching on Venice Beach, and the celebrity lifestyle in Beverly Hills; it was all a whirlwind of new experiences and unforgettable sights. Martin and I were eager to experience everything the city had to offer, so we made sure to hit some of the most famous spots.

Disneyland

Our visit to Disneyland was like stepping into another world; it was already a well-established destination, having opened its doors in 1955. We started our adventure on Main Street, USA, where the charming, turn-of-the-century architecture set the stage for the day. The sight of the Sleeping Beauty Castle at the end of the street was awe-inspiring, a true symbol of Disney magic.

We wandered through Fantasyland, where classic rides like Peter Pan's Flight and It's a Small World whisked us away to whimsical worlds. In Adventureland, we rode the Jungle Cruise, a humorous boat ride through dense jungles filled with animatronic animals and corny jokes from the skipper.

But the real thrill came in Tomorrowland. Space Mountain was the big draw back then – a roller coaster in the dark that made you feel like you were rocketing through space. It was innovative for its time, and the park's energy was great fun.

Knott's Berry Farm

Just a short drive from Disneyland, Knott's was different from Disneyland, with a more rustic, old-timey feel that paid homage to the Old West.

The park had started as a simple berry farm in the 1920s, but by the time we visited in 1979, it had transformed into a fully-fledged theme park.

The Ghost Town was the heart of Knott's Berry Farm. Here, we walked through a re-creation of a Wild West town, complete with cowboys, gunfights, and old wooden buildings.

One of the highlights was the Corkscrew rollercoaster, which opened in 1975, and was one of the first rollercoasters in the world to feature a full 360-degree loop, and we could not pass up the chance to experience that. The whole place had a more relaxed, homely feel compared with Disneyland, but it was just as much fun, with its mix of thrill rides, live entertainment, and good old-fashioned Americana.

Hollywood Wax Museum

The next day was a visit to the Hollywood Wax Museum. Located right on Hollywood Boulevard, this was the place to go if you wanted to get up close and personal with lifelike versions of famous stars like John Wayne. Well, at least the wax versions.

We wandered through the halls, taking in the eerily realistic statues of stars such as Marilyn Monroe, Elvis Presley, and Steve McQueen. The museum also had a section dedicated to horror movies, where figures of Dracula, Frankenstein and other monsters lurked in the shadows. It was a little kitschy, sure, but we enjoyed it. We were living the dream, America was larger than life, bursting with energy and creativity.

Now, we were ready to head back to Huntington Beach, we felt like Los Angeles was the perfect capstone to our road trip, and it was time to make our way back to the house and see Dale and the boys and tell them of our adventures.

CHAPTER 26

BACK TO FLORIDA

With about three weeks left on our 90-day visas, Martin and I knew it was time to start planning our journey back across the country. We wanted to make the most of our remaining time, and spending more in Florida before we left was appealing.

But before we returned to the Sunshine State, we had another stop to make – Blaine's place in Birmingham, Alabama.

Dale had suggested that we visit his brother Blaine on our way back to Florida. Blaine lived in Birmingham and, when we called him, he was more than happy to have us over.

He sounded excited on the phone, welcoming us to stay in the spare room of his two-bedroom condominium that he shared with his girlfriend.

It felt like the perfect way to break up the long journey, and we were eager to see another part of the country.

Planning the Greyhound bus trip back was almost as much of an adventure as the trip itself.

This time, we wanted to take a different route, to see unexplored places and experience more of America's vastness. The first stop on our new route was Phoenix, about 350 miles away, and we were looking forward to it.

From Phoenix, we would head to Dallas – a long haul of 1,065 miles across the vast, open desert. I remember how the bus would rumble across that seemingly endless stretch of land, with nothing but sand, cacti, and the occasional tumbleweed to break up the monotony.

It was the kind of landscape that made you feel small, just another traveller in the vastness of the American West.

Cowboys

During our stopover in Dallas, Martin and I had a few hours to kill, so we wandered around and checked out some of the local shops. We stumbled upon this fascinating little place that was a mix of an Army surplus store and a boot and leather shop. The place had that unmistakable smell of leather and old fabric, and the walls were lined with all sorts of gear, from military jackets to rows of boots that looked like they had seen some serious miles.

We could not resist diving into the racks of used military shirts and T-shirts. Something about those worn-in clothes, with their history and ruggedness, appealed to us. We each picked out a few items, feeling like we were getting a real piece of Americana to return home.

Then we moved on to the boots. The place had an impressive selection, but what really caught our eye were the cowboy boots – genuine leather, tough as nails, with those pointy toes they called "shit kickers."

We learned from the store owner that the pointed toe was designed to kick the dirt out from a horse's shoe, but it was clear these boots had a reputation that went beyond practicality.

Martin and I looked at each other, and without saying a word, we knew we had to have a pair. We splashed out on them, knowing these boots would be a perfect memento of our time in Texas. They were heavy and solid and made us feel like we were channelling some of that cowboy spirit.

Walking out of that shop with our new gear in hand and those boots on our feet, we felt like we were bringing a piece of the Wild West back with us.

It was one of those small, unexpected moments that added another layer to our journey across America.

After Dallas, the plan was to head to Jackson, Mississippi. It was another long stretch of road, but by that point, we were used to the marathon bus rides and the strange mix of exhaustion and exhilaration that came with them.

The final leg of our journey would take us from Jackson to Birmingham, Alabama – another 640 miles.

Birmingham, Alabama

By the time we arrived in Birmingham, we would have covered a lot of ground and seen a lot of new places. But the thought of staying with Blaine, meeting new people, and experiencing life in yet another part of the United States made the miles ahead seem more like an adventure than a burden.

It was one more chapter in our American road trip, and we were ready for whatever it had in store.

We spent a couple of days mostly hanging out at Blaine's condominium complex. The place had a fantastic swimming pool, and with a few pretty girls around, it was easy to stay put and enjoy the laid-back atmosphere.

Blaine and his girlfriend were lovely hosts, making us feel at home. They even took us out to dinner at a local pub in the city, where we had a wonderful time laughing, sharing stories and soaking up the local culture. But soon enough, it was time to pack our bags and continue our journey back down to Pensacola.

We called Jane to let her know we were on our way, and true to form, she was at the bus station to pick us up as soon as we arrived.

Returning to Pensacola felt like coming home. The familiarity of the place was a comfort after our long, exhausting trip across the country. It was good to be back with Jane and Martin's family, where we could finally kick back and relax after days on the road.

Those last couple of weeks in Pensacola were much more settled. We spent most of our time around the house, enjoying the slower pacc of lifc.

I even dusted off my painting gear and started working on some acrylic pieces – surrealistic and fantasy stuff I had been thinking about for a while. One picture I did was of a lizard on a moonscape in space. Jane loved it, and I decided to give it to her as a gift. She insisted on paying for it, knowing that we were running low on cash, but it was clear that she really appreciated it. She hung it up in her condominium, and soon after, one of her friends who visited the condominium saw the painting and admired it.

He told Jane to let me know that if I wanted a job designing and creating T-shirts for his business, which he ran from a beach house down at the shore, I was more than welcome to join him and his team.

The offer was incredibly enticing. I could easily picture myself living in Florida, working as an artist, and enjoying the beach life. But I was with Martin, and we both had responsibilities back home.

Our visas were due to expire, and I knew that if I wanted to pursue this dream, I would need to return to England first and look into getting a green card, so I could come back to the USA legally.

Eventually, the time came for us to leave the United States and return to the United Kingdom.

In three months, we had covered over 6,000 miles on this epic journey. It was the adventure of a lifetime, but it was over.

The family in Pensacola had been so wonderful to us, and saying goodbye was hard. We had bought a gift for Frank and Joanne with the rest of the money we had left, just a small trinket, but they were so pleased. There were many tears at the airport as we hugged and said farewells.

With one last wave, we turned and pushed our trolleys through to baggage control, leaving behind a chapter of our lives we would never forget.

CHAPTER 27
ENGLAND

Martin and I walked into the Crooked Billet pub in Maidenhead. After three months in the USA, it felt like a homecoming. Our friends greeted us like heroes, eager to hear our tales. We had spent the previous few weeks in Florida, so our deep tans stood out in May's early days, making our friends look pale and envious.

I scanned the pub, taking in all the familiar faces. But Anne and Ingrid were nowhere to be seen.

The next morning, I sat down for breakfast with my mum and dad. They were so relieved I was home and unharmed. Before I could start sharing my stories, my mum, with an unusually stern look, said she had news for me.

"Yeah, what's the news, mum ?" I asked.

"Anne came to see me shortly after you left," she began.

"When I told her you had a three-month visa to the USA, she began to cry. She said it was clear you didn't want to be with her."

I laughed, "What a silly girl. She knows I love her. No girl in the world comes close. I told her I just needed some space for a while. I'll call her, and hopefully, she'll calm down."

Mum replied, "Oh, she calmed down, my boy. Two weeks after you left, she got married. She is now living in Australia with her new husband."

"What? You're kidding, right?" I said in disbelief.

My father chimed in, "You missed out big time, son. She was the best thing that ever happened to you, and now she has slipped through your fingers. Serves you right for being such an idiot."

I drove the mile to her mother's house and sat in my car, staring at the front door, hoping to see her. Finally, I summoned the courage to walk up the path, knocked on the door, and held my breath. When Anne's mother opened the door and saw me, she put her hand over her mouth, feeling as awkward as I did.

She told me to step inside. I followed her down the hall and sat at the kitchen table. She made me a cup of coffee and joined me. I could not tell if she was angry or sad as she silently sipped her tea.

"I can't believe it. Did she really get married?" I asked.

She put her cup down with a thump and answered, "Yes, and it's your bloody fault, you silly boy. She is gone, gone to bloody Australia, of all places. Why did you clear off and leave her like that?"

She wiped tears from her eyes and looked at me. I could not hold back any longer and we both cried together.

Back home, lying on my bed, my world felt like it was falling apart. I realised just how much I loved her, the pain tearing through me like my guts had been ripped out. I kept asking myself why I had been so selfish and not called her. The regret was overwhelming.

Highs and lows

Just a few weeks before, I had been living high in the USA, not in a care in the world, and having the time of my life. Then, suddenly, I had lost the only girl I ever loved. I had not realised how much I loved her until she was gone. The bottom fell out of my world. I was heartbroken. Not only was I feeling sorry for myself and the loss, but I also wondered if I had hurt her so much that she could marry a guy she only knew for two weeks. Her mum explained that she had been working with him. He was Australian and had to return to Australia, so he married her to take her with him.

I drove past her house every night, hoping she would return from Australia. I could not sleep; I could not do anything. I was so unhappy. I parked outside her house every night for weeks, but she did not come home. I felt empty and alone.

After a couple of months, I gradually accepted the fact that she was gone. I had made the biggest mistake of my life, but it was done. It was time to accept, adjust, and move on.

That pain stayed with me for years, a space inside me; it took years to get over Anne.

CHAPTER 28

CAROLINE

She was just 18 when we started going out together. I had just returned from the US a few weeks before. I had seen her around several times. She was often in the local pubs. I always thought Caroline was a good-looking girl, but she was three years younger than me. By now, she had grown up quite a bit.

One evening, she walked into the pub with Tom Scott. They had been dating since before I left for the USA.

We all sat around a table, drinking and talking and I noticed how she kept smiling at me. Tom was also 18, a lovely lad, but a wimp. Caroline knew what I thought of him and seemed to enjoy teasing him.

Eventually, I asked her to come out with me for a drink and she accepted. She dumped Tom, and soon, Caroline and I were an item. She was not a pretty girl; she was striking, though; she had her own style, which was quite different from the crowd, which attracted me to her. But I could not get Anne out of my head. She would not leave me; she would not go away.

My dad parked his car and came in, heading straight to the sofa, which was unusual for him. Usually, he would go to his bedroom, change his clothes, wash up, and then help my mum in the kitchen. I said, "Hi, dad. How is it going?"

"All right, son," he replied, hesitating. "I've got an annoying pain in my hip. It's been bothering me all day, coming and going ever since we returned from holiday."

That was a couple of months ago. I asked, "What sort of pain is it?"

"A real nagging pain, on and off again, quite sharp," he said. "I think it's from the flight back from Malta. The seats were tight, with no space to move. We were squashed in those seats for hours."

Later, I went to pick Caroline up from her father's house to take her out for the evening. All was not well at her home. Her mum had left to live in Spain with her new boyfriend. Her father, Ken, was crushed and did not handle her infidelity and desertion well.

I had witnessed the breakdown of her father and the family over the past couple of weeks. I liked him, but he had turned to drink and was becoming an alcoholic; his business was in trouble and the home was a mess, his life disintegrating around him.

I knocked on the door and walked into the kitchen. Ken was angry, screaming at Caroline, her younger brother standing in the corner looking shell-shocked. Ken, in his drunken anger, was comparing her to her mother, calling her a cheap slut, and telling her to leave the house for good.

Caroline was not crying; she did not argue. She stared at him with an icy cold look, her hatred for him evident. She went upstairs, and Ken ignored me, going outside to his garage. Her brother looked at me and said, "Welcome to the madhouse," then went into the living room and switched on the TV.

I sat at the kitchen table and waited for Caroline. She came downstairs with a large travel bag in her hand. Seeing I was alone, she sat at the table and began crying. She was upset, clearly struck deep and in shock, struggling to find her words.

I said, "Come on, let's get out of here. You can stay at my place."

She looked at me with tears and asked, "Will that be okay? Will your parents mind? If I can stay for a few days, it will give me time to find a place."

She was working and earning her own money, so she felt confident it was time to escape the turmoil.

We walked into my parents' kitchen, where they were watching TV. My mum saw Caroline's bag and knew something was up. As always, my mum was fantastic. She came into my bedroom and Caroline started crying. My mum hugged her and told her she needed not to worry about anything; she could stay at our house, in my room, for however long she wanted. Caroline could not hide her relief and hugged my mum and dad, thanking them both.

My father replied, "Don't be silly, Caroline. You're Roger's girl;

you're one of us now." And I watched him limp back to the living room.

Moving out and moving up

After a few weeks, I decided it was time for Caroline and me to move out and get our place. My parents were great about it, but being in the bedroom next door to them felt strange.

My father told me about a caravan for sale in Bray, on a farm near Windsor Road, about five miles from my parents' home. It was advertised for £1,600 for the freehold of the caravan, plus £5 a week for the site rental. My parents took Caroline and me to look at it. It was one of four caravans on an orchard smallholding. Pomona Farm was in Monkey Island Lane, a very exclusive postcode and home to millionaires and celebrities.

The caravan was about 30 years old, a bit scruffy, painted yellow and white, with an old wooden outhouse and a chemical toilet. It was quite a shock. Caroline and I looked at each other and laughed, unable to see this as our future home. My father reassured us, saying it was a better choice than renting. It would be ours, and we would only have to pay monthly site rent.

"Don't worry, kids," he said. "It will be easy to make this nice and comfortable. Look at the plot; it is quite large. You have a private parking space surrounded by fruit trees and hedges. You've even got a quaint cottage-style front gate with a rose arch." He smiled encouragingly.

It was quite picturesque, and we began to see his vision. We decided to buy it.

I walked into the betting shop and saw Burt Farr for the first time since before I went to America. The punters turned to look, some of them remembering me. I said, "Hi, Burt."

He was behind the reinforced glass counter, still in his worn-out tweed jacket, his cigarette dangling from his bottom lip as usual. He looked at me and, without smiling, said, "How much?"

Surprised, I said, "I just came by to say hello."

He smirked and said, "How much do you want to borrow?" Everyone laughed.

I laughed and said, "Please lend me some money."

We all chuckled, and he said, "Come inside." He unlocked the security door and took me behind the counter. He made me a cup of coffee. I told him about the caravan, about Caroline, about my father not being well, and how I wanted to get out of their house and get our own place.

I explained that I had money in my savings account, but could not access it for six months. I promised to repay any loan then.

Burt picked up the phone and called his solicitor. He told him we would be arriving at the law firm's office later that afternoon and to prepare a contract to loan £1,600 to Roger Warner. Later that day, I signed the contract, and his solicitor handed me an envelope with the money I needed.

I said, "Thank you so much, Burt. I won't let you down."

He said, "I know you won't, boy. I am happy to help. Good luck."

We moved into the caravan, decorated it, and made it comfortable. Little did we know what we would be facing in the winter to come.

CHAPTER 29
BACK TO BAKER ST

I parked my Mini on Crawford Street, displayed my disabled parking badge, and paid for the meter just to be sure. I walked about 80 yards to 104 Baker Street. It was terribly busy, with queues of big red buses, black taxi cabs and many pedestrians.

This place was special to me; the Jerry Rafferty song *Baker Street* inspired me to get out of my boring life and see the world. And I had been to Europe, the USA and Mexico since then.

Now, here I was, at the home of Sherlock Holmes, the famous detective. I had read most of his books, so I knew this part of London well.

I had a 10:00am interview with Pelling & Cross, the professional photography equipment supplier. I made my way up two flights of stairs, fortunately finding a good bannister rail to use with my left hand, my walking stick in my right hand. I wore my best suit, a colourful tie and a new haircut.

Mr Pelling greeted me and took me into his office. I sat down at his leather and mahogany desk, with Baker Street visible through the window behind him. He glanced through my CV and saw my address: Pomona Farm, Bray.

"Oh, I see you live in Monkey Island Lane?" he said, clearly impressed.

I smiled inside, knowing Terry Wogan lived just down the road. There was no way he could know I lived in a caravan. "Yes, do you know it?" I asked.

"Yes, it's a genuinely nice part of the world. We have dined at the Monkey Island Hotel a few times. It's beautiful there, lovely views of the Thames."

He looked at my previous employment and seemed more than happy that I could tackle the job of Assistant Designer. He showed me around the art studio and introduced me to the other two staff members.

"OK, then, Roger. Welcome on board. You start next Monday."

I was so excited. This was my first job in the West End of London, a step up. I was looking forward to it. I reached out my left hand, which always confused right-handed people, but he adjusted, and we shook hands. I made my way down those stairs and out onto the famous Baker Street. I could not believe my luck again. When going for a job interview, the dice fell my way, but I thought I would not be able to invite Mr Pelling around for coffee.

Caroline was working, I now had a decent job, and we had our own home. My father was not well and had tests at the hospital. Caroline suggested, "Why don't we get married?"

My career was underway

I had not planned to get married. It was several months since I returned from the USA. Anne was always on my mind, and I wondered if her hasty marriage would soon break down and she would return home.

I also dreamed of returning to the United States. I was confident I could find a job there and excited at the prospect of living abroad. However, since I returned, things have not gone as planned. Caroline's situation forced her to become my partner in a very tangible way, and my father's illness meant I could not leave the country knowing he was unwell.

Caroline seemed very keen to tie the knot, and I was in a good place. We were having fun and enjoying our modest home. We were both earning decent money so we could go out and buy things. Life was wonderful. So, I agreed to an October wedding, which, being nine months away, seemed like enough time to get used to the idea.

I was fit; my body had grown stronger, as strong as it was ever going to be. I still needed a walking stick to get around, but I was pushing myself hard.

I woke up early and drove my car to Maidenhead bus station,

where I parked. I had to climb the stairs to the platform, take the train to Paddington, disembark and take the stairs down to the underground. Then came the battle with the crowds to board the underground tube train to Baker Street station, climb the stairs to Marylebone Road, and get a taxi to the Pelling & Cross office in Baker Street before 9:00am. It was quite a workout for me twice a day.

In the following months, we applied for and were given a new house in Radcot Close by a local housing association. My mother made the application on my behalf without me knowing. One of her friends at the bowling club, who was involved with the housing association trustees, also nominated me for the Sportsman of the Year trophy. Somehow, I went straight to the top of the waiting list, and within a couple of weeks, we were moving into a brand-new three-bedroom house.

After a couple of months working in the West End of London, the first excitement wore thin. The costly and difficult commute every day was too much. I responded to a job advertisement for a paste-up artist at the prestigious advertising agency Harrison Cowley in Maidenhead. Thanks to my experience working in London, I got the job working on the Renault cars account. My salary increased, and my commute was down to 10 minutes.

At last, I felt normal, confident and positive. I did not think about my disability or about getting better – only about what I was achieving in my career, my relationship, my own home and my future.

CHAPTER 30

MICK AND SAM

y father, Mick, was confined to home, unable to get out of bed because the pain had become so severe. My mum insisted he see a doctor.

I did not know exactly what was afflicting him, but I knew he needed tests and treatment. He had problems with his prostate gland, but now it was clear his condition was profoundly serious and things were gradually getting worse.

I could see my mother under incredible stress, with my sister doing everything she could to support her. I felt helpless. I made a point of visiting my father every day, but it became noticeably clear that this was aggressive cancer. He had lost weight and looked 20 years older than just a few weeks before.

Caroline suggested we move the wedding date to 12 April, just a few weeks away. Even though nobody said it, we all knew my father would not make it to October. So, I went to Maidenhead Town Hall and booked the registry office.

The wedding went as planned, but my father was too ill to attend. He stayed home, dressed in his best suit, so we could take photos with him when we returned.

Caroline's mother thought giving her a few gin and tonics would steady her nerves before the ceremony. I had to hold Caroline upright in front of the registrar as she swayed and giggled, the smell of alcohol on her breath embarrassing. Looking at her tipsy mother, I suddenly realised I had made a terrible mistake.

We returned to my parents' house to see my father. With help, he was able to stand with us for some photos. He was frail and in a lot of pain, but he smiled and hugged me tight.

I took Caroline back to our house to change out of her wedding dress and into our evening clothes. I complained that she had gotten drunk before the wedding. She did not like that and responded by throwing an alarm clock at me. It just missed my head, smashed into the wall, and disintegrated into pieces on the floor. I held my head in my hands and thought, "What have I done?"

We returned that evening for our wedding reception at the Swan restaurant in Maidenhead, where all our guests were waiting for us. We had an evening meal, made speeches, read the cards and thanked our guests for all the gifts. Around 11:00pm, we left for our honeymoon hotel.

The final days

My father's cancer was advancing quickly. He lost even more weight and became very weak. They moved him to Saint Mark's Hospital, a small cottage hospital close to the main hospital building. It was quite close to my parents' home, just a 10-minute drive away. My mum and sister were usually there to feed him and I would see him most evenings after work. I read books with him. His love was sailing and I bought him a big photo-illustrated book, The World's Greatest Yachts.

He loved it. I brought him his binoculars so he could watch the birds. It was spring and the garden was beautiful.

Saying goodbye

It was 16 May when my mum called and said, "You'd better come to the hospital."

I sat by my father's bedside. He was gaunt and grey, unconscious from the painkillers, his body still except for the weak rise and fall of his breathing. My mum, sister and I talked to him, but he could not hear us. He was slowly slipping away. I held his big, hard left hand in mine and squeezed it, hoping he would feel it.

His breathing became uneven, and he was fighting for breath. We knew what was coming and were all weeping. I leaned down close to his face, so my warm breath brushed his face, and said, "I love you, dad. It is okay to let go now. Please know I love you so much."

His chest wheezed and he struggled for air. There was a stutter in his breath, which made his chest rise slightly, and then he was quiet. He had gone. He was finally out of pain.

I couldn't believe it. My dad, Mick Warner, dead? I had never felt a pain like this before. I pulled his hand to my face and held it tight; I was screaming inside. I kissed it and said goodbye for the last time.

My father's passing left a massive hole in all our lives. My sister was devastated; she had always been daddy's little girl. My mum had married my dad in 1949 when she was just 19. They had not been separated in 31 years of blissful marriage. She was destroyed, certainly not capable of living on her own. Fortunately, she still had her mum, my 78-year-old nan, my sister and her three daughters, and, of course, me. We would all support each other.

Unexpected news

"I'm pregnant," said Caroline.

It was just a few weeks after my father died. I was shocked because we had been taking precautions. Caroline was on the pill, and we had not planned to have kids; we never even discussed it.

"What?" I said in surprise.

"I'm pregnant. Aren't you happy about it?" she answered.

I was stunned and spinning. After my accident, the doctor told me I might never be able to have children. Yet here I was, being confirmed as man enough to breed and create the next generation. It was incredibly satisfying.

But I had never contemplated being a father, certainly not for the next few years, and I was convinced we were taking precautions. I was so confused, angry, terrified and happy all at the same time. I did not know what to think.

"I thought you were taking the pill?" I spoke.

"Well, I stopped taking the pill when we got married," she said.

"So, when was this baby conceived?" I asked.

She looked at me and smiled. "I think it must have been on our honeymoon, looking at the dates."

"Why didn't you tell me you were going to stop taking the pill? Surely this is something we should agree on together, isn't it?" I asked.

She looked angered and said, "I thought you'd be happy about it."

"Of course, I'm happy that I'm going to be a dad. I would love to have a baby, but I am unprepared. This has come as a terrible shock to me," I replied.

"So, what are you saying? You do not want this child?" she snapped.

"No, of course, I'm not saying that. I am not saying that at all. Of course, I want this child. I am extremely excited that I am going to be a dad. It is just very sudden, OK?" I replied.

Samuel was born on 1 February, 1981. He was late and the birth had to be induced. I took an active role, holding Caroline's hand and shouting encouragement during her arduous labour. I had an up-close view as Samuel's head gradually emerged. His little face pointed directly at me, and as he opened his eyes, I was the first thing he saw. I was close enough to have blood splattered on my arms and shirt. But it was not scary at all. It was the most fascinating thing I have ever seen in my life. Witnessing birth is incredibly inspiring.

I was so excited, thinking about all the adventures I was about to have with this little blond-haired boy.

CHAPTER 31
ETON

We made a good profit when we sold the caravan. We bought it for £1,600, and just a year later, we sold it for £3,500. My dad's hard work decorating, and new curtains and furniture covers made it look nice. Together with the rest of my insurance money, we now had enough to put a deposit on a house. I was working at the advertising agency, receiving a good salary and, even with Caroline no longer working, it was quite easy for me to get an 80% mortgage.

We found a small two-bedroom end-terrace house for £21,000, on the same road as my parent's old house where we were living when I had my accident. It was just a coincidence. The house was in awful condition and needed decorating from floor to ceiling in every room, but we had the time and motivation to turn this little house into our very own cosy new home.

My life was swinging back and forth like a pendulum. Losing my dad was, without a doubt, the worst thing that ever happened to me.

I thought my accident was terrible, but seeing my dad shrivel and turn into a faint shadow of his former strong, handsome, life-of-the-party self, then literally slip through my fingers, was devastating.

Then, just a few weeks later, to learn that I beat the odds again by fathering a child was an extraordinarily scary high.

"Roger, did you see the ad in the *Maidenhead Advertiser?* They're looking for a Senior Graphic Artist for a magazine publishing and design studio in Eton," Annabelle, one of the three other graphic artists in the studio, asked me with a sparkle in her eye. I was not looking for a change, so I barely gave it a second thought. "Yeah, I saw it. Are you interested?" I asked.

She grinned, "I think I am. Imagine working in Eton, all those handsome, rich boys parading up and down the High Street."

She giggled, the thought amusing her. The ad was from Group Typesetters, a company on Eton High Street, right where the famous school was, with its boys in top hats and tailcoats.

"Why don't you give them a call?" I suggested.

Annabelle hesitated, a bit of shyness creeping in. "I don't know what to say. Could you call them for me? Just to get more details?"

I agreed, figuring it was the least I could do. I dialled the number, and after a few rings, a voice answered, "Hello, Group Typesetters, Ben speaking."

"Hello, Ben. My name is Roger Warner. I saw your advertisement for a Senior Graphic Artist and was hoping to get more details – like what the job entails, the benefits, salary, that sort of thing," I said.

"Sure, Roger. But first, can I ask what you are currently doing and where you are working?" he replied.

That caught me off guard. I had not expected to be the one answering questions. But I had no choice. "I'm a Graphic Designer and Paste-up Artist at Harrison & Cowley in Maidenhead. I work on the Renault Cars account," I explained.

"Oh yes, I know them," Ben said, sounding interested. "When can you come in for an interview? How about tomorrow at 5:30pm?"

I was floored. I had not planned on this, but I found myself saying, "Yeah, sure. I'll see you then." Annabelle laughed, "Looks like I got you a new job, Roger!"

I was one of four graphic artists in the design studio at Harrison & Cowley, with a studio manager who was also a designer and artist. I would have ranked myself about third best – still learning, still finding my feet.

So, I was stunned when Ben Burton offered me not just a position as a Graphic Artist but as a Senior Designer as well. In the world of graphic design, that was a significant step up. Typically, Graphic Artists bring other designers' visions to life, interpreting their concepts into finished artwork. For instance, my work on the Renault account left little room for creativity – I followed a strict design specification, turning instructions into art. But a Graphic Designer?

That role was for someone who dreamed up the concepts and created them rather than just executed them. And Ben wanted me to do both.

Ben had just contracted to produce layouts for two monthly magazines: *Defence* and *International Broadcast Engineer* (IBE). The magazines were a mess – ugly, outdated, amateurish. Ben wanted me to set up a magazine production department within the design studio, bringing these publications into the modern era. I would redesign them, handle the page layouts, and streamline the entire production process. It was a thrilling opportunity, a clear step up the ladder, and I eagerly accepted the challenge along with the better benefits package that came with it.

The studio, as it stood, was a relic. Two lady typographers worked on IBM typewriters, the old golf-ball models with special ribbons and unique fonts. They typed on black carbon paper that could be cut and pasted onto magazine forms, which were then passed to the Paste-up Artist, a young girl named Marion. She used Letraset for headlines and larger text, following the editor's instructions to design the page. It was a slow, labour-intensive process.

But I knew things could be better. I had seen the advances in cold-type processes and how they had developed into computerised systems. I quickly realised we needed to upgrade our equipment if we were to succeed. I met with Ben and laid out my vision. I wanted to bring modern CG typesetting equipment – specifically, the EditWriter, an innovative machine from an American company. This machine could create type in sizes from six-to-72 points, store information on eight-inch floppy disks, and image onto photosensitive paper with incredible precision. It would replace the outdated chalk, carbon and Letraset process, making everything faster and more exact.

Ben was intrigued, but cautious. It was a significant investment, more than we could justify based on our current contracts. "So, what do you think, Ben? Can we get a couple of these CG machines and revamp the whole production department?" I asked.

Ben looked at me, his face serious. "How can we make it pay?" he asked.

"What do you mean?" I replied, unsure of where he was going.

"Well, you can have the machines, but they have to make a

profit. I need to see a financial return that covers the investment and the salaries of the staff," he said.

I was taken aback. "How am I going to do that?"

"You're going to have to go and get some new customers," he said matter-of-factly.

It was a new challenge for me. Until then, I had been a junior designer, focused solely on artwork, posters and business cards. The idea of being responsible for studio equipment, hiring staff and, most daunting of all, finding new clients was overwhelming. But I knew it was the only way forward. The company needed to evolve, or it would not survive.

Ben was willing to take the risk, so I dove in. I managed to find two used CG machines for the price of one new one. The printing company selling them even offered us a deal on printing prices if we used their services for our magazines. They also began sending us small design and artwork jobs, which helped us build momentum.

The quality of our magazines improved dramatically. Soon, Ben secured a third contract for a magazine called *Miltronics* (military electronics), followed by another for the British Racehorse Owners Association magazine, *Owners, Trainers & Breeders.* Then came *Majesty*, a magazine about the royal family. We were doing well.

But I needed to bring in more business to keep the momentum going. I had no formal sales training, only my design, artwork and printing knowledge. So, I started cold calling. I remembered something my father had once told me: "If you want to make money, go where the money is. Talk to the people who have it."

Considering that, I drove around Slough Trading Estate, looking for offices with the most expensive cars parked outside – Jaguars, Mercedes, Range Rovers and the occasional Rolls-Royce.

I parked my Lancia on the curb, grabbed my walking stick in one hand and my folder of samples in the other, and approached a printing factory. I pushed open the blue steel door and walked inside. To my left was a glazed office where a smartly dressed man in his 30s waved me in.

"Hello, yes, what can I do for you, sir?" he asked, thinking I was a customer. In my naïve way, I introduced myself. "Hello, I'm Roger from Group Typesetters in Eton. We offer a range of design services." I began to show him my portfolio.

He raised his eyebrows, set his coffee cup down, and said bluntly, "Fuck off, mate. I have not got time for this. Not now, not today. Call and make an appointment." He waved me away dismissively.

I was stunned. Speechless. Gutted. I sheepishly backed out, hurried to my car, and sat gripping the steering wheel, wondering what I had gotten myself into. Was this what I would have to face every day? It was a nightmare.

Back at the office, I told Ben what had happened. He burst out laughing, put his arm around me, and said, "Chin up, Roger. Nothing ventured, nothing gained. You will be all right. Just keep knocking on doors; eventually, someone will say yes."

I mentioned where I had been thrown out, and Ben said, "Do you know they print the packaging for Commodore computers? They are a big player. If you could land a contract with them, you would be laughing. Why don't you call and make an appointment?"

The next day, I looked up their number in the Yellow Pages and dialled. "Hi, you might remember me. You told me to fuck off yesterday," I said.

The voice on the other end chuckled. "Yes, I remember you. Sorry, you caught me at an inconvenient time. What can I do for you?"

"I'd like just 10 minutes of your time to show you what we're doing. It may or may not interest you, but surely, it is worth 10 minutes to find out if I can save you some money?"

To my surprise, he agreed. "Why not? Come by at 3:00 this afternoon. I look forward to seeing you."

I pulled up again, parked beside his shiny black Mercedes, and walked into his office. This time, he smiled and offered me a seat. He even asked if I wanted a drink. I declined politely and asked for his name.

"Simon O'Connor, Managing Director," he replied.

"Nice to meet you, Simon. I am from Group Typesetters in Eton. We are a small, but excellent, design studio. We work on a range of things, including labelling and packaging design. We also produce five significant magazines and have recently invested in new equipment to offer top-notch typography and packaging."

He seemed interested. "OK, sounds interesting."

I continued, "Plus, we're just around the corner, so I can get here in 10 minutes if you need anything quickly. It might be worth giving us a try."

Simon got up, retrieved a board from a cabinet, and placed it on the table in front of me. "How much would you charge me to do something like this?" he asked.

It was packaging for a Commodore computer box, about three by two feet, with various illustrations and text panels. I had no clue how much to charge, so I asked, "How much would you expect to pay for it?"

"If you can do it as finished artwork for £175, the job is yours," he said.

"Sure, I can do that," I replied without hesitation.

"Great. Can I have it back within the week?"

"Of course, no problem, Simon. Consider it done!" I said, my excitement evident.

I made my way back to the office, feeling triumphant. I walked into Ben's office and proudly presented the folder to him. "Bingo! We got our first job – Commodore packaging."

Ben took a step back, clasped his hands together, and said, "Well done, Roger! I can't believe it."

Ben, being a talented designer and typographer, took the reins from there. He marked it up for the typesetters and turned the job around in a couple of days. Simon was thrilled with the result, and soon, a steady stream of work started coming in.

The studio was buzzing, busier and more productive than ever. For me, it was a completely new view of the world. I had always focused on typefaces, designs, and colours, content when my work pleased clients. But now, I have discovered a new thrill – being a sales associate.

CHAPTER 32
WAR

he nuclear submarine *HMS Conqueror* sinks the Argentine cruiser *General Belgrano,* killing 323 sailors, blared the headline in the *Daily Telegraph* on 2 May, 1982.

Mike Jenkins, the Editor of *Defence* magazine, was practically buzzing with excitement as he sipped his pint of Guinness and bit into his egg and bacon sandwich.

"Look at this!" he exclaimed. "There is going to be so much interesting product news coming in. Our advertisers have spent fortunes testing their munitions and weapon systems to prove their effectiveness in battle. Now, thanks to this most fortunate of wars, they will have real data, battle-tested evidence every day. This is great for the defence industry, my boy."

Defence magazine was one of the five publications I designed and helped produce in our studio. The Argentinian forces had invaded the British overseas territory of the Falkland Islands on 2 April, 1982, having claimed sovereignty over the islands for years.

Its military junta had gambled that Britain, being more than 8,000 miles away, would not attempt to reclaim the islands by force.

But they had not reckoned with Margaret Thatcher's resolve. She undertook the extraordinary feat of assembling and sending a task force of warships and hastily refitted merchant ships to the Falklands.

Thatcher later wrote in her memoir 'Downing Street Years', "When you are at war, you cannot allow the difficulties to dominate your thinking: you must set out with an iron will to overcome them. And anyway, what was the alternative? That a common or garden dictator should rule over the Queen's subjects and prevail by fraud and violence? Not while I was Prime Minister."

The massive Argentinian battle cruiser, *General Belgrano,* was sailing within the UK's exclusion zone, defying Thatcher's threat to sink any ship that entered. Even though it was on course to exit the zone within 30 minutes, some insiders believed that Thatcher gave the order to the captain of *HMS Conqueror* to fire and sink the enemy ship. It set the stage for the rest of the war, with the British forces relentlessly pounding the Argentinians by air, sea, and land. Despite suffering brutal losses, the British Navy prevailed, and the Argentinians surrendered on 14 June.

"Yes, great news, Mike, lots more weapons adverts for me to design," I said, half-joking, as I grabbed my walking stick from the bar. "Anyway, some of us have to get back to work." I began the 50-yard walk from the Christopher pub on Eton High Street back to our office on the first floor of the old, converted fire station. The stairs were tough, but the broad steps and solid bannister made it easier. I treated each ascent as a workout, pushing myself to reach the top as quickly as possible.

As soon as I walked in, the office phone rang. Ben answered and then looked at me, "Roger, it's for you."

I took the phone, "Hello?"

"Roger, it is Stuart. You need to come home now," said my brother-in-law, my sister's husband. His voice was tense, and the urgency in his tone confused me. Why would Stuart be calling me at work?

"Stuart? What is wrong? What is the problem?" I asked, my confusion turning into anxiety.

"Just get back here now. It is urgent," he insisted and hung up.

A shudder ran through me – a sudden, paralysing fear of the unknown. My heart pounded as I stared out the window, trying to imagine what could have happened that required me to rush home immediately. The darkest thoughts began to swirl in my mind. My son, Sam, was just a year old. Had something happened to him? Or to my wife? Was there an accident? Panic gripped me, and without explaining anything to my colleagues, I grabbed my stick and hurried back down the stairs.

Moments like these, when I could not run, cut deep. The 50

yards to the car park behind the old fire station felt like a marathon. I was terrified of falling, knowing it would only slow me down. I thrashed my old white Lancia HPE the six miles back to Maidenhead, driving far too fast, praying I would not crash.

As I pulled up on the street outside my small end-terrace, I saw my sister Lesley standing at the front door, tears streaming down her face, shaking her head in despair.

"Oh my God, what's happened?" I thought as I rushed into the hallway. I did not even notice Lesley getting into her car and driving away in tears.

Inside the living room, my mum was wailing incoherently like a banshee, her face crimson and wet with tears, swaying in a frantic, trance-like state. She looked horrified. My wife was sitting on the sofa, sobbing uncontrollably into a white handkerchief, her face red and swollen. Stuart, my brother-in-law, sat beside her, his arm around her shoulders, comforting her.

I looked around the room, but I could not see my son. Panic surged through me again, and I screamed, "Where's Sam? Where's Sam?"

Stuart looked at me and said, "Sam's okay. He is upstairs, sleeping."

Relief washed over me like a tidal wave. My darkest fears were extinguished. My beautiful boy was fine, sleeping through the chaos. But confusion quickly replaced my relief.

"What the hell is going on here? Will someone please tell me?"

Stuart looked up at me, his eyes serious. "We are in love," he said.

I froze, the words hitting me like a punch in the gut. I had been bracing for something far worse, so initially, I felt a strange calmness. But then the pieces started to fit together – the women in a frenzy, Stuart's urgent phone call, the two of them sitting side by side on my sofa. My mum's rage and sorrow, my sister's tears of disbelief and anguish, my wife's desperate attempts to disappear, and this long-haired, bearded imbecile announcing that he and my wife were "in love". The absurdity of it all stunned me.

Stuart spoke again, his tone stern, "I'm very sorry, Roger, but we're in love, and we're planning to live together."

I looked into his eyes with disdain and disbelief. "Oh, for fuck's sake, you absolute moron. Fuck off now. Get out of my house," I said, pointing to the door. "Thank God it was not my son. Thank God it is just you two fucking idiots. You're welcome to each other, so go on, fuck off. Both of you, fuck off now, get out of my house!"

My mum stepped back into the room. Stuart stood up, but my wife remained seated. "Go on, get the fuck out of here!" I shouted again. As Stuart walked out, he glanced back at Caroline, but she did not see him, her face buried in her hands. He left, and I looked at her, feeling a foul taste in my mouth that I wanted to spit out, but did not. Instead, I stayed composed and asked, "What on earth have you done?"

She cried, "I am sorry, but we just fell in love. You would not understand."

I snorted in disbelief. "Oh, where did you fall in love? In my bed? In my sister's bed?"

She shook her head, still sobbing. "No, it was not like that. We love each other."

The situation was ludicrous, and my anger flared. "So where, then? In the back of his fucking filthy old Volvo estate?" I paced around the room, shouting, "And where was Sam? In his Moses basket on the front seat?"

"No, no," she cried.

"You disgust me. You are unbelievable. It is my sister's fucking husband, for Christ's sake. They have four children. What did you think was going to happen?"

My mum put her arm around me, trying to calm and comfort me. I looked at her and said, "I am sorry, mum. I cannot stay here. I am going to throw up. I have got to leave. Please take care of Sam. I will see you later. I cannot stay in the same room as this bitch."

I drove the half mile to the local park, lit a cigarette, and stared out at the playing fields, the playground, and the procession of schoolchildren walking home with their mums.

My thoughts raced. Here we go again. My life was torn apart once more. Is there no end to the torture? But this time, I did not cry. I screamed in anger, my mind spinning as I tried to make sense of what was happening. I had learned to take the blows – to accept, adapt, and move on. My rational, pragmatic mind took over, and I began to plan my next steps.

After a couple of hours, I went back to the house. Mum had left, and my wife was upstairs with Sam. I did not speak to her. I picked up my son, kissed him and told him how much I loved him. Then I called my friend Dave. "Hello, mate. I just want to check if you are at home. I have had a bit of a situation. OK, if I come over for a chat?"

He could tell something was up from my voice. "Of course, friend. Come over. You can crash here for a while. See you soon," he said without hesitation.

I called my mum next. "Hello, mum. It is me."

"Oh, my darling, I am so sorry. This is all so crazy. My whole family was smashed to pieces by those two disgusting, selfish pigs. My poor Lesley is alone at home with the children. That idiot Stuart has gone to stay with his parents. Can you believe it? What a mess. What will you do, my darling?" she asked, her voice breaking with tears and fury.

"I will be staying at Dave's for a while. I cannot stay in this place. I need to sort my head out. Do not worry about me, mum, I am OK. I will pop around and see you tomorrow. I am so sorry you must see all this. I love you, mum."

As much as I hated it, I knew I had no choice but to leave Sam with Caroline for now. She was sitting on the bed, crying, when I went upstairs. I did not want to talk to her. I did not care about her feelings or emotions – she had not cared about mine, my sister's, or anyone else's. She had brought this on herself.

I was too angry to feel any empathy for her or anyone else except my son, my poor, distraught mum, and my sister, who was devastated with four young daughters. Even my grandmother, our matriarch, was in shock at this mess. I packed a bag, knowing I did not plan to come back anytime soon, and slammed the door behind me.

When I told Dave what had happened, he listened intently, his face a mixture of disbelief and anger. He insisted I stay with him for as long as it took to sort myself out.

For me, this felt like the end of the marriage. How could we ever get back together after this? She had declared her love for him, and he for her, killing any hope of reconciliation. My marriage was over, dead. There was one thing I could not abide – a liar, let alone someone who deceives and transgresses in such a way as to have an affair while married. The infidelity was terrible enough to have a relationship with my sister's husband. It was incestuous, revolting, and hurt so many people in one vile act. We were a close-knit family with five young children involved. It was utterly despicable.

"How could we ever look at each other in the eyes again, knowing what is in there? Things will never be the same," I thought. Not to mention, I never wanted to see his bearded face again, and for sure, my sister would never want to be near Caroline again.

Trying to lighten the mood, Dave said, "Cor blimey, Roger, here you go again, son. You do go through it, don't you, mate?"

I smiled at him and said, "It is another test, Dave. I have just got to sort it out. Besides, I have only got myself to blame. I married the girl, and I knew she was a bit screwed up. I have always tried to be there for her, to be supportive, to give her love. I thought we could make it work. How wrong I was."

CHAPTER 33

CARRY ON

Caroline was just 16 when I first met her. A rebellious schoolgirl, she was a bit mixed up, cutting her hair short like a boy and wearing jeans, a shirt, and a tie most of the time. But she could not hide her hips and breasts.

We got to know each other over the next couple of years and finally got together after I returned from my travels around the USA in May 1979. I was 22 and she was 18.

She had had an awkward adolescence, her parents' break-up following her mother's affair, and the subsequent divorce was difficult for her. Her mother left to live in Majorca, Spain, with her new man, leaving Caroline at home with her broken father and younger brother. Her sister, two years older, had already left home.

Caroline had had a pregnancy with a previous boyfriend that ended in abortion. She was self-harming, cutting her forearms with razor blades, often bandaging them like war wounds. Her father, who had attempted suicide himself, finally threw her out, and she came to live with me at my parents' house.

"She was a fruitcake, mate, and you did your best," Dave said, his voice filled with anger. "Look at how well you have coped after your dad died. You have bought your own house, got an excellent job, and had your son. For fuck's sake, what does she expect?"

"I am over her, Dave. I just hope my sister can find a way out of this mess without that fucking demented husband of hers. It is going to be so difficult for her, with four daughters, the youngest not even two years old. What were those two thinking? What did they think would happen with five children involved? It is absolute madness. Not to mention the age difference – he is 10 years older and should have known better."

Dave, now fuming, said, "As for that fucking Stuart, what a piece of shit he turned out to be. I want to go around there and kick the fuck out of the prick!"

"Nah," I said. "He would love that – to be the poor victim. He is a natural loser."

All I could think about was my son. I could bear leaving her, but not him. He was my pride and joy, and I did not want to be separated from him. I started to plan my next steps in my usual pragmatic way. I did not want this to turn into something hostile. I would take the high road and focus on how to continue with a clear divorce in the future. I stayed at Dave's place for a few months while the dust settled.

Ben, my boss, was very understanding during those difficult weeks. The whole company was incredibly supportive, even giving me a pay rise to help with the mortgage and rent. Dave never asked for money, but I tried to pay him whenever I could.

Against my advice and much to my chagrin, my sister took her pathetic, lying husband back after he grovelled and begged for forgiveness. She decided to forgive him despite my warnings that their relationship would never survive this calamity. But she was terrified of being alone with four girls and figured she could handle it. Time would tell if she was right.

Meanwhile, Caroline was alone, stuck at home with no one to support her. Her father was disgusted and would not talk to her. Her mother preferred the sunshine of Majorca. Her brother was off at university in Liverpool.

My mum would visit, but only to pick up Sam for the weekend – no words were spoken. With no chance of a future with Stuart, Caroline eventually prayed for my forgiveness and begged me to take her back, blaming him for her stupidity and naïvety. She tried to justify her actions, then realised she still loved me. I did not believe her for a moment, but after a few months, my anger cooled, and I could think more clearly.

One thing Caroline said that I believed was that Sam needed his dad. He was coming up on two years old – those crucial months of learning to talk and run around.

My dream of being a good father and raising my son became my priority, gradually overcoming my negative feelings toward her. I figured I could handle it and, against the advice I had given my sister, I decided to move back home. I could tolerate Caroline as my wife. I could always find my pleasures elsewhere if necessary. But I needed to be a hard-working husband and a loving father – that was the best I could hope for.

Apart from those few months we were separated, I never strayed with another woman. My family upbringing had instilled in me the importance of honesty, loyalty and faithfulness. I could not contemplate having an affair while being married and being a father.

She sat on the sofa, and I sat in the chair opposite. She tried to look vulnerable as she said, "Roger, I am so sorry for all the hurt and pain I have caused, especially for what I have done to your sister. But I want us to make this work. I do."

I looked into her eyes. It was difficult for her to be submissive, but I saw a young woman with two faces. There was no doubt she had suffered too. She was hurting, and her intentions were sincere.

"We've been through a lot," I replied. "I wasn't the perfect man, but I accept that. You supported me through my father's illness, and I appreciate that. I hope you also recognise what my family and I did for you when your father threw you out?" She nodded.

"Look, there is nothing I want more than to be a dad to my boy, but this will always be there in the background. It will be hard."

"I know," she said. "I will wipe it from my memory if I know we can carry on as if it never happened. I promise I will be a good wife and mother. Please, give me another chance."

So, we made a pact to rebuild our lives. We promised each other we would forget what had happened, never bring it up again, and work hard at our relationship and at being good parents to our son.

Surprisingly, things went well. I focused on my work and renovating our house. A year later, in August 1983, our daughter Stephanie was born. I was still at Group Typesetters, designing magazine layouts, packaging, product labels and corporate branding. My new role as a sales representative had gone particularly well. I had acquired several new clients, and our productivity and profits rose, as did my salary.

With inflation at 18%, I had to push my bosses for more money at least twice a year.

Derek McGuire, one of the shareholders and directors of Group Typesetters, was also the owner of *Owners, Trainers & Breeders* magazine, a horse racing publication. I enjoyed working on this magazine – lots of pictures of jockeys in colourful silks, beautiful horses and wealthy people collecting trophies.

Horse racing was an exciting and romantic world, one I knew well from my days with Burt Farr in the betting shop. Aware of my enthusiasm, Derek brought me several horse racing-related jobs in addition to the magazine.

He owned racehorses himself and was involved in horse breeding. He was constantly launching new businesses, and I often worked late preparing presentations, business plans and investment prospectuses for him. Occasionally, he would ask if I wanted to join him when he was going to the stables or the races. I enjoyed riding in his Rolls-Royce or his Daimler Double Six Coupé; he even gave me money to place bets at the racecourses.

Derek had great relationships with all his advertisers and we often met them in pubs and restaurants to discuss upcoming advertising and sponsorship contracts.

One day, we were in Antiqueos Italian restaurant, wining and dining with the boss of an international electronics company that worked for the military. He explained to Derek how they were expanding into the ever-growing private and civil security markets.

Derek looked at me and said, "Wow, now that is a coincidence. Roger here has been working on the design of our new cover for *Force & Security* magazine, a new project we are working on."

I smiled, realising what he was doing. There was no such project; Derek had produced it on the spot. He quickly saw the opportunity and told the client we were about to launch a new publication covering civil security, police forces, firefighters, and private and industrial security products and services.

By the end of lunch, Derek had sold them the back cover for a year – a contract worth enough to underwrite the launch of this new magazine. Back at the office, he hugged me, laughing, "Quickly,

Roger, you better design me some front covers and a rate card so I can make more presentations."

He had conceived the idea over lunch, and it went on to be an enormous success.

One day, the phone rang, and I picked it up. "Hello, Group Typesetters. How can I help you?"

It was Derek. "Roger, are you wearing a tie?"

"A tie? What do you mean?" I asked, confused.

"If you are not wearing a tie, go up to my office, borrow one from the chaps in accounts, and then come over here to meet me in the restaurant. I am dining with the ambassador of Ghana, and I need you to be my Creative Director. Do you understand me?"

Sure enough, I borrowed a tie and walked to the restaurant, an arduous 100-yard trek with my walking stick. When I arrived, Derek introduced me to the two African gentlemen at his table as his "Creative Director".

The only other thing he said to me was, "Choose what you like from the menu and what you want to drink." My role that day was to be part of his sales story. Derek was a fantastic entrepreneur and I learned so much from him.

No matter how much I enjoyed my job and working in the shadows of Windsor Castle on the River Thames, Caroline's affair with my brother-in-law was a constant embarrassment I could not shake. It was public knowledge among my colleagues, friends, and family. It was like an awful lingering smell I could not escape. I desperately wanted to tear my life up and start all over again.

CHAPTER 34
STEPHANIE

The final episode of my favourite Sunday night drama was on. It was 9.30 in the evening, and Caroline was stretched out on the sofa. Her night dress was wrapped comfortably around her and she propped her feet up. We were halfway through the final episode of this six-part series, and I was thoroughly absorbed in the unfolding climax. Suddenly, Caroline turned to me, her face tense. "I think the baby's coming," she said, her voice strained.

"Not now," I groaned, my eyes still glued to the screen. "Let me see the end of this episode, please."

She screamed at me, "It's not up to me, is it? The bloody baby comes when it comes! Can you check my bag, please?"

Resigned, I got up, grabbed the bag and checked on Sam. He was fast asleep, blissfully unaware of the commotion. My mother was away on a bowling tour, so I quickly decided to fetch my 81-year-old grandmother to come and babysit. I told Caroline to sit tight while I raced out to get nan.

I jumped into my white Alfa Romeo GTV and sped up the road. It was a mile to her bungalow, which sat back from the road across a manicured lawn. I did not have time to park and walk up the path with my stick, so I drove right across the lawn and parked outside her front door, knocking loudly.

Nan finally answered the door, her hair dishevelled, dressed in her pink dressing gown and slippers, without her teeth. "Nan, the baby's coming," I blurted out. "Mum's in Gloucester, can you come to watch Sam while I take Caroline to the hospital?"

She looked shocked but nodded, her toothless grin showing her surprise. "Oh, of course, love. Let me just grab my handbag."

I helped her down into the low car. She was still in her pink fluffy slippers and woolly dressing gown as I revved the engine and sped back home. The wheels screeched, and the engine roared, probably the fastest my nan had ever travelled. She gripped the door handle, her knuckles white, her mouth slightly agape in a mix of fear and excitement. But nan was a trooper. She had lived through two world wars and knew how to handle emergencies. I parked with two wheels on the footpath outside my front gate and helped nan out of the car. "Well, did you enjoy the ride, nan?" I asked, half-joking.

She laughed, slapping my arm lightly. "Oh, you are a cheeky one, Roger Warner."

With nan settled on the sofa, I helped Caroline to the car. She was in visible pain, writhing as I buckled her in. "Hurry, for God's sake, hurry – it's coming!" she moaned.

I slid into the driver's seat, but as I went to put the key in the ignition, I realised it was not there. I checked again, panic rising. This was my bunch of keys, but the ignition key was gone.

"For God's sake, give them to me!" Caroline snapped, snatching the keys from my hand. She frantically went through them, one by one, then screamed. "For fuck's sake, Roger, where's your bloody key?"

I could not understand it. The key was just gone. "I'll have to call an ambulance. Come on, let us go back into the house," I said, feeling utterly defeated.

Caroline could barely stand. "Oh, for fuck's sake, you have to be joking?" she yelled.

I dialled 999 and requested an ambulance. Caroline stood in the doorway, moaning and squirming, too afraid to sit down. The ambulance took about 10 agonising minutes to arrive. We rushed to Cliveden Hospital just before 11:15pm. There was no time for any preparation. Caroline's labour was advanced; I held her hand, coaching her through each push like a trainer urging on an athlete.

Stephanie was born about an hour later, on 8 August, 1983. Seeing my first daughter born was incredible; I was over the moon. The doctor suggested I go home to rest, as mother and baby were well, but exhausted. I said goodbye to Caroline and Stephanie and walked out to the car park, spending a good five minutes looking for my car before remembering it was back at home.

I found a phone box and called a taxi. Still in shock, but overwhelmingly happy, I realised I was now a father to a little girl. I felt like a new person, a different man.

The following day, nan woke me with a cup of coffee and some Marmite on toast. She sat at the end of my bed with Sam, and I told her everything that had happened. She was thrilled. I glanced out the window and saw something black on the white line in the middle of the road. Curious, I went outside, and there it was – my ignition key, the black plastic fob broken. "Thank you, Alfa, for your excellent build quality," I muttered, laughing at the absurdity of it all.

After taking nan home, I told her I would bring the new baby by tomorrow. "What are you going to name her?" she asked.

"Stephanie," I replied.

Nan looked puzzled. "Stephanie? That is not one of our family names. Where does that come from?"

"Stephanie Powers, nan. You know, the actress from *Hart to Hart*. I think she is gorgeous," I said with a grin.

I dropped Sam off at my mum's house and recounted the drama of the night before. Then I drove into town, parked on the double yellow lines, and headed into Mothercare. I bought Stephanie a tiny yellow and white dress, like a doll's dress, for £12 – the first thing I ever bought for my daughter.

I was filled with excitement about the happy times I knew were ahead. But despite the joy, I knew that drastic changes were needed if we were to make a go of this family life. I was more determined than ever to move far away and start over somewhere new, where no one knew us.

By this point, the accident and the damage it had done to my body and education no longer dominated me. That was nine years ago. Since then, I had grown into a man. I had seen a lot of tragedy, travelled a good part of the world, and now, I was a father. I was beginning to find a new self-confidence and a new presence as a businessman. I was starting to understand commerce and the dynamics of business. I was far from merely having a job. I was beginning to see my value as an asset, my potential to build a stable career and even my own business one day.

CHAPTER 35
LINCOLNSHIRE

Jerry Foley, one of our clients, invited me out to lunch. I designed brochures and advertising for his company and managed all their printing. Jerry was a charming Irishman in his early 40s, relatively short, always impeccably dressed in a three-quarter-length Camel Crombie coat and a chestnut brown trilby hat. He spoke with the smooth confidence of a London city gent, his Irish accent only adding to his charm. His beautiful Indian wife, Jess, looked at least 10 years younger than her actual age and was just as well-turned-out as her husband.

We met at Shoppenhangers Manor Hotel in Maidenhead. I parked my white Alfa Romeo GTV in the car park, noting Jerry's black Rolls-Royce with Douglas, his chauffeur, sitting in the driver's seat. As I walked into the dining room, Jerry raised his hand to get my attention, and I joined him at the table, where Peter Bromley, a photographer, was already seated. Jerry introduced us, but we already knew each other.

"Can I buy you a drink, young Roger?" Jerry asked with his usual politeness.

"Yes, please. I will have a pint of Guinness," I replied.

Menus were passed around, and we ordered our food. Jerry ordered steak and chips, and so did Peter, though he asked for his steak 'blue'. After we ordered, Jerry leaned back in his chair and began, "Now then, Roger, over the past six months of working with your firm, I've found you to be a nice fellow to deal with and a most efficient and productive contractor. I think your design work is excellent and I also appreciate your management skills."

I felt my excitement rising, suspecting where this conversation was headed. Was fate finally about to open a door for me?

Jerry turned to Peter and continued, "Peter here was recommended to me as probably the best photographer in this business. I've already spoken briefly to him before you arrived."

He turned back to me, "As you know, Roger, we've been working on several publications for the City of London, and we've decided it's time to go out on our own and publish a niche magazine. The cost of doing such an enterprise here in the Thames Valley or London is prohibitive. Frankly, our location will not change our business, so, with efficiency in mind, we have got modern offices in the north of England. I already have my editor, Mr Bill Shakespeare, whom you have met, and I have an advertising sales director currently working for Paul Raymond in London who will be joining us. My wife will run telesales and HR.

"What I need now is someone like you to run the entire design and production side of the business. I want Peter here to be our photographer. He'll be snapping some very high-profile and prominent characters in the business world, and I think he's the best."

Peter grinned like the Cheshire Cat that had just found a fish.

"Where up north are you planning to set up this business?" I asked.

"Well, we decided on Lincolnshire, Lincoln City, for several reasons. It is just over two hours from London St Pancras, and there are several trains each day. By car, it is only 160 miles, straight up the A1, from here in Maidenhead. It is an easy and relatively quick commute, yet the difference in property prices, office leases and, especially, salaries is enormous!" Jerry replied.

I nodded, acknowledging his points.

"This makes it much more affordable for a start-up like this. It becomes a workable project for us to undertake and much easier to attract investment," he continued.

I looked at him, somewhat surprised.

"Have you been to Lincoln before, Roger?" he asked.

"No, I haven't. I have never been to that part of the country, only north of Oxford to the Lake District on holiday with my parents when I was young," I replied with a grin.

Jerry smiled. "Well, Lincoln is nowhere near the Lake District. It's not the North at all. It's in the East Midlands."

I laughed and said, "The only thing I know about Lincoln is they have a pretty hopeless football team near the bottom of the fourth division, and, of course, in the Robin Hood movie, the 'merry men' wore Lincoln Green tunics."

That was the extent of my knowledge of Lincoln.

Jerry laughed. "Well, I can assure you it's a beautiful part of the country. Did you know the city was originally a Roman fortress, a Viking settlement, and later a major trading city in the Middle Ages? It was always a prosperous place, even having a large Jewish community at one time. There's lots of history there."

He continued, "However, the past few years have not been kind to Lincoln as the UK's manufacturing industry has declined. The city has taken a beating. It was always home to several heavy industries. Did you know the first tanks were built there for World War I?"

He went on, "But now, things are changing. I predict a boom. This city will turn around and grow significantly in the next few years. Now is the perfect time to move there and take advantage of the low property prices."

"It sounds intriguing, Jerry," I replied.

Then he asked the question I had been waiting for, "Well, would you be interested in considering a position with our new company?"

I did not want to appear too eager. I could sense he was committed, and I was in an excellent position to bargain. "Can you tell me more about the magazine? What is the publication called?"

"Not at this stage," Jerry replied. "What I would like to do is for you both to come to our home in Lincolnshire next weekend. Bring your wives and stay for a couple of nights in a hotel. I will book that for you. Give Jess and me a chance to tell you more about our plans and why we think this opportunity will be a great chance for you both.

"You can see first hand our new offices in the city centre and maybe check out some of the residential properties available in the surrounding countryside."

"So, what do you think?" He looked at both Peter and I.

I turned and glanced at Peter, and it was pretty clear he had made up his mind and wanted to go. I was also convinced I would like to see this place. So, I looked at Jerry and said, "I'd love to come."

Peter said, "Yes. Sounds very interesting."

"Excellent. Let's do it. I'll book the hotel for Friday and Saturday nights," Jerry said.

I was not too confident about taking my old Alfa GTV on such a long round trip, so Jerry suggested he would rent a car for me. He did not want me to drop out at the last minute. It was the new Ford Sierra, an entirely new type of car. The motoring press called it a jelly mould, but it made the trip a much more pleasant experience, knowing we could relax on that long journey in a brand-new car.

We spent the first evening with Peter and his wife at the Bishops Hotel in Lincoln. Caroline came alive. My mum had Sam and Stephanie so Caroline and I were enjoying a rare trip to a new place, staying in the hotel, dining and drinking with friends. We had a lovely evening and were off to a great start. We woke up early and had breakfast in the hotel restaurant. Then, the four of us drove to the city centre offices in Peter's Daimler to meet Jerry.

Eastgate Publications Company had leased offices in Brayford Wharf, a tall glass building with open-plan office spaces and glorious city views. There were several elevators and a large multi-storey car park, all just a short walk into the heart of town – perfect for me.

I had been working in a listed Victorian building on Eton High Street. I also spent quite a bit of time in Derek McGuire's office, which was also in Eton, a 14th-century house so old you had to duck to pass through the doorways. If you put a tennis ball on the floor, it would roll to the far corner of the room. It was luxuriously furnished and extremely expensive.

So, this 1970s-style Lincoln city centre office block would be quite a change for me. It was motivating to see the space we would soon fill.

Jerry knew that much of what we had seen in the newer part of the city would have been less than impressive. There were many empty factories and boarded-up shops, so the canny Irishman took us for lunch at the expensive White Hart Hotel, facing the Cathedral and Lincoln Castle. The ladies went for a walk around the medieval Bailgate area. There was no arguing with the fact that old Lincoln was quite enchanting, and our wives could not wait to do their shopping in Lincoln's old town.

We all drove the 20 miles back to Jerry's house in a small village south of Lincoln, close to Sleaford. It was a delightful location, and their large bungalow was situated next to the village church, surrounded by charming old stone cottages. I looked in surprise as I saw two splendid pheasants walking across his lawn. It was a world away from the red brick urban sprawl of suburban Maidenhead.

Jerry delighted in showing us around his dazzling home. I could not help noticing his fridge was full of bottles of champagne. We all sat beside his indoor swimming pool, and his wife poured us drinks as he talked in more detail about the business. *Money Monthly* magazine would be the first publication to target the City of London's financial sector. It would be similar in size, format, and style to *Campaign* magazine, which served the advertising and media industries. He then explained that he wanted to launch two more publications soon after.

It all seemed very attractive indeed. Then, the canny fellow presented us with several property brochures his wife had collected from local estate agents. He was astute, knowing how much my terrace house was worth. He knew the increase I would soon have in salary and had picked out some beautiful properties that would now be in our price range. The properties were far more illustrious and extensive than anything we could ever afford down south.

The higher salary meant we could afford a mortgage to buy a house double the price of the one we had. The 160-mile move to Lincolnshire meant we could upgrade from a small, shabby old two-bed terrace in town to a modern, luxurious four-bedroom detached bungalow in the countryside.

The opportunity to move to a nice area far away from Maidenhead, combined with his slick presentation and the financial incentives he offered, was compelling, and it was an easy decision for all of us.

I now had a new and exciting career challenge far away from the stench that engulfed us in Maidenhead. I could not get to Lincoln quickly enough.

I explained to Ben that Jerry was opening new offices up north and that his goal was to hire his in-house staff so he would not need our services any more.

Ben said, "Well, that's unfortunate to lose a good client, but I understand why."

I took a deep breath and said, "He's offered me a job, Ben."

Ben sighed and replied, "Ah, I see. And are you interested?"

"Yes, I am, Ben. You know I've loved my time here, but with all that's happened to me this past year, I think this will be the perfect move for us, an opportunity to restart our lives."

Ben smiled, put his arm around me, and said, "Roger, go for it with my blessings. I hope it all works out for you; truly, I do. We'll miss you, of course."

I laughed and said, "Nah, you've got young Marion over there. She is a far better designer than me, and everybody knows what they are doing now. You'll be fine."

CHAPTER 36
HELPRINGHAM

I stood in my new kitchen, glancing out over my freshly cut lawn, my early morning coffee in hand, before I set off for work. A horse cantered around in the meadow next door. Alfie, my beautiful pedigree Black and Tan Gordon Setter, was chasing blackbirds and, at the end of my enormous back garden, I could see the small stream that separated the village from the farmer's fields beyond.

I watched my wife prepare breakfast for Sam and Stephanie and could not help feeling a tremendous sense of accomplishment. Not only had I managed to move us from a tiny suburban two-bedroom terrace house, but I had also extricated us from the torturous aftermath of the affair in Berkshire. I had set up myself in an exciting new job with excellent career prospects at a new publishing company in Lincoln city centre.

My new company car, a silver Ford Escort XR3i, was parked beside my wife's new white MG Metro outside my double garage. Mature trees overhung the driveway, and flowers and hedges surrounded the front garden.

It was perfect.

My wife and our young family could now enjoy life, growing up in the countryside in our beautiful new home, which sat imposingly at the end of the enchanting Vicarage Lane in the shadows of the enormous medieval church in the beautifully named and wealthy village of Helpringham in Lincolnshire.

I never really felt at home in Maidenhead. It was a lovely town, and I had many wonderful friends. The glorious River Thames was my playground as a young lad, but I had no roots there. My family were all born in London; they were East Enders. My mum was born in West Ham and my father in Stepney. They were immigrants to the suburbs. My dad's brother, sister and cousins all lived in London, so we often visited.

I worked in the West End of London for a while and enjoyed the novelty and excitement. It helped me understand the importance and role London plays in the UK. But I was happy to leave. I knew I did not want to spend my career in 'the big smoke'. I realised what made me happy was discovering new places and travelling.

Peter and his young family also moved to a small village near Lincoln city. By late autumn 1983, we were all settled in our new homes and getting started in our new jobs.

I was 26 years old. It was 10 years since my accident. I had since lost my father – he was way too young. I had nearly lost my marriage, but survived that. Our new daughter, Stephanie, was born in August '83, which was thrilling for me and gave us a new lease on life. We were happy at last.

What more could a man want? This was, indeed, my dream coming true.

CHAPTER 37
MAJORCA

Jerry Foley was a true entrepreneur and a visionary. I remember him saying, "The economic development of the British service industry and commerce is inevitable. Improvements in communication systems and computing will make low-cost places like Lincoln an obvious choice for businesses wishing to expand."

And he was right. Looking back now, I can see how much of what he predicted has come true. He foresaw Lincoln becoming a boom town, urging us to move in while it was still cheap. Sure enough, with the completion of the M25, the A1M, and other road improvements, the commute became easier. Lincoln got a new university, and the city flourished.

The first few months at Eastgate were exhilarating. Setting up the offices, recruiting and training new staff, and planning the development of *Money Monthly* magazine was both challenging and exciting. Life was good. Sam started at the village school, Stephanie was growing fast, and Caroline enjoyed her coffee mornings with the ladies in the village. I loved my 25-mile commute through the Lincolnshire countryside to the city in my silver XR3i. Coming home to my beautiful bungalow, wife and kids, what could be better?

Sam was a toddler running around now, and Stephanie was still a baby in a pushchair.

Caroline's mother, now living in a luxury condominium on a private beach in Majorca with her new husband, Bruce Nelson, a former publisher, invited us to visit. She was excited to see her grandchildren.

Bruce, who had made a fortune by selling his electronics magazine, became a great advisor on publishing issues. He also taught me a valuable lesson about liquidity. One of his neighbours,

Cyril, was in financial trouble with an unexpected tax bill. Desperate, Cyril offered to sell his beautiful three-bedroom condominium for £65,000. Bruce offered £50,000, which Cyril initially refused. But Bruce presented him with cash in a bag. Desperate and pressed for time, the instant payment was hard to refuse.

Bruce sold the condominium a short time later for £75,000, making a quick profit. He said, "If you've got liquidity, you've got buying power. Opportunities like this will arise, and you need to be ready."

It's always disappointing when a marriage falls apart, especially when it tears a family in two. Caroline's mother had clearly been unhappy for a long time, and she finally found a man who adored her and who could give her the lifestyle she felt she deserved. She confided in me once, after a few too many drinks, that one of her conditions for leaving Caroline's father and moving to Majorca with Bruce was that she would be wined and dined with champagne every other day.

No matter what you think of the people involved, their personalities, and their relationships, it's hard to escape the allure of a place like Majorca. Sun-soaked and exotic, the island was a jewel in the Mediterranean, full of excitement and intrigue. For Caroline, it became her mum's new home, a place we could visit with our kids for a sunshine holiday whenever we wanted. Spending time with Bruce and his wealthy pals was an education for me. I wanted to see the world and understand how successful people built wealth and lives.

One day, I was sitting on the balcony, enjoying breakfast, when Bruce joined me in his shorts and silk dressing gown. He squinted out at the bay, trying to focus on a boat moored in the distance. Without a word, he went back inside and returned with a massive pair of binoculars. He sat down, elbows on the railing and zeroed in on the cruise boat. Then, with a sudden burst of excitement, he called out, "Linda! Linda, come here quick!"

Caroline's mum, Linda, put down her utensils in the kitchen and came out to the balcony. Bruce handed her the binoculars. "Look! He's gone and done it, the bastard. That must be 45 feet; it's bloody huge." It took me a moment to realise what was happening. Bruce and Linda's neighbour had bought a new boat that was a few feet longer than Bruce's.

In that moment, it hit me. Even if you own a beautiful condo and a 35-foot cruiser, you can still feel bitterly disappointed when someone outdoes you by just 10 feet. It reminded me of how I'd recently been jealous of a friend with a Golf GTi, which was generally accepted as being better than my XR3i.

I realised then that no matter how much you have, if you're a plonker with no money, getting more money only makes you a bigger plonker. That day, I learned a huge lesson.

As if to drive that lesson home, I had another encounter on the beach in Majorca. I was carefully making my way across the sand with my walking stick, heading toward a small beach bar, when a tall, white-haired man with leathery, deeply tanned skin and brief white swimming shorts approached me.

"Hello, son," he said. "Don't mind me asking, but what happened that left you needing a walking stick?"

I smiled and replied, "No problem at all. I had an accident playing rugby 10 years ago and broke my neck."

"Crikey," he said, "you're lucky to be alive, aren't you?"

"Yes," I replied, "I was lucky to survive, and I appreciate every day, especially days like today." I looked up at the blue sky and raised my hand.

"Let me buy you a beer, young man," he offered, and together we walked into the shade of the beach bar. There was a pool table, and he challenged me to a game. At the time, I was quite proficient and confident, thinking I'd probably beat this older man.

We downed a few bottles of San Miguel, and after a couple of hours of shooting pool, we were slightly drunk and jolly good mates.

As we walked back to the condo together, he told me how he had injured his back severely in a waterskiing accident a few years before and so appreciated my guts and determination not to give in to my injury.

He shook my hand and said, "Maybe see you on the beach again tomorrow."

"Sure," I replied, "have a good evening, mate."

When I returned to the condo, Bruce asked, "How do you know that man? Do you know who he is?"

"No," I said, "just some old fella from Manchester, I think. He owns a villa nearby."

Bruce's eyes widened. "That's Thomas Barclay, a multimillionaire industrialist. He's a director of Barcelona Football Club and owns several companies in the UK and across Europe."

I was taken aback. "Wow, I didn't know that. He's a good pool player and likes to drink. Yeah, we did talk about football – he's a big Maradona fan."

I met Tom again and asked him about his businesses. He joked, saying, "I'd much rather be here and leave it all to my directors. It's all a bit of a farce, you know? I've got a Rolls-Royce Corniche in a Stockport garage, and I haven't seen it in over four years. So, what's the point?" he continued, "Believe me, son, your health is the most important thing," and he put his hand over his heart.

Later that week, Thomas invited Caroline and me to a party he was hosting, but he didn't invite Bruce and Linda. Bruce's look was priceless, and his jealousy was palpable. Once again, I saw the ugly side of wealth and the bitterness it can breed.

CHAPTER 38

EASTGATE

ack in Lincoln, I was busy organising printers and distribution contractors, working with interesting people, and developing new products. 1983 and 1984 were great years.

Jerry's next innovation was a computer database to pair job seekers with employers, a precursor to online job platforms. We launched *Joblink* magazine to advertise jobs and provide useful editorial content for job seekers.

The concept was strong enough to attract significant investment. My role as Production Director involved managing all aspects of design, production and marketing. Peter, an innovative photographer, brought Jerry's vision to life with dramatic magazine covers and creative presentations of people.

We contracted out our typesetting to a local company, Lincoln Typeset, run by Mike Jones, an ex-RAF pilot. The publishing operation was running with a significant client base and staff. We were thriving, and as any successful publisher knows, it is wise to use in-house resources by publishing multiple magazines.

Our next venture was *Prosper* magazine, a lifestyle publication for successful men. It focused on luxury, achievement, and success in business and sports. With connections from Paul Raymond's Soho entertainment empire, the Sales Director was confident in securing advertising for the first 12 issues, which would generate enough income to support the magazine.

Our *Money Monthly* magazine was doing well, and we successfully launched *Joblink* magazine, with its integrated database of job opportunities and employers.

The work was exhilarating, the team was incredible, and we were all having an absolutely fantastic time.

Life seemed perfect. At 27, I could not believe how much I had achieved since leaving the hospital.

But on a wet Monday afternoon, everything changed.

Jess, Jerry's wife, called us into the conference room. We were excited, expecting good news. Jerry walked in, smiled, and then, looking out the window towards Lincoln Cathedral, he said, "I'm sorry, guys, but it's all over."

Silence filled the room. He rambled on about how some investments in Hong Kong had gone wrong and how when he discovered the deception, he tried to secure further investments. A venture capital syndicate had promised significant funding, but that fell through unexpectedly, leaving no way to save the business. He rambled on, making excuses, but I don't think any of us really heard what he said. We were all in complete shock.

Jess began handing us our P45s and telling us to immediately take them to the Jobcentre and sign on for social security.

I was owed about £2,800 in salary and expenses, but Jess said there was nothing they could do. Jerry explained that our Sales Director had falsely promised advertising contracts, yet no cash had arrived in the bank account.

I went to the Jobcentre, desperate. They arranged an interview for me and gave me an emergency payment. Standing at the petrol station, filling my car, I realised I had only £100 left to last the next 10 days. My world had fallen apart. Peter was in the same situation.

Driving home, I dreaded telling Caroline what had happened. Our dream was over. Those 25 miles were the longest of my life.

CHAPTER 39
FOR SALE MAGAZINE

It was now early 1985. I was relaxing in my bungalow in Vicarage Lane, looking out of my leaded-light living room windows to my front garden, when a big American car rumbled up and pulled onto my driveway. Peter Bromley stepped out, a big grin on his face, with the song *19* by Paul Hardcastle booming from his car stereo. "So, what do you think of my new car?" he asked, proud of his latest acquisition.

The car was a 1978 Cadillac Seville, light powder blue with a dark blue padded vinyl roof. It was ghastly, loud and ostentatious, typical Peter, who had a history of owning big American cars.

"Very nice, but it is a bit dull, mate. Couldn't you find a pink one? Anyway, what is it?" I replied, half-joking. Peter laughed, undeterred by my sarcasm. "This, my boy, is a 5.7-litre luxury and power machine, a gentleman's car."

After we lost our jobs at Eastgate Publications, Peter and I asked Jerry what to do with our company cars, the two Ford Escort XR3i's. To our surprise, Jerry told us to keep them. They were on a lease, which was already paid for.

I contacted the motor leasing company to tell them we still had them, and they were relieved that I had let them know. The truth was they had not received a single payment on either car in nearly a year. They were grateful but said we could continue using them for the time being, as they were insured. Six weeks later, the finance company from Essex finally came to collect my lease car, so I bought an old 1974 Ford Cortina 2.3 Ghia Estate from Marty, my Irish friend in Maidenhead. It was cheap and did the job.

Peter and I sat in my living room, contemplating our next move over coffee that Caroline had made for us. Just two weeks after

Eastgate closed, Jerry had opened new offices in Stamford and asked us to join him for a new, smaller venture. We went to see him, but we were not convinced, and due to his own troubles, that venture did not materialise.

We both signed up for benefits at the Jobcentre. During my appointment in Sleaford, I explained that I would probably have to start a business.

It was a new experience for me, so I asked several questions: Was I allowed to write business plans and do presentations to banks and investors? The lady at the Jobcentre said yes, as long as I was not being paid for my work.

"So, if I have an appointment at the bank, do I need to declare that?" I asked.

"No," she replied, "as long as you're not earning, you can continue to receive support until you have a paying job."

I asked, "If I try to set up a business with a partner, and they get paid, but I don't receive anything, is that okay?"

She said, "That sounds like a good plan. Just keep us informed."

With that in mind, Peter and I discussed our options and kicked around some ideas. We decided our best option was to start our own business.

"What can you do in Lincolnshire that doesn't involve farming?" I asked Peter.

He laughed. "I may have had a sheep as a pet, but I'm no farmer."

"I think we will have to start our publication, mate. How about a Lincolnshire *Auto Trader* magazine?"

Back down south, the *Thames Valley Trader* had launched in 1977 as a small, classified publication. The *Southern Auto Trader* followed in 1981. Peter had done some snap ads for them. The concept was simple: an agent would come, take details and photos of your car, and collect your £5 fee.

It was an A4-size weekly, black-and-white publication full of classified car ads. It was growing in popularity and quickly becoming financially successful.

Peter said, "Can you imagine driving 20 miles to Boston for a £5 snap ad?"

"No, not really. And if we stick to just Lincoln, with a population of about 76,000, there is no way we can make a car publication pay," I replied.

Peter added, "Plus, you've got the daily *Lincolnshire Echo* and the weekly *Chronicle* to compete against."

"What about a *Farming Trader*? Tractors, farm machinery, livestock, and other farming stuff. There is not much in the local newspapers serving farmers, is there?"

We lived in rural villages surrounded by farmland, so we were familiar with the types of agriculture and equipment used. Peter's eyes lit up. "Now you might be onto something, Roger. *Farming Trader*?"

We decided to test the waters. We went to the Newark cattle market, about 20 miles away, where Peter mingled with several farmers, showing them the dummy magazine I had made as a sample.

The response was encouraging; they wanted to know what equipment was available locally. I sat in the café with farmers from Lincolnshire, Nottinghamshire and Cambridgeshire. They all agreed that the local newspapers were not particularly useful to them. The only influential publication was *Farmers Weekly,* a national magazine, but advertising was expensive.

On that one excursion, we learned so much about the vast scale of farming in the area. The marketplace covered several counties, with substantial investments in machinery and equipment. The types of agriculture varied from small sheep and dairy holdings to 4,000-acre cereal farms.

They liked our dummy issuc and the idea of something dedicated to farming, covering the relevant local areas but much cheaper to advertise in. High-quality printing was not necessary, and a free issue delivered by mail was appealing. We also spoke to dealers, auction companies, and tractor traders – all were interested and supportive.

We returned home motivated and confident that we were onto something. The farmers liked our concept, and the response was positive. Now, all we had to do was put everything into a business plan.

All those late nights working for Derek McGuire in Eton High Street, producing his business plans, were about to pay off. He was constantly raising investments for various ventures, and I had learnt how to present the correct information properly, creating a physical plan with all the elements, including spreadsheets. Derek showed me how to present a concept that quickly and simply transfers the ideas while highlighting the salient points for investors.

"What's in it for me?" Derek would say. "Investors are not really interested in your idea – whether it is horse breeding or printing. They want to know how much you need, how you will use their money, how long you will need it, and how much interest they will get back in return. You must show them this."

He continued, "If they like what they see, they'll want to know more: what skills, expertise and resources you have, how you'll overcome the competition, and what personal investment you have in this plan."

We chose the local National Westminster Bank, Smith's branch in Lincoln, because it was the country's most prominent farmers' bank, or so we heard. The bank manager reviewed our presentation, asked questions, and seemed impressed.

He put the folder down, drank his tea, and then said, "Gentlemen, there is no doubt you have done your homework. Your previous experience and research are excellent, and your proposed concept is impressive."

But then came the kicker: "However, one flaw in your plan prevents me from lending you the money. Farmers are notorious for not paying their bills on time. I am sure you could make the sales targets, but you might struggle to collect the revenue. This will impact your cash flow, and bad debts will likely rise far above your expectations."

Peter and I were reeling. It was true; we had not calculated for that scenario, and the bank manager had more experience in this area than we did. We could not argue.

He continued, "I'm sorry, gentlemen, but the bank will not be forthcoming with a business loan for this project. However, this needn't be the end of your idea. I'm impressed with your concept and your commitment. I suggest you rethink the magazine idea. Don't rely just on farmers. Come back with something more comprehensive, encompassing other products, and then let's talk again."

Disappointed but not defeated, Peter and I went straight to the pub. Peter started downing Carlsberg Special Brew bottles while I sipped on Samuel Smith's draft bitter. "Well, that went well," I said, half-joking.

Peter looked at me, surprised. "Really? Do you think so? No money."

"That was a yes, Peter. He educated us there."

Peter smiled, raising his bottle. "Are we going back?"

I raised my pint. "We most definitely are, Bromers."

Private customers had to pay cash in advance at the office to advertise in the *Lincolnshire Echo,* the paid-for daily newspaper. And if you wanted a response, you needed to buy more than one day because today's paper was in the bin tomorrow. It was large, broadsheet and difficult to handle.

So, our brilliant plan was to make our publication smaller, easier to handle, and free to advertise. By giving it away, we believed advertisers would quickly fill the classified pages, ensuring people would pick it up, read it, and use it. Once they bought something from the magazine, they would start selling things in the magazine, creating a cross-fertilising cycle.

We came up with the name *For Sale Magazine.* It was an A4, stapled so it did not fall apart, black and white on newsprint, with colour front and back covers to make it stand out. It was a local newspaper without any news, just a big, classified advertising section organised into a few simple categories. The significant difference from the competition was that it would be much cheaper and user-friendly, with fun bits like horoscopes, games, and a colouring page for the kids, plus crosswords and puzzles.

We were confident in our plan but had to consider loan terms. We did not have cash to invest and did not want to use our homes as security. We needed to set up offices and buy equipment if we expected to produce a magazine.

I suggested to Peter that we meet with Mike Jones, who owned the small firm Lincoln Typeset. Mike had been our contractor for artwork and typesetting at Eastgate. I proposed that he join us as a partner, bringing his office space, staff, and equipment as his collateral for a 33.3% share of the new business. The three of us could then present our plan to the bank as a troika – a far more solid proposition.

Mike immediately saw the potential and was keen to be involved. We returned to National Westminster, where we met with the bank manager, Mr Batley. He was a portly man in his 60s with slightly balding white hair, a reddish nose, and gold-rimmed glasses. The three of us presented our new partnership team and *For Sale Magazine* idea. The bank manager pawed through the plan, looked at us, and said, "Looks like you are in business, gentlemen, a very solid plan. I am happy to support you."

He offered us an unsecured loan of £16,000 and agreed to provide further investment funding if we met our revenue targets over the coming year. The deal was done, and we left the bank with huge smiles, shaking hands with Mr Batley.

As we stepped outside, Mike said, "Well done, lads. I will see you later." Peter and I stood beside his outlandish light blue Cadillac, throwing up high fives and laughing. The bank manager came out the door and almost bumped into us. We turned to him and said, "Thanks again." The look on his face was a picture.

"That was easy," Peter said.

"Yes, almost too easy," I replied.

We formed a new company, Oak Publications Ltd., and published the first issue of *For Sale Magazine* a few weeks later on Friday, 24 May, 1985. *For Sale Magazine* was an instant success. The public liked the convenience of size and free advertising, and we quickly built up an extensive classifieds section with hundreds of free ads every week.

We hired three sales staff who sold ads to businesses, while Mike's team handled pre-print production. I worked a few days in the office doing accounts, invoices, and banking. Peter dealt with the printing and distribution on Thursdays and Fridays. Only Mike worked full-time and was paid; Peter and I were not yet full-time employees because the company could not afford it.

The magazine became so popular that people queued on Friday mornings, waiting for copies to be dropped off by the printers at our office. Private advertisers wanted to be the first to get their copy to pick up bargains. The success of the private free ads built a vast readership, and dealers and traders could not ignore our success, so they soon bought advertising space on contract. Revenue started pouring in. Our success became a problem for the local newspapers, especially the daily *Lincolnshire Echo,* as we had put a massive dent in their classified ads revenue.

CHAPTER 40

SAMSON

I was in my office when the phone rang. One of my customers, Danny Hart, had become a good friend over the previous year. Danny was about my age, with a black father and a white mother, and he looked the spitting image of Olympic gold medallist Daley Thompson, except Danny was even bigger. As he liked to joke, "I'm much better looking, and I can run faster."

Danny had served in the Royal Air Force as a Military Policeman and was an accomplished boxer, having been a heavyweight champion. Later, in Lincoln, he became well-known as the chairman of the Lincoln Boxing Club. He also owned several businesses, including an elderly care home, an in-car entertainment business, and a second-hand car dealership.

I picked up the phone. "Hello," I said.

It was Danny, and he sounded upset, his voice unusually high-pitched.

"Roger is that you?" he asked.

"Yeah, mate. What's up?" I replied, sensing something was wrong.

"I can't believe it. The court has put a destruction order out on Samson. The fuckers want to kill my dog," he said, his voice laced with desperation.

Samson was a magnificent Rottweiler about five years old who lived at Danny's car dealership. He was a huge and handsome guard dog whose job was to look and sound ferocious, which he did very well. But Samson was always happy and friendly with Danny and his friends.

According to the official complaint, Samson had bitten someone on the foot while chained up. The man had been wandering around the car lot, uninvited and unescorted. Samson barked and looked mean and did what he thought was his job. The man, shocked, apparently kicked Samson, only to have his boot caught in a bite that Danny described as the equivalent of a three-ton vice.

"That's awful, Dan," I said. "That's so unfair. The dog was provoked, surely?"

"It doesn't matter, mate," Danny replied. "He's now considered a dangerous dog, and they want him dead. I can't let that happen. Can you help me out?"

"What do you have in mind?" I asked, bracing myself.

"Can you come round now and steal him, you know, when I'm not looking? Put him in your car and drive off with him," Danny suggested.

"And take him where?" I asked, incredulous.

"Home. You'll have to keep him. He can't ever come back here," Danny said, sounding desperate.

"Danny, I've got two young kids. He's a big, scary guard dog. My wife will never go for it. We've already got a big dog," I said, thinking of the potential chaos.

"He loves kids, and your wife loves dogs. She'll love him, and so will the kids. Please, mate, your place is miles away and perfect for him," Danny pleaded.

I called Caroline and explained the situation. She wanted to come with me to see Samson first.

We arrived at Danny's place, and I parked my big old Peugeot 604 in the backyard. Danny came out with Samson on a short leash. The dog was large, muscular, and immediately won over my wife. She went straight to him, and Samson started wiggling his big bottom back and forth, his excitement evident despite his docked tail. I couldn't go near him; his enthusiasm would have easily knocked me off my walking stick.

My wife made up her mind quickly. "Yes, let's have him. He's so gorgeous," she said, beaming.

My son Sam was at school, and my daughter Stephanie was in the car. At the time, I had a 1978 Peugeot 604, a large executive car with a boot. Danny suggested it might be best if we put Samson in the boot. I thought it sounded extreme, but Danny said, "He'll be OK. He'll relax in the dark. You don't want a 14-stone dog jumping around on the back seat with your little girl in there."

Danny added, "I should tell you there are three things Samson doesn't like, things that make him bark. First are motorbikes; he hates motorbikes. Then sirens – police cars, ambulances, and fire engines, anything like that. And he doesn't like other black dogs for some reason."

I hesitated. "Alfie, our Gordon Setter, is a big black dog, Danny. Is that going to cause a problem?"

"Nah, no problem. If Samson's your dog and they live together, they'll quickly become great friends. It'll be great for Samson to have a mate," Danny assured me.

Samson was not inclined to jump into the boot, so Danny lifted him, placing his front paws on the lip of the boot while my wife helped lift his back legs. Samson gave them a look as if to say, "This is very undignified, and I don't approve!" But he settled down quickly, and we closed the lid, ready to drive home.

On the way home, we were stopped at a traffic light when an ambulance sped past us with its sirens wailing. Suddenly, the car began to rock back and forth as Samson reacted angrily to the noise, barking and moving around violently in the boot. Thankfully, the ambulance passed quickly, and the siren's noise faded, allowing Samson to calm down for the rest of the 20-minute drive.

When we got home, we hesitated before opening the boot. It was silent, no sound at all. We thought it best to stand to the side of the car when opening the boot just in case Samson decided to bolt. But when we slowly lifted the boot, we found Samson reclining comfortably as if nothing had happened. We coaxed him out, and with gravity on our side, getting him out of the car was much easier.

Alfie, our Gordon Setter, was not impressed when this huge black dog entered the hallway. He barked loudly and viciously at Samson, who stood confused and statuesque, looking at Alfie. Alfie quickly realised that this was a fight he would never win, so he stopped barking, went immediately to his bed in the kitchen, and lay down. Samson followed him, stood over Alfie's bed, and, once Alfie vacated it, promptly made it his own. From that day onwards, the two dogs became like brothers, enjoying each other's company.

Samson quickly became a devoted guardian to our three children. True to the Rottweiler personality, he considered them his responsibility. The kids loved him, too, treating him like a big teddy bear. Samson always kept them in sight while they were outside, following them around to ensure their safety.

He also became very fond of me. He would always get up to greet me when I got home, his large bottom shaking amusingly from side to side in an uncontrollable wobble. He seemed to know I was unsure on my feet, always careful not to knock into me. Once I was seated, his colossal head would land in my lap like a giant boulder, the weight heavy on my legs.

We developed a deep bond. Samson loved it when I talked to him and gave him attention. We became best friends, enjoying each other's company immensely.

My village pub, the Nags Head, was about 100 yards down the lane. I could just about make the distance with my walking stick in one hand and Samson's lead in the other. We would slowly walk to the village green. Once inside the pub, I would remove Samson's chain, and he would wander to the corner of the public bar and lay under a table. The locals loved him, feeding him crisps and giving him a stroke. He became a bit of a celebrity.

One evening, after maybe one pint too many, I was walking home with Samson. The lead never pulled tight as he constantly watched my slow gait. Slightly drunk, I fell, fortunately, onto the grass. No harm was done, but that big black face looked disapprovingly down on me. Samson's long pink tongue hung between his huge white fangs as if he were laughing at me. He stood close, stable as an oak table. I was able to put my arms around his back, pull myself up to my knees, and then, by leaning on his shoulders, stand up straight. Samson looked up at me as if to say, "OK, but are you ready to get going?" and we strolled home, none the wiser.

Years later, when Samson became ill with cancer in his shoulder, it was heartbreaking to see this once-powerful dog reduced to a limp similar to my own. The poor boy was in incredible pain. One evening, he was lying next to the sofa on his right shoulder, with his painful side facing upwards. My son Harry, about six months old, was lying on the couch when his mother went to get him a new bottle of milk. Suddenly, Harry rolled over. Before I could stop it, he fell from the sofa and landed directly on Samson's bad shoulder. The poor dog yelped in severe pain, but quickly got to his feet, turning his head toward baby Harry. Before I could react, Samson's big tongue was licking the crying baby's face. That was the guardian role he had with the kids.

Sadly, Samson's days were numbered. The cancer took him just four years after we rescued him, but those were great formative years for my children. For me, losing Samson was incredibly tough. He had brought so much happiness into our lives, and he and I had shared a unique friendship. Saying goodbye to my best friend was one of the hardest things I have ever had to do.

CHAPTER 41

MARGARET THATCHER

It was 1986, I was 28. There was a seismic shift in the newspaper publishing industry, a change driven by Rupert Murdoch that would forever alter the landscape. The National Graphical Association (NGA) and other unions held a stranglehold over the industry. Without a union card, getting a job in the print industry was nearly impossible, and union agreements dictated pay and working conditions.

Murdoch's response to this union power was nothing short of revolutionary. He secretly built a new publishing centre equipped with modern computer facilities. These latest technologies allowed journalists to input copy directly, bypassing the need for NGA typesetters who had previously been required to use the old "hot metal" Linotype printing machines.

News International, Murdoch's media empire, closed its operations in Gray's Inn Road and Fleet Street, firing 5,500 workers. On 26 January, 1986, they moved to the new Wapping plant in East London, a run-down area that soon became the epicentre of a nationwide strike. The strike's failure was catastrophic for the NGA and other print unions, leading to the widespread adoption of modern newspaper publishing practices and a significant decline in union influence across the UK.

Unfortunately, this broader battle between unions and modernisation was about to impact us directly.

Not long after Murdoch's move, we started receiving visits from the local NGA shop steward, Bernard Rutter. Bernard worked at the *Lincolnshire Echo,* a newspaper we were challenging by taking a significant share of its classified ad revenue with *For Sale Magazine.*

Bernard accused us of using illegal labour, explicitly pointing to the interns we had working on our modern typesetting machines. According to him, these young people were not members of the NGA, and that was a problem.

However, our interns were part of a government-subsidised apprenticeship scheme, with 50% of their income covered by the government. Mike explained this to Bernard, noting that the programme was backed by the TUC (Trades Union Congress) and the government. We thought that would be the end of it, but we were wrong.

In April 1986, the world faced another crisis, the Chernobyl nuclear disaster. The *Daily Express* front page screamed: "Nuclear Nightmare is Here," with reports of 2,000 dead and thousands more in peril from the atomic cloud. It felt like another disaster was piling on top of the challenges we were already facing.

Peter, ever the pessimist, said, "Jesus Christ, here we go again. We have just managed to survive the collapse of Eastgate Publications, worked our nuts off to establish *For Sale Magazine,* and now we have to survive a nuclear cloud!"

I replied, "I know, I can't believe it. Is there no end to the disasters we have to cope with?"

But while the world was worrying about nuclear fallout, we had another challenge – one that came in the form of Bernard Rutter.

One day, Bernard stormed into our office, accompanied by a large, intimidating man in a denim jacket that was clearly too small for him. They looked like they had just walked out of a bad sitcom about socialist workers' rights.

Mike, ever the calm ex-military man, asked, "Hello Bernard, what can we do for you today?"

Bernard launched into his usual spiel about protecting union jobs, saying, "I warned you a lot to get rid of your non-union labour. I told you you had to sign up for the NGA if you want to stay in business, but you ignored me, and now you are going to pay the price!"

Mike replied, "Bernard, I do not understand. These young people are working on an apprenticeship scheme, and their salaries are subsidised 50% by the government. It is an employment scheme to help young people get into work. This scheme is perfectly legal and endorsed by the TUC and Margaret Thatcher's government, so please do not come here again, and stop intimidating us."

But Bernard was not having it. "Listen up, I run the print union in this city, not the fucking TUC, and I do not give a fuck what Margaret Thatcher has to say about anything. In this town, we make the rules, and I am telling you for the last time: get rid of those kids and employ proper union members on union salaries, or I will close you down by the weekend, and I will have you blacked by the NGA. Do you understand me?"

With that, he stormed out of the office, leaving us all in shock. It felt like a shakedown straight out of a Mafia movie.

Mike decided to call our local MP, Tom King, to find out where we stood legally. We could not afford to have trouble with the unions or employ union labour, which was prohibitively expensive.

Our MP confirmed that we were within our rights. Our use of trainees was in line with government and TUC guidelines, and we had nothing to fear from the NGA – or so we thought.

The following week, just as we were about to go to print, I got a call from our printer in Norfolk. He sounded panicked.

"Roger, what the hell is going on at your office?" he asked.

Confused, I replied, "What are you talking about?"

He explained, "I have had a visit from the NGA shop steward here in Norfolk, and he has told me we are not allowed to print your magazine any more. The union has blacked you."

I could not believe what I was hearing. "That is utter nonsense! We have some trainees here who are on a government training scheme, that is all. The NGA does not like it, but we have checked with the TUC and our MP. We are not breaking any rules or agreements."

But my words fell on deaf ears. "Sorry, Roger, but we can't print you this week or any week until you resolve this issue," the printer said, clearly distressed.

I was livid. "Do you realise the damage you could be doing to us by refusing to print? I will have no choice but to sue you!"

But the printer was equally desperate. "I am deeply sorry about this, Roger. I know it is unfair, but I cannot afford to have the NGA walk out of my print shop. It will destroy my business, so it is you or me. I am sorry, but that is it." And with that, he hung up.

This was devastating. Just as *For Sale Magazine* was gaining momentum, it felt like the rug had been pulled out from under us. We managed to get printed the following week by paying cash upfront in a brown envelope to a group of NGA workers who were quite happy to break the rules for cash in their pockets. But this was unsustainable, and we were running out of money fast.

The NGA's blacking had a concertina effect on our business. Advertisers refused to pay for their ads, and our debtor list grew along with our overdraft facility. The bank manager called us in, explaining that we had reached our overdraft limit. We would have to sign bank guarantees if we wanted a larger facility. Reluctantly, we did, hoping the NGA would eventually leave us alone.

But they never did. They gradually squeezed the life out of our business. The bank foreclosed, and both Peter and I lost our homes. That is when I realised that Mike, who never had to repay anything to the bank, must have been a Mason. Peter and I were left to swallow all the losses.

Caroline was devastated. After everything we had been through, it seemed like we were finally on the verge of success, only to have it all come crashing down. To make matters worse, she was pregnant with our third child, and we had 90 days to move out.

I did not sleep well. I was still in shock, sliding into a deep depression. This was not just mismanagement on my part; it felt like outright evil. A group of people had set out to destroy us, and they succeeded. We had worked so hard, created so much, and employed 10 staff, all of whom were now unemployed.

Our MP, Tom King, raised our plight during Prime Minister's Question Time in Parliament. Margaret Thatcher responded, "I am incredibly disappointed to hear of the foreclosure of a small publishing business in Lincoln, Oak Publications. Yet another young flame of British entrepreneurism, snuffed out by the tyranny of the unions." Her statement was later published in the *Daily Telegraph* and the *Lincolnshire Echo.*

This experience taught me several harsh lessons. Being kind and being right is not enough. Believing is not enough. Trusting other people is risky. Being honest and courteous will not save you. You have to be tougher than everyone else if you want to survive or at least avoid being trodden down.

CHAPTER 42
HARRY

had lost every penny I had. We were still living in the bungalow in Helpringham, but it was on the market for sale by the bank.

I learned a lesson, and with new determination, I told myself, "I've been down before and got back; it's nothing; I must focus on the future, rebuild, and start again."

With our third child on the way, I was driven; I started applying for any job I could find within a 40-mile radius. I even applied for jobs that paid half of what I had been earning just a year before at Eastgate Publications.

Caroline's contractions started very early one Monday morning; she was prepared and had her go bag ready by the door. I couldn't believe it was such thick fog when we stepped outside the house. We got into the car, and we rushed to the hospital. Boston was 16 miles, and the fog was so dense we could hardly see the road. I had to drive with the window open at about 10 miles an hour. It was tedious and torture for Caroline.

Despite the challenges, we arrived safely, and she gave birth to a healthy baby boy, just as I was there with her when she gave birth to Samuel and Stephanie, so I was for Harrison Warner, on 13 July. It was one of the happiest days of my life, a moment of pure joy and celebration amid so much turmoil and pain. I knew then I had to succeed for this little chap. We debated names and decided on Harrison, after Caroline's uncle and my uncle Harry, a WWII hero.

My mother and stepfather Roy came to stay with us in Helpringham to help with the new baby and support us through this challenging time. They were fantastic, covering many of our expenses as we struggled to get back on our feet. But, even as we celebrated the birth of our son, the reality of our situation weighed heavily on me. We had no choice but to move back to Maidenhead as soon as the house was sold.

We did not want to leave. We had fallen in love with Lincolnshire and wanted to stay there if possible. But to do that, I needed to find a job.

I relocated my family back to my mother's house, including Samson and Alfie, our dogs. Leaving me free to focus on finding employment.

I responded to a job advert for a sales rep position at *Boston Target,* a small free newspaper owned by the *Lincolnshire Echo.* The interview was uncomfortable. My interviewer was younger and less experienced than me, and we both felt the situation's awkwardness. As I left, she thanked me for coming and said they would be in touch, but I did not expect to hear anything.

At 29, my life was tumbling down around me. I was a new dad again. I had a beautiful little boy with dark hair like mine, but we were also losing the roof over our heads. I had no source of income. I was terrified.

CHAPTER 43
THE *ECHO*

It was Friday. I was back in Maidenhead for the weekend with the family. The phone rang, and my mum answered it. "Hello, Warner residence. Yes, he's here. Hold on, please." She looked at me excitedly and said, "It's the *Lincolnshire Echo*."

I took the phone, my heart racing. "Hello, Roger Warner speaking."

A voice on the other end said, "Hello, Roger. My name is Tom Park. I am the Assistant Managing Director of the *Lincolnshire Echo* Group. How are you?"

"Hello, Tom. I am very well, thank you. What can I do for you?" I replied, trying to keep my voice steady.

Tom continued, "Roger, I understand you attended an interview at our *Boston Target* newspaper a couple of weeks ago. The advertising manager there passed on your application to me. You were too highly qualified for that position. However, we think we might have something for you in Lincoln. Would you be interested in learning more about it?"

I glanced at my mum, who was practically vibrating with excitement. I tried to contain my own. "Yes, Tom, of course, I would be very interested to know what's happening at the *Lincolnshire Echo.*"

"OK, when is a good day for you to come in? How about Monday afternoon, say at 2 o'clock?"

"Yes, of course, no problem. I will see you there at 2," I agreed.

"Excellent. I look forward to meeting you, Roger. Goodbye."

As I hung up, my mum started jumping up and down in the kitchen like a teenager, grabbing me in her arms, saying, "Yes, yes, well done! I knew you would find something."

I had forgotten how much stress all of this had put on her. Naturally, I leaned on her like I always had, but I had not realised how much she had worried about me.

"Hold on, mum. I have not got anything yet," I said, trying to temper her enthusiasm.

"Don't be silly. Yes, you do. You have an interview, and you will get this job; I am certain of it," she replied, her confidence in me shining through. Caroline looked relieved, though still a bit shell-shocked by everything.

When Monday came, I went to meet Tom Park. He was in his 30s, unusually bald for his age, with a thick dark moustache that seemed to compensate for his lack of hair. He was a short, barrel-shaped man who seemed hyperactive. He was always walking fast, busy with things in his hands, looking around, and never sitting still. Despite this, he was obviously talented and had a cheerful, upbeat demeanour.

The interview was brief, but promising. "Great to meet you, Roger. Very interesting. You will hear from me very soon," Tom said as he shook my hand.

Another week passed, and I began to worry that perhaps it was not going to happen after all. It seemed to be taking too long. But then, I was asked to attend another interview, this time with Ted Stevens, the Managing Director of the *Lincolnshire Echo* Group.

Ted was an ex-guardsman. Tall and broad, he wore an unusual light grey suit and had long, wavy grey hair. He was about 55. He was a calm, relaxed, and gentle soul who exuded command without needing to assert it.

Ted asked many questions about my work at Eastgate Publications. He was especially interested in my business publications and how we created *For Sale Magazine.*

The interview went well, and as I left, Ted said, "Well, thanks for coming in, Roger. I am pleased to meet you finally. I think Tom and I need to have a discussion now, and we'll get back to you in a couple of days."

A very long week later, the phone rang again. This time, it was a woman. "Hello, Roger, I'm Sharon, Ted Stevens's secretary. He would like to know if you could attend a meeting tomorrow at 9:30am?"

"Yes, of course," I replied, trying not to sound too eager.

The next morning, I walked into Ted's office. He stood and reached forward to shake my hand, gesturing for me to sit in one of the armchairs. I sat down, placing my walking stick on the floor. Ted sat behind the desk, which was set slightly higher, making him appear even more commanding.

A couple of minutes later, Tom Park came barrelling in. He was not wearing a suit jacket, and his sleeves rolled above his elbows. He looked like he had been rushing around. He shook my hand enthusiastically; and then both men began to explain their ideas.

Ted started, "Roger, as you know, we have an influential daily newspaper that covers the county and several free newspapers in the towns around the county. However, we feel that we could do much better with our business section. We want to open a new department, which we will call Special Publications. From there, we will produce a range of specialised supplements for daily use in the paper. We would like you to run that for us. We will make you the manager of that department. To start, we will provide you and one assistant. You will have full access to our editorial resources. I'd like you to start by creating a monthly *Business News,* a tabloid pull-out supplement of the main paper."

I took it all in, feeling a surge of excitement. This was exactly what I needed: an opportunity to build something again and create new publications with the support of a large company.

Tom Park looked at me with a big smile and asked, "So, Roger, what do you think? Can you handle it?"

"I think this is an excellent idea, Ted," I replied, "but you've made one mistake."

They both looked at me, surprised. Tom raised his eyebrows. "Oh, really, Roger? And what is that?"

"One of the things I realised while competing against you across the city with *For Sale* was the amazing strength of your brand, *The Echo.* Everyone knows and trusts *The Echo.* So, if we are going to do a business publication, we should call it *The Business Echo,* not *Business News.*

Tom looked up at Ted, and Ted looked down at Tom. They both laughed, turning back to me. Ted said, "Perfect, Roger. When can you start?"

The opportunity I had been waiting for had finally arrived. I had a new job with a great company and a good salary.

For my first week, they sent me on a Northcliffe Newspapers Group management training course in Leicester. Meanwhile, back in Lincoln, they arranged office space and workstations for my new department. The management training course was excellent – educational and rewarding. I was there with eight other young managers from within Northcliffe Newspapers across the country. I could not wait to return to Lincoln and create *The Business Echo.*

With a respectable job in hand, I could now start looking for a mortgage. Ted Stevens was incredibly supportive, offering references for my mortgage applications. It was not long before I secured a 100% mortgage with a 10% interest rate, and we set about buying a new house.

Caroline and I started house hunting in the city of Lincoln. This time, we moved closer to the office and the schools as the children grew fast. After looking at several houses, we settled on a large four-bedroom terraced house on Mount Street, close to Lincoln Castle and a short distance from the city centre. It was a rather old Edwardian style, particularly superior quality with many attributes, and although untidy, we felt it had a lot of potential for improvement.

In September, we moved out of my mother's house in Maidenhead and into our new home. It was a significant comedown from where we had been, but we were back together as a family, our future safe and secure once more, and back on the road to making progress.

CHAPTER 44

BUILDING STUFF

He was sceptical when I first approached Ted Stevens about printing *The Business Echo* on better-quality white paper with full colour covers and centre spreads. The *Lincolnshire Echo* has always been printed as cheaply as possible, in black and white on plain old newsprint. "Do you realise the increase in cost? It will be quite significant. I do not think it will be possible," Ted said.

But I was prepared. "Yes, Ted, it will cost an extra £800 a month, but we can recover that by making a colour ad surcharge for the back cover and four small ads on the front cover. Any additional ads sold on the other six pages of colour will be pure profit," I explained. I had done my homework, analysed production costs, and compared ad rates in other publications.

I also suggested direct mailing *The Business Echo* to a business leaders' mailing list, getting it directly into the hands of people who might never buy a regular *Echo*. "This will be a great selling point for advertising sales, and it could even boost the *Daily Echo*'s circulation," I continued. "I'm confident we can sell the extra advertising and profit more."

Ted hesitated, clearly taken aback by the boldness of my plan. But he knew he had brought me in to do a specific job and stopping me at the first hurdle would not set a good precedent. Reluctantly, he agreed.

The Business Echo was a hit from the first issue, making a profit right out of the gate. The success was undeniable, and a couple of months later, my ex-partner and best mate, Peter Bromley, was struggling. I suggested he might want to work for me at the

Lincolnshire Echo. I was already planning my next special publication, the *Farming Echo*, and it seemed like the perfect project to bring him on board.

I prepared a comprehensive business plan for *Farming Echo,* building on the work Peter and I had done previously with our *Farming Trader* concept. I included Peter as a new Senior Sales Representative, who needed to supervise the publication and report to me. I discussed the idea with Cliff, the editor of the daily newspaper, who was thrilled with the success of *The Business Echo.* The project's prestige had spilt over to him and his team, and he was eager to take on a new challenge.

"So, what do you think, Cliff? Can we do the farming one as well?" I asked.

"Yes, absolutely," he said. "We have loads of agricultural-type material that does not make it into the main newspaper because of space constraints. This is a great idea. Let us do it."

With Cliff on board, I presented the plan to Ted, following the same format as *The Business Echo,* but with a mailing list of 5,000. Ted was happy to go ahead.

"By the way, Ted, can I have a personal computer, an Apple Macintosh?" I asked. "I will be able to build a database for the farmers' mailing list, print out sticky labels, and use the spreadsheet for projections and reports. Plus, with the word processor, I will no longer need a secretary to type my letters."

"Where did you get this idea?" Ted asked.

"A friend of mine, James, who owns some care homes and flies aeroplanes, showed me his Apple Macintosh. It is brilliant. He uses it for flight plans and running the care homes."

Ted was not convinced. "I am not sure we can justify that sort of expense right now. Maybe we can talk about it again another time."

I knew this was a lot of new thinking and technology for Ted to absorb, so I let it rest for a couple of weeks. Then I brought it up again at the next management meeting, this time with the IT manager, John Devon, present.

"Ted, it is taking us a huge amount of time to write all the sticky envelope labels for the 5,000 farmers each month. I think we could save a fortune and increase profitability if you let me have this PC," I argued.

Ted looked at me sternly. "Let me think about it. I will talk to you tomorrow."

The following day, he called me into his office. "Okay, you can have your damn PC," he said, grinning.

"Wow, well, thank you, Ted. What changed your mind?" I asked.

"Nothing changed my mind. I do not like to shell out money so easily. But the fact that you kept coming back jumping all those hurdles I put in front of you, proves to me that you probably do actually need this PC. You cannot get the Apple Macintosh, which costs about £900. But John said he could build you a PC for £400, so I am prepared to spend that. It seems reasonable."

"This is the beginning of a new era," I said as Ted rolled his eyes and waved me out of his office.

I went straight downstairs to the IT workshop, where John Devon was excited at the prospect of building a new PC. He confirmed this was a new policy from Ted; no one at the *Lincolnshire Echo* had previously been given a personal computer. I was to be the first in *Lincolnshire Echo* and the entire Northcliffe Newspapers Group. John had also found some MS-DOS-based software called Delta 3, which has a database, spreadsheet, and word processor.

He said, "I'll bring my PC in tomorrow and teach you how to use it." DOS was a command-line operating system. There were no graphical windows, just a black screen with green letters and numbers. You had to know the commands to type at the prompt to launch programmes, run utilities, and do anything on the computer.

Peter Bromley soon joined us, and we launched *Farming Echo.* It quickly became a success and a vital publication for the local farming industry.

I was on a roll, looking for more supplements to create. My next target was the motors section of the *Lincolnshire Echo,* which was weak and uninteresting, especially compared with the thriving motors advertising in the *Lincolnshire Chronicle,* a weekly free newspaper. I saw an opportunity to do much better.

I made a dummy issue of a new supplement, *Auto Echo,* and took it to Tony Wood, the Group Advertising Manager. "Tony, your motors section is crap. It's dull and uninteresting. You publish less than a page daily, sometimes twice on a Friday. There's no editorial. All the main dealers advertise in the *Chronicle.* How would you like to kick their arse?"

Tony was intrigued. "Okay, explain your plan and how you'd make this work."

I laid it all out for him. "If you let me run it, I guarantee I can increase your ad revenue." I had already shown the dummy to some motor dealers, and they loved it. Many offered to provide cars for us to do local road tests.

Danny Hart, my friend who ran a motor dealership, suggested I poach Lynn and Sharon from the *Lincoln Chronicle,* the two top motors salespeople in city. Lynn and I were great friends. She had worked for me at *For Sale Magazine* and, after its collapse, gotten a job at the *Chronicle*.

I drove to her house and knocked on the door. Lynn, who was taking a sick day, opened the door in her dressing gown. We laughed, and I got straight to the point. "Would you like to come and work for me again? I am starting a new publication called *Auto Echo.* It is going to be fantastic, but I need you."

She agreed, and she also brought Sharon on board for telesales.

I updated Tony on my progress. "Tony, those two guys you have got selling motors are useless. The dealers do not get on with them. They are part of the problem. They are not interested in cars."

Tony grinned. "Go on?"

"I have headhunted the two top auto girls from the *Lincoln Chronicle*. The A-Team," I said, laughing.

"We move the two guys to the Property section and revamp that as the *Property Echo*."

Tony was thrilled. "Bloody well done, Roger. This will put the cat among the pigeons. Let's do it."

Auto Echo and *Property Echo* were born in the same week: *Property Echo* on Thursdays and *Auto Echo* on Fridays. Both became instant successes. Over the next year, I launched *Health Echo* monthly, *Home & Garden Echo* monthly and *Crimewatch Echo* monthly, in cooperation with the BBC Crimewatch TV programme. During those years, I won three national Newspaper Society Awards for best supplements. I increased the company's agricultural income from 1.7% to 17% a year.

CHAPTER 45

BREAKING STUFF

One day, I was in the *Echo*'s NGA Union-run production department waiting for proof of a full-page Jaguar ad that I needed to get signed off by 5:00pm. The artwork was finished, but when I asked the compositor to make a proof, he grinned and said, "Can't you see I'm doing something?"

"I just need you to help me out here. If I do not get the page signed off, it will not go in the next issue, and we won't get paid," I said, trying to keep my cool.

"When I finish this, I'm on a break anyway," he replied, walking away.

Frustrated, I reached over to his workstation to take the artwork to the copy machine myself. He turned back and shouted, "What are you doing? You cannot take that!"

"If you're busy and about to go on break, I'll do the copy myself," I said.

He whistled loudly, and the shop steward shouted, "Stop work!" The shop steward came over and asked, "Do you have a card?"

I knew what he meant – he asked if I had an NGA union member card, which I did not. "Do not be ridiculous; you know I don't have a card," I said.

"Then put the artwork down and wait until it's been done by an NGA member," he replied.

"You're joking, right?" I said, incredulous.

"No, I am not joking. Put it down and wait."

I put the artwork down and stormed straight to Ted's office to report this ludicrous situation. Ted was annoyed. "This will not be going on much longer. Just wait; plans are in place to sort this mess out once and for all soon."

Northcliffe Newspapers Group, part of *The Daily Mail,* owned the *Lincolnshire Echo.* By this time, Rupert Murdoch had already moved to eliminate the unions. All the print unions, including the NGA, were in a massive battle for survival.

Northcliffe Newspapers had started making secret preparations to drop the unionised labour force. Middle management staff from sales departments were sent on "training courses" to the USA, but in reality, they were learning how to operate the printing machines, plating, and scanning equipment – union members' jobs. Northcliffe also created mobile production units in articulated lorries, equipped with press production equipment, ready to be sent to any newspaper facing a union dispute.

As expected, negotiations with the unions broke down. The union's collective bargaining system was unsustainable. If one member worked late and got a bonus, everyone else in the union got the same bonus, even if they were asleep at home. This situation was financially crippling for companies.

When negotiations in Lincoln broke down, the management immediately fired every production employee while they were all in a meeting room, so they could not return to their workstations. They were offered a warning – return to work the next day, and they would be re-employed on individual contracts. About 20% of the Lincoln staff returned, but the others vilified them as scabs. The rest stayed out and began picketing the premises, trying to stop staff entering.

My role in the contingency plan was in the production department, doing artwork at the same workstation where the NGA members had dismissed me a few months earlier. Many of us brought sleeping bags, and the company made provisions for us to sleep in the building as long as needed.

A combination of returning production staff and trained middle management allowed us to print a paper every day. Ted made a point of handing a copy of the *Echo* each morning to Mr Rutter, the infamous Lincoln shop steward, outside the office.

Driving into the office car park was intimidating. The strikers crowded the entrance, waving banners and banging cars with their poles. One morning, I decided to take Samson, my Rottweiler, with me. He sat in the back seat, curious about the commotion. When one of the picketers kicked my car, Samson threw himself forward, hitting the glass with such force that blood and saliva covered the window. The striker stepped back, and I drove through into the secure parking zone.

These were crazy, scary times, but after a few weeks, the unions' fight ended, and the company won. I took immense pleasure in getting revenge on Rutter and those in the NGA who had killed my business and lost me my family home a couple of years before.

The print unions eventually collapsed, losing their grip on power. Their downfall came from failing to recognise how technology was transforming the industry. Instead of adapting, they positioned themselves in opposition to management, viewing the union as their true allegiance rather than seeing themselves as team players and integral members of the company they worked for.

CHAPTER 46
AGAIN

I saw Dennis Leigh walking into the office. He had been Tony Wood's assistant and was now the new Advertising Manager at the *Lincolnshire Echo.* I was at my desk in the Special Publications department, and we worked closely together. Dennis, eight years my senior, seemed more experienced. He had been a professional footballer for Doncaster, ending his career after six years and with Lincoln City. Well-known and respected around the city, his reputation likely helped him land the job at the *Echo.*

Dennis acknowledged me and said, "Hey Roger, can you pop into my office for a quick chat?" I grabbed my walking stick and walked to his office, a glass box in the corner of our open-plan space. Inside, he motioned for me to close the door, so I did and sat down in one of the executive-style chairs, leaving my walking stick leaning on the other.

Dennis looked concerned, rubbing the stubble on his chin and staring at his empty desk. After a long pause, I asked, "What is it, Dennis?"

He looked up and said, "Roger, mate, you know several of us at the *Echo* drink at the Duke William, where your wife works in the evenings as a barmaid."

I knew many people, including the *Echo* guys, frequented the Duke William. It did not please me that my wife was serving beers there. Caroline had been working a couple of nights a week for about a month. She wanted to earn her own money, even though we had agreed she would be a full-time mum to our three kids. Her working evenings meant I babysat our children, including our baby son Harry.

"Yes, what about it?" I asked. Dennis looked uncomfortable, finally saying, "I'm sorry, mate. You seem to be the only person in

Lincoln who does not know. Your missus is shagging another bloke."

His words hit me like a punch. Betrayal, lies, and humiliation flooded my mind. I was first in disbelief, then in shock. The thought of her coming home late and getting into our bed after being with another man made me sick. As I thought about her excuses, anger swelled inside me. I covered my face with my hands, trying to control my emotions. When I looked up, I asked, "Who is it, Dennis? Who is she fucking?"

Dennis replied, "His name is Phil Dickson. He's in there most evenings."

"Thank you, Dennis," I said, standing up. "I appreciate it, mate. I will go for a drive and get some space to think; I'll call you later." Dennis opened the door for me, patting my shoulder as I left.

Driving out of the office car park, I could not make sense of it. I had been working so hard to get us back on our feet – I was even doing it every Saturday and getting paid overtime. Things were finally moving in the right direction. We had a lovely home; she had a new Ford Fiesta, and we had a good life, or so I thought. I decided to confront Caroline later after the kids were in bed.

I went to Shirley Johns' house, a classy lady in her 50s who worked at the *Echo* with me as the classified advertising supervisor. She welcomed me in; she knew why I was there, and when I broke down, she held me and let me cry it out. She offered me a spare room to stay in, and I accepted gratefully.

Later that evening, I went home. Caroline asked where I had been, but I just got a beer and sat down. I waited for her to start talking about trivial things before I asked, "How is Phil Dickson?" Her shocked reaction confirmed everything.

Furious, I snapped, poured my beer over her head, and said, "You've done it again? What is wrong with you?" You are disgusting, wicked. She tried to deny it, but I told her not to bother; everyone in Lincoln knew what she had been doing, and she had disgraced me and my children. There was no possibility of us ever being together again after this; I forgave you once, but not again. I told her I was leaving. I packed a bag, kissed the kids goodnight, and told Caroline I would be back for my things.

I stayed with Shirley for about two weeks, during which Caroline moved in with Phil Dickson. I moved back into my house and rented out my old bedroom to a lady friend who had just got a new job in Lincoln and was happy to pay me rent. I was so upset and disappointed, but I just tried to continue with life. Eventually, Caroline and I agreed on shared custody of the kids; I would pay maintenance money for them.

Months later, I got my divorce papers. We had a 50-50 financial settlement; I was officially a single man, hurt by Caroline's betrayal, knowing my life plan had been destroyed and things would never be as I had dreamed, a family man with my children.

I was determined to get over this and to move on. I had enough cash to put a deposit down and I bought a new small one-bedroom bungalow in Roman Wharf near the canal in the city, starting a new chapter in my life.

Despite the pain and sadness, I focused on my work and my children. I accepted that I was a weekend dad now. I adapted and moved forward, living on my own for the first time and finding yet another new beginning.

CHAPTER 47
IBIZA

I had some holiday due from the *Lincolnshire Echo,* and Danny recommended that I go on an 18-30 holiday to avoid being on my own. I was 31 and felt a bit awkward about it. "No need to be concerned, mate. You still look like you are in your early 20s," he reassured me.

I parked on the double yellow lines, displayed my disabled driver parking badge on the dashboard, and walked into the travel agents opposite Lincoln railway station. Taking a seat, the girl behind the desk asked, "Where do you want to go?"

"I have no idea. What can you recommend for a single guy travelling alone?" I replied.

"Do you like Spain?" she asked.

"Well, I've only been to Majorca a couple of times. I liked it there. My friend suggested I go on an 18-30 holiday so that I'm not on my own."

She suggested, "Have you ever been to Ibiza? It's buzzing right now."

I knew of Ibiza's reputation as a party island. Pikes Hotel was famous after Wham recorded the video for their song *Club Tropicana* there in 1983. And in 1987, Freddie Mercury performed live with Montserrat Caballé to record the epic song *Barcelona* in the famous nightclub Ku. Excitedly, I said, "Yeah, I can go for seven days."

She replied that it's not an 18-30 holiday, but in the same hotel they use, so it should be busy with young people.

I replied, "Brilliant, that sounds perfect. Thanks."

She booked me into the Arenal Hotel on the beach in Sant Antoni de Portmany, near Pikes. The island had rocked to the sounds of George Michael's Wham, Duran Duran, and Queen during the early

1980s. By the time I went there in 1988, it was the dawn of the second summer of love, with the methodical thump beats and synthesisers of acid-house music taking over. The best band at the time was Amnesia, with Pascal Pante (known as Plastic) and their album *Hysteria,* which was rocking all the clubs in Ibiza that year.

I did not know it then, but Pascal and I would become good friends many years later.

This was my first time travelling alone, and I was incredibly nervous. With my walking stick, carrying bags and rushing to make connections between buses and planes was a struggle, but I thought, "I've got to try. Let's go for it and see what happens."

When I arrived at the hotel, it was heavy with 18-30 groups. Boys and girls were everywhere, and the place was electric with life. The hotel sat on a beautiful beach, surrounded by sunshine, bars, and clubs.

I wandered into the hotel's restaurant, sat at a small table by myself, and ordered my evening meal. Planning to walk out to the main street later, I hoped to bump into some people. I noticed another single chap sitting alone at a nearby table. He looked over, acknowledged me, and saw how my walking stick hindered my progress from carrying my plate from the buffet.

"Can I help you carry that?" he asked.

"Yes, please. Thanks," I replied.

We returned to a table and sat together; two lonely blokes surrounded by groups of youngsters who knew each other. That first evening, we spent time on the sun loungers by the hotel pool, listening to the music from the bar, drinking beers, and talking.

"Do you mind me asking what happened to you?"

Here we go again, I thought. This is a common question, but I never really minded. I appreciated him asking. I know it is not easy to do. I feel people should know rather than wonder. So, I told him my tale of accident and recovery, verbatim from many times past. He was suitably impressed by my determination and independence, and we moved on to more typical topics like jobs and cars.

I have never been a big drinker. I cannot consume vast amounts of beer, partly because of my weak bladder. I could not hold my beer, and if the toilets were far away or on the other side of a crowded pub or bar, I could quickly lose control because I could not walk fast enough to get there on time.

A few beers in, the alcohol was taking effect, and I was feeling sorry for myself. I started telling Christian about my woes – how my despicable wife had just had her second affair, cheating on our children and me again, and how hard it was to be a weekend daddy and see my kids living in another man's house. I let it all out, and he was a sympathetic ear.

Christian shared that he was 30 and worked in his father's motor business. He drove an Aston Martin, which I was envious of, as it sounded like he was living well.

I asked him, "What brings you here alone?"

Christian said, "Early last year, my wife fell ill quite suddenly. We did not know what it was. It was like a vicious flu; she was always tired and had no energy. We went to our local doctor, and she had abnormal results on a routine blood test. He referred her to a specialist in London. We found out she had a form of acute leukaemia. She started her treatment, and we got married soon after, but she declined rapidly. A year later, she died. She was only 26."

I saw he began to get emotional, the pain stabbing him in the guts once more.

"I'm so sorry, Christian. That is awful. I should not have asked," I said.

He sobbed and looked at me. "I have to learn to talk about it. Do not be sorry. It helps me come to terms with it. Not knowing you made it kind of easier."

"Can you tell me more about her? I bet she was gorgeous," I asked.

He chuckled, tears in his eyes, and said, "Yeah, she was a stunner, a true soulmate. We were a wonderful team. We had a lovely life. I'm so lucky I ever met her and had her for the time I did."

Suddenly, my troubles felt so insignificant. The world seemed vast. We drank and talked until early morning. I was so tired and drunk that Christian had to help me to my room. I could hardly stand, let alone walk. He was a big lad, and we were in fits of laughter as he tried to carry me up the stairs on his back.

I managed to make it down to the hotel restaurant before the end of breakfast. It was a buffet, and I made a few trips back and forth, having only one hand to carry my food. Two pretty young girls offered to help me and joined me at my table. One was tall with short blonde hair and very white skin. I could tell she was Scottish by her beautiful accent. The other girl was shorter, had very dark, short hair, and had an exotic Mediterranean look. Their names were Olivia and Isabella.

Olivia asked, "So, Roger, are you going to Ku tonight?"

"Where?" I responded.

"Ku, the nightclub in San Rafael. You must have heard of it. It is the biggest dance club in the world. There is an 18-30 tour bus taking us all tonight. Are you going?" asked Olivia.

"I'm not part of the 18-30 group. I'm 31," I laughed. "I just happen to be in the same hotel as you guys. Besides, it's not my cup of tea. Massive places with many people are usually difficult for me – long walks, busy, bustling crowds, all a bit risky for me to negotiate on a walking stick."

Olivia replied, "Don't be daft. You can come with us. We will look after you. I will get three tickets. We can go on the bus together, okay?"

Isabella smiled and nodded encouragingly. "Come on, Roger. We are all here to have fun. Don't you want to step out with two beautiful girls?" she laughed excitedly.

"OK, I'm in. How can I say no to you two? My lucky night, I think," I laughed.

Getting on the bus was a caper. I needed help up the step, which was quite high. The girls grabbed my arse and pushed me up like they were loading a bag of sugar onto a truck. We all laughed as we stumbled to our seats.

1988 was the second summer of love, and acid-house music was the scene. I had to pinch myself. The girls were all dressed up for clubbing, looking fabulous with striking make-up and glittering sexy outfits. There I was, in jeans and a T-shirt, feeling incredibly lucky.

The bus parked next to about 100 others in an enormous car park. The path to the club entrance was long, downhill, and gravelly. I could not have made it alone in the dark, not on my walking stick. But the girls grabbed me, one under each arm, and we marched into the entrance like a troika.

We showed our tickets and walked into the symphony of laser lights and the rhythmic boom of acid house music. I felt like Mick Jagger. It was an incredible feeling.

Thousands of beautiful people were bouncing rhythmically to the music on the dance floor. Exotic people were draped around swimming pools and lounging under palm trees, all bathed in coloured lights. Waiters in amazing costumes delivered drinks to tables, and multiple bars with performing bartenders added to the spectacle. High stages with podiums were full of exotic, half-naked dancers, and entertainers mingled around the dance floors. It was all-consuming, like nothing I had ever seen before.

We made our way to a table and ordered drinks. I stuck to gin and tonics to avoid frequent trips to the toilets, which were miles away. I figured I would not drink too much that night, as I had had a skinful the night before and was still recovering.

Across from us was a table where girls surrounded three wealthy-looking young men. I thought they must be celebrities. Club staff were waiting on them; trolleys with ice buckets and champagne were coming and going at quite a pace.

Now and then, I could see one of these guys; he kept looking over at our table. He was very handsome, with his long blond hair, a gold watch that looked expensive, and those Scandinavian looks. Who was he? I recognised him but could not place him. A pop band, I thought.

I told Olivia, "That guy over there keeps staring at you."

She turned, took a brief look, and said, "Really? Well, we are here with you," she giggled.

I could tell he picked her out from the crowd and was interested. Olivia and Isabella looked at me, reached over with their drink glasses stretched out together, and said, "Cheers."

We were extolling the virtues of this fantastic place, and I said to

Olivia, "That guy over there can't take his eyes off of you."

This time, she turned and looked right at him, held him in her stare, and smiled at him. She raised her glass to him, then turned back towards me and asked, "Is he still looking?"

I said, "Oh yes, definitely, you've scored there, Olivia."

A few minutes later, a waiter came to our table, pushing a silver trolley containing a bottle of champagne in an ornate silver ice bucket. He indicated by looking over at the blond guy's table that it was sent to us from him. We all three looked at each other in amazement and gasped. We looked over to his table; the blond guy had his arm out, his glass raised as if to say cheers. We reciprocated with cheers, raising our drinks.

I told the girls, "Come on, we should go to his table and join him there. It would be rude not to."

They agreed, so the waiter took the champagne trolley, and the girls dragged the chairs over to his table. The group made room for us, ensuring Olivia sat beside him.

We all spent the evening together around that table. The champagne flowed all night, and I was careful not to drink too much. When it came time to leave, we all gathered at the exit. The blond guy's car and driver arrived, and he invited Olivia to join him. We all hugged and kissed in that European way and said goodnight, even though it was morning.

Isabella and I waited for the bus. A man I assumed was the club manager came over to say goodbye. He said it was great to meet us and that, as friends of Johan, we were welcome back any time, free, of course. It was awkward when we returned to the hotel. I am not strong anyway, and after a long night out, I was exhausted and slightly drunk. I wanted to sleep with Isabella but knew I could not perform as I wanted to.

Isabella returned to my room, and we just talked for a while. We were both dead tired. She said, "Let's sleep now; you'll be stronger in the morning."

She was correct. When we woke, we were both naked. She was incredibly gorgeous, with big brown eyes, full lips, a sexy body with impressive breasts, her small behind, and her brown skin. She was perfect in my eyes. We made love; she was so unrestrained, so uninhibited. She knew I had been married for several years and that she was my first since that divorce. After we showered together, she soaped me all over, and I returned the favour. It was terrific.

Isabella returned to her room, and I met her on the beach later that morning. I was used to topless beaches from Majorca in the ’80s; it was the norm. But this Ibiza beach was packed with gorgeous young women, nearly all of them topless. I did not know which way to look; it was extraordinary.

I got used to the incredible surroundings. Then, Isabella came over with two cold beers. She handed me one. She was topless; it was not an issue for her. It was weird for me and fantastic at the same time. She sat with me, and we talked and reminisced about the night before.

“Where is Olivia?” I asked.

“I don’t know; she hasn’t come back yet,” she replied.

I concentrated on getting a suntan. I was only there for six nights and was determined to go home nice and brown. After a few hours of the intensely hot sun beating down on me, I retreated to the shade of the bar and drank with Christian.

Olivia spent the remaining days of her holiday with the blond guy while Isabella hung out with her 18-30 group. She invited me to various places, including Pacha, another famous club, but as much as I liked her, I could not face night after nightclubbing until dawn. Instead, Christian and I went on an old-fashioned pub crawl, enjoying the variety of bars and street life of Ibiza town.

The group organised a day trip to Formentera, the smallest of the Balearic Islands, close to Ibiza. This time, Christian joined us. The boat trip to the island was the tour guide’s opportunity to get everybody drunk. The cruise boat carried about 40 people.

The music was blasting, and tour guides poured the sangria, ensuring everybody was loaded and happy by the time they got to the island’s beaches.

I discovered I had a new talent that day. They were competing on how long you could take a continuous stream of sangria while being poured into your open mouth by a guide. We were lined up four at a time as four tour guides tipped their jugs into the competitors' open mouths. To my astonishment, I won pretty easily, having found a rhythm of how to swallow and gulp after gulp continuously. This achievement gained me great applause from the drunken group, and I was heralded as a great drinking leader.

By the time we got to the beach, we were all paralytic, and the beach games began. The sun was fiercely hot, and after a brief time, I sat at a table in the shade with Christian. Together, for the next couple of hours, we drank beers and watched the topless girls sunbathing.

Teams were set up and had relay races up and down the sandy beaches. They had to bend over with their foreheads touching a stick to the ground, spin around the axis 10 times, then stand up and run back to their teams. By this time, they were all so dizzy they could hardly stand up, let alone run in a straight line. The spectacle of team members' pathetic attempts to reach each other was hilarious, resulting in bilious laughter all over the place. It was a fantastic day out, even if I had a steaming headache.

Christian said, "Roger, thanks for making me come today. I have had a fantastic time. It has been ages since I laughed so much. I simply have not been able to have any fun since my wife died. Today was terrific. I even spoke to some girls without feeling guilty. I probably would have stayed at the hotel and read my book if you hadn't forced me to come with you, so cheers, mate."

I replied, "Thanks for coming, Christian. It was terrific. I enjoyed it, too. I felt a lot more confident with you here, getting on and off the boat and moving around, knowing that you were there to help me, especially coming back home if I was too drunk."

Christian laughed.

I entertained two or three ladies on that holiday. My walking problems became an advantage, not a hindrance. Meeting and getting to know Christian helped me put my problems in perspective. Isabella had taken me to a place I had only dreamed of previously. The sexual encounter built my confidence as a man again. The whole

Ibiza experience rejuvenated my belief in myself and my prospects. I realised I would only be alone if I chose to be so and that it would not take long to find a new partner if and when I was ready.

I returned happy to Lincolnshire, my interesting job and my beautiful children.

You could say I'd "found myself" that week. I had taken myself off alone to another country, of all things, on an 18-30 holiday at the age of 31. I managed the physical obstacles, and I met lovely new friends. I'd grown in confidence and had a wonderful time.

Another new chapter of my life had begun.

CHAPTER 48
SINGLE

Danny was single, but he lived with one of his girlfriends and her daughter in a large five-bedroom house he owned on the banks of a lake. He had a Rolls-Royce and a Mercedes SL Convertible. He was doing very well. Now that I was a single man, Danny thought I'd be his new sidekick; he was keen to get me out and have some fun.

I walked into his in-car entertainment business office on Tritton Road industrial estate and sat down.

"Hello, mate. How's things?" I spoke.

Danny asked, "Do you want a cup of coffee? I've got a new coffee machine."

"Yeah, nice, thanks," I said.

That's real ground coffee, espresso, no rubbish here," he joked.

"I was gutted to hear about poor old Samson," he said.

Samson had cancer in his shoulder the year before. He was such a heavy dog that it became difficult for him to get up from a laying-down position. It was obvious he couldn't cope with the pain. While I was away from home for a few days on a management training course, Caroline had arranged for him to be put down.

Coming home and not being welcomed by my beloved dog and learning of his fate was very upsetting. People who have had faithful dogs for many years and then lost them understand the pain.

"Now you must be enjoying life as a single man. You must be getting loads," laughed Danny.

"Leave it out, Danny. All I do is work and sleep. I have got child maintenance payments plus the mortgage for that bloody overpriced bungalow you sold me, you bastard!" I roared.

"Don't blame me, mate. I sold that bungalow to you at a fair price. It's not my fault the markets crashed!" he laughed loudly.

He continued, "Let's go out tonight. Fancy a trip to Nottingham? We can go in the Merc, put the roof down, and take some girls. It will be classic."

"No, thank you, mate. I can't keep up with you. I can't drink the way you do, let alone the rest of the stuff. I'm not interested if you're doing gear!" I said firmly.

"All right, all right, old man. Let's go to Cinderella Rockefeller's here in Lincoln. We can just have some drinks and a laugh, mate. Loosen you up a bit, meet some ladies, and have some fun. Come on, fella," he pleaded.

"Yeah, all right then. Cinderella Rockefeller's it is. That sounds more like it," I said.

"I'll pick you up from your place at 9 o'clock. Don't forget to bring that disabled parking badge of yours so we can park in the street outside the club," he said.

Danny's Rolls-Royce Silver Spirit was a good one, just a couple of years old, but it was post-office red with a cream leather interior. It really stood out. He parked it on the double yellow lines in front of the club, with two wheels on the pavement, so I did not need to walk too far. He put my disabled parking permit in the front window and said, "OK, partner, let's go for it."

The club was banging, and the music was loud. The place was packed and full of gorgeous ladies. Danny and I had done our customary walk around, seeing who was in tonight and saying our hellos. We laid eyes on two very sophisticated girls sitting at a cocktail table near the dance floor. One girl had blonde curly hair and wore an expensive-looking white suit; the other had long dark hair and wore a skinny little black skirt and vest-like top, showing off her impressive breasts. They both looked in their 30s.

I looked at Danny and said, "That's more my style, Danny, a bit of class. You can tell they're ladies from a long way away." I noticed the YSL handbag, the smart shoes, and the gold jewellery. They were very well turned out.

Danny sent over a big smile, and those perfect bright white teeth shone out from his dark coffee-coloured skin. They looked back and giggled and immediately turned away. I looked at him and said, "Oh, poor Danny, looks like you're out of luck already, mate."

Danny answered, "I'm not done yet. Follow me." He started to walk towards their table; I followed close behind him. They did a double take, seeing me hobbling along slowly behind him on a walking stick. They looked and looked again to see I was Danny's partner in crime. I stood there while handsome Daniel said, "Ladies, good evening. You're both looking amazing tonight. Can my friend Roger and I buy you two lovely ladies a drink?"

Simultaneously, they both looked up, gave him a stare, slowly smiling, and then in unison, saying, "No dear, piss off."

Danny replied, "Well, girls, that's not very ladylike, is it?" He looked at me. "I thought you said these were two classy ladies, Roger. You were mistaken."

The blonde girl looked again, smiled, and said, "We only drink champagne. To be precise, we only drink Moët Chandon." And she turned her back on us again.

We stepped away. Danny grabbed me by the arm and said, "Come with me to the bar."

Danny was a regular and knew the barman very well. He called him over and said, "Michael, please give me four bottles of Moët Chandon, with the tops off, by the neck. No ice bucket and no glasses needed."

I laughed and said, "Are you serious, Danny?"

He said, "Yes, mate, you heard the girls. They only drink champagne, so Moët Chandon it is."

The price in a nightclub was astronomical, but he was having fun. We walked back to the table, Danny with two bottles in each hand. "Ladies, your drinks," he said.

The girls turned around. Danny thumped the four bottles down on the table; he passed one to me, picked up one himself, and said to the girls, "Cheers, ladies."

They couldn't keep a straight face; they both burst out laughing. We sat down with them, and the evening progressed from there. It was a great night. Niamh, the blonde, happened to be the daughter of an Irish hotel magnate. At the time, she was the General Manager of the Eastgate Hotel, which overlooked Lincoln Cathedral. The other girl with the dark hair was her assistant. I did not find Niamh that sexy or attractive. It was not a lustful relationship, but she was a lovely, funny girl with a seductive Irish accent. She was a girl that knew how to have a fun time. We had a great night, exchanged phone numbers, and went home.

I called her a few days later, and she invited me to her hotel bar for a drink. She had a new Toyota MR2, which was quite impressive then. We got on well and went out several times over the coming weeks. On warm evenings, we would drive to pubs and restaurants with the roof off. It was a lovely summer.

As the General Manager of the Eastgate Hotel, she lived in a special house within the hotel grounds. When she was not working, she had room service from the hotel. I would spend her off days and holidays at her place. This significant luxury house was fantastic. She had her staff for room service. She would pick up the phone and order champagne, port, single malt whiskey, beef steaks and chips, ice cream, whatever we desired.

We spent most of our time watching TV and eating. She did not turn me on sexually; she was fun and lovely. I think it was the lifestyle that attracted me; comparing my spartan, solitary home with oven-ready freezer meals from my microwave oven to this luxury, it was easy to spend time with her.

It was quite an experience. It only lasted a couple of months. Niamh was soon on her travels back to Ireland to work for her daddy, but it was great while it lasted.

CHAPTER 49
LETTERBOX

Now that I just had a tiny, one-bedroom bungalow, having the kids stay overnight was challenging. I was just two miles from where they lived now. So, my weekend routine was to collect them on a Friday evening and drive the 165 miles to my mother's house in Maidenhead.

While down there, we also had the chance to visit Caroline's father, who also lived in Maidenhead, just a mile away from my mum's. He had been shattered at our breakup, so disappointed in his youngest daughter, embarrassed by her betrayal of me. He saw me as a good dad and did what he could to support me. He had fallen out with Caroline after her first affair; they hadn't spoken for years, and this latest episode of her selfish behaviour had cemented his disappointment even further. Caroline would not talk to him, so the only chance of him seeing the grandkids was when I took them to his house.

The kids loved their weekends in Maidenhead, and we had some beautiful times. We would leave Sunday afternoon, and I would return them to their mother's by 7:00pm. Caroline could not conceal that she looked forward to her weekends alone or with Phil Dickson if he were home and had no kids around his feet. She would make the excuse that the kids were such demanding work all week that she deserved some time to herself.

This particular weekend, my mother and my stepfather Roy were driving up to York, his home city, to see his family. So, we agreed to meet in Lincoln en route to York on Sunday. I arranged with Caroline to pick the kids up Sunday morning and return them around 6:00pm. I took them home, and they were watching cartoons on the TV.

But when my mother and Roy arrived around midday, there was hardly enough space for us in my tiny bungalow. It was such an awful day; it was pouring rain, so we decided to go to McDonald's. Once we had finished our meals and drinks, we chatted for a while, but there was not much else we could do. The children were getting bored. I had arranged with Caroline to take the children back at 6:00pm. It was about 3:00pm when I called. The plan was to drop the children off earlier so mum and Roy could continue their journey to York and get there before 6:00pm.

I called, but there was no answer, so we waited a while. Then I phoned again and let it ring longer. Finally, Caroline answered. I said, "Hi, is it OK to bring the children back early? It is pouring with rain, and they are getting bored."

She replied, her speech slow and muffled, "No. Please do not bring them back now. Can you bring them back tomorrow?" She hung up. I called again, but she did not pick up. She sounded hesitant, her speech a bit slurred. I thought something was not right. She did not sound like her usual controlling self. Odd?

I explained to mum and Roy that this was not the typical response I would expect. Something was wrong. I should go there now and see what is going on. Roy said, "OK, Roger, your mother and I will follow you around there."

I parked outside Phil Dickson's house. It was still raining heavily. I told the children to wait in the car in case mummy was not home yet. I knocked on the door, but there was no answer. So, I knocked again. Still no response. I went back to my car phone. I called Caroline's house number, and there was no answer. This was strange, as her Ford Fiesta, which I had provided for her, was parked on the driveway. I knew Phil Dickson was working overseas, and I did not think she would have gone out in the rain.

I left the children in the car, stepped back into the pouring rain, and hurried back to the shelter of her porch, careful not to let my walking stick slip on the wet concrete. Back at her front door, I rang her doorbell and then rang it again. I knocked again as loudly as I could, but still no answer. I managed to bend over, flip the letterbox open, and look through it. I could see down the hallway and into the kitchen. The door was open, and I could see her lying prone, face down, on the kitchen floor.

I shouted through the letterbox, "Caroline, Caroline." She did not answer, and she did not respond at all. She looked dead. I stood up, and by this time, my mum and Roy, still sitting in their car, had guessed something was wrong. Roy started walking down the driveway and came to join me at the front door. My mum got in my car and sat with the kids.

"Roy, I can see her. She is lying on the kitchen floor. She looks like she is unconscious," I said.

Roy tried banging on the door again, ringing the bell, but nothing could stir her. Roy went around the side of the house. I followed him, and he reached up and opened the latch to the tall gate that led to the back garden. It opened, and we went into the backyard. The kitchen door was not locked, so we went inside.

Caroline was lying on her front, wearing just her underwear. An empty bottle of sherry and three empty bottles of paracetamol tablets stood on the kitchen table. I sat on a kitchen chair and tried to wake her. She was semi-conscious and utterly unaware of what was happening or who I was. Her eyes were half-open, her eyeballs rolled back and glazed.

I told her, "Caroline, we must call an ambulance and get you to the hospital. Can you move?"

She did not respond, and I was extremely concerned. I said, "Roy, can you call 999? We need an ambulance. The phone is in the hall."

On the table with the pill bottles, I noticed a small notebook. A message was scribbled in it: a few heart-wrenching and sad words to the children and her mother.

The ambulance arrived and took her to the hospital, and I followed in my car. Roy and my mother stayed behind at the house with the children and waited for the news. The children did not understand what was going on. My mum told them their mummy was not feeling well and would come back later. I sat in the waiting room for a couple of hours when the doctor came out to see me.

He said, "Caroline has consumed a lot of alcohol, together with a considerable number of painkillers; this is a lethal combination.

She is fortunate you found her when you did. We first induced vomiting to remove as much of the substance from her stomach as we could. We gave her activated charcoal to absorb the drug, and we pumped her stomach to remove the rest of the substance. She is now getting intravenous fluids to help speed up her body's recovery."

"Oh dear, is she going to be all right?" I asked.

He replied, "She is stable now, but we must keep her here for a few days to watch her progress. Hopefully, she will be OK. You should know that this amount of paracetamol could quite easily send her blind. She has liver poisoning because of this, which could well have dangerous side effects and even cause liver failure, if not now, later in life."

I went in to see her. She was reclined in the hospital bed, hooked up to IV drips. She was very sullen; she started to cry when she saw me. I sat beside the bed and held her hand.

I said, "What on earth do you think you are doing? You nearly killed yourself."

She cried some more, looking pathetic. I felt sorry for her. What could have made her do such a drastic thing?

I said, "You have three beautiful children who love you so much. I do not know what is happening with Phil and you, but you now have a responsibility to the kids."

She thanked me and apologised again, explaining that she was very depressed and that she had broken up with Phil. Her mother was supposed to come up from London to stay with her that weekend, but she cancelled her visit at the last minute. It was some flimsy excuse, and it had all gotten a bit too much for her. This final rejection was enough, it seems, to tip her over the edge.

She was in the hospital for about a week. I went back to work as usual, and my parents cancelled their trip to York so they could look after my kids while I was at work.

During that week, we had this bizarre situation. My mum and my stepfather were living in my two-timing ex-wife's current lover's house, sleeping in her bed, looking after my children, getting them up, taking them to school, cooking their dinners in his kitchen, with me visiting in the evenings, while she was lying in a hospital bed.

Having saved her life, it was all bonkers.

My mother was convinced that Caroline felt she had made a colossal mistake. She explained, "The stupid girl, she got caught out. I guess she never planned to be with this new man, only have some 'fun' with him. And now she is stuck in a relationship with a man who does not want her, especially not the children."

She continued, "She regrets it. She can see you are progressing with your career, making more money, having a nice house and car, travelling to places she only dreams about, and having your choice of pretty girls. And she feels she is stuck with the kids and the housework."

That was the case. My new single-man lifestyle, the fact that I was able to work, travel, and meet new women. But I was not happy and enjoying life; I missed my children, putting them to bed, just being a full-time dad. The truth is, I had an ideal vision of being a family man, a good husband, and a father, but it was just a dream. It was never going to be a reality. And while I deeply regretted losing full-time responsibility for my three kids, I was relieved to be rid of her. Regretfully, we were never meant for each other.

Her disappointment with her situation was evident, as her life seemed not to be going smoothly. She was often moody and inattentive with the children, and there did not appear to be much love and affection in her mothering. Fortunately for me, she was glad to be free of the children at any opportunity and rarely turned down a chance for a weekend, or even a Christmas, without them.

However, there were many occasions, mostly those that involved money, when she would use the children as hostages, as bargaining chips, trying to manipulate me, and even hurt me, regardless of the effect that may have had on our growing children.

I did not recognise it back then, but now I know how much it affected them. Those sweet little souls were collateral commodities used in negotiations. I do not think she cherished and loved them the way they deserved.

I know it is wrong, but it is the truth. It's human nature, and I defy any of you to say, "It wouldn't happen to you," but when the sparks were flying in those situations. She was telling me what a terrible father I had been, what a piece of shit I was; I have often thought, "What if I had not looked through her letterbox that day?" I am reasonably sure she would not have survived her attempt to end her life; the drugs would have killed her.

She would have inadvertently gifted me my children, and life would have turned out to be vastly different for all of us; it could have been wonderful.

CHAPTER 50
CORNWALL

Christmas of 1988 brought with it a momentous change in my life. I had just been handed the keys to a new company car, a Ford Orion Ghia 1.6, a significant upgrade from my old Ford Escort 1.3L. This car had previously belonged to our Assistant Managing Director, Tom, but it was passed down to me after he received his new company vehicle. It felt like a reward from my boss, Ted Stevens, for all the vigorous work I had been putting in, which was finally showing results.

With the new car, I took my children from Lincoln to Maidenhead to spend the Christmas holidays at my mother's house. Caroline and I had agreed that it was the best place for the kids to be for their first Christmas since our divorce a few months earlier. My mum's house was perfect – a large detached, four-bedroom home with a big garden that opened onto the countryside. She had decorated it beautifully for Christmas, making it a warm and welcoming place for the kids, who seemed to enjoy a regular, loving family holiday with nanna and grandad Roy. They never missed their mother.

Amidst our celebrations, the news was still buzzing with the tragic story of the Pan Am Flight 103 bombing. On 21 December, 1988, the flight from Frankfurt to Detroit via London and New York City was destroyed by a bomb over Lockerbie, Scotland. All 243 passengers and 16 crew members perished, along with 11 people on the ground. It was a horrific event, the deadliest terrorist attack in the UK, and it cast a shadow over our festive season.

Opportunity knocks

Returning to work in January, Ted called me into his office. His demeanour was unusually cheerful, and he offered me coffee and biscuits, which immediately signalled that something significant was up. After we settled into the comfortable armchairs by his office window overlooking Brayford Wharf and Lincoln Cathedral, Ted asked, "Do you think you'll miss Lincoln?"

Confused, I responded, "What do you mean, Ted? Miss Lincoln?"

"Your progress here has not gone unnoticed," Ted said. "A couple of our other offices were interested in offering you a position, but I think you might be very pleased to know that Tony Wood wants you to join him at Cornish Weeklies Newspapers."

Tony Wood had been my boss until a few months before. As the Group Advertising Manager of the *Lincolnshire Echo,* he had recently been promoted to Managing Director of the Cornish Weeklies Group in Truro, Cornwall.

Ted continued, explaining how Tony saw me as one of his own and believed I was the right person to help him achieve his ambitious goals in Cornwall.

I was shocked and flattered.

"This comes as a bit of a shock, Ted. I thought you might be sending me on a management training course or something," I said, trying to process the news.

Ted smiled, acknowledging my surprise. "Roger, you've done an excellent job with the special publications department. All seven publications are now well-established, and you have built a good team. Peter Bromley is probably ready to take over from you."

It was clear that Ted had my future in mind. He encouraged me to take the next step in my career, even if it meant moving far from Lincoln and my children to Cornwall. The opportunity was too good to pass up, and I felt excitement and apprehension as I prepared for the move.

The drive to Truro was long – 350 miles from Lincoln – so my thoughts naturally turned to my children. I will not be able to have them every weekend; it may have to be every other weekend or even once a month. I will have to see how this works out, but I am guessing I will only be in Cornwall for a year or two, and then I will be moving somewhere else anyway. Who knows where I will be over the next few years? I thought.

Burning surprise

I was determined to make it to Truro in one go, but by the time I reached Newton Abbot, about 270 miles in, I had to pull over and consult my map. As I sat there, I noticed that Orion's bonnet started to rise; suddenly, it popped like a balloon. I was confused and saw smoke coming from the car's engine.

I realised it was blistering paint; the engine was on fire. Panicked, I reached into the back seat for my walking stick and my briefcase; just as a red van pulled up, the driver ran over and pulled me away from the burning vehicle.

The fire quickly engulfed the car; an Esso petrol tanker pulled into the lay-by. The driver had a fire extinguisher and was trying to extinguish the flames. The van driver had called 999, and soon, a fire engine arrived to put it out.

A police patrol car also arrived, and officers placed orange road cones to prevent other vehicles from parking. After a few minutes, they sent the petrol tanker on its way, and the van driver left. I sat on the grass, verge shaken and concerned about my situation. Once the fire was extinguished, the police removed their cones, and all the traffic resumed. I could see the police were about to leave, so I struggled to get up from the ground; I walked carefully with my stick on the bumpy surface over to the stationary Ford Granada police car.

I asked one of the police officers, "Would you be able to give me a lift into Newton Abbot, please, so that I can arrange a rental car? "

To my surprise, he said, "No, sorry, we are not a taxi service."

I looked at him and asked, "Do you intend to leave me here alone? What am I supposed to do?"

He answered, "Do not worry, sir. We have called a recovery vehicle, and you can go back to town with your car."

Bewildered and exhausted, staring at my black, burnt-out car, I waited for the breakdown truck. I did not want to sit back on the grass as I might not be able to get up again.

When it arrived, I had to ride in a dirty cab, and the driver took me to a car rental in town. There, I managed to get another vehicle and finally reached Truro, albeit three hours late, for my meeting with Tony Wood. Tony laughed at my ordeal. Given my record of accomplishment with company vehicles, he joked about getting me multiple second-hand cars instead of one new one. Despite the rough start, I was eager to begin my new role as Group Advertising Manager for Cornish Weeklies Newspapers, overseeing 12 publications and a staff of 160.

Mobile advantage

My new remuneration package was very generous. It included not simply a significant pay rise, but also six weeks of paid holiday per year, a Peugeot 405 GR company car, an interest-free bridging loan to purchase a new house in Cornwall, to be settled when my home in Lincolnshire was sold, and £2,500 towards new furniture.

When the time came to collect my new company vehicle, Tony informed me the London office HQ had organised it, and they had designated a cheaper GL model. Embarrassed by the mix-up, he allowed me to add any accessories I wanted to the car and to bill them to the Cornwall office; that way, he said with a wink, London would not know of the additional cost of the extras, and no one's feathers would be ruffled.

At the Peugeot showroom, there was not much in the way of accessories. I ordered a front air dam, colour-coded wing mirrors and alloy wheels, but that was all they had to offer. I saw in the corner of the showroom a car mobile telephone display. The new 'Nokia Hutchinson' carphone was now available; it was the first digital car phone in the market. Thus, it was extremely expensive, so I told the sales manager,

"I'll have one of those as well, please." I thought, be bold, "He who dares wins."

A few days later, my new car arrived, and I drove it back to the office. Tony Wood came out to look. He walked around it admiringly; it was white with nice alloy wheels. He checked out which accessories I had included when he saw the car telephone installed on the dashboard; he looked surprised. He turned to me and said, "What have you done here? This is not an accessory; this is not what I agreed to."

I answered confidently, "Of course, it is from the Peugeot showroom, Tony. You said it would fit whichever accessories I wanted."

He replied, "Yes, but not a bloody telephone. You'll be the only employee in Northcliffe newspapers with a carphone, including the Chairman and board of directors in London."

I answered, "It is the future, Tony. We are ahead of the curve. We set the trends, we do not follow them." I laughed.

He replied, "Christ, you're going to cause some noise in London when they hear about this."

Tony was a small, slight man; in my experience, such men like to be called boss.

I said, "Boss, think about this logically: it's a perfect tool for my job as Group Sales Manager if I'm to be out on the road travelling around the entire county of Cornwall, visiting any one of six offices, some over 50 miles apart, with this handy business device, you'll still be able to contact me anytime anywhere, no excuses. You always have me firmly under your control. You can remind them that we lead the way in innovation and technology development in Cornwall," I laughed.

He looked at me out of the corner of his eye with a sarcastic grin. He said, "You're a crafty bastard, Warner, but you have a good point."

Embracing common sense and innovation

For me, all this was common sense. I was always a big-picture manager, not one to get bogged down in the minutiae of micromanagement. My strength lies in forecasting potential scenarios, identifying problems and opportunities, and introducing innovative solutions. This pattern repeated itself throughout my career.

It began when I left ML Aviation, quickly realising that the future I saw there wasn't for me. At Group Typesetters, I knew we had to modernise our equipment and production processes to survive. Moving from Berkshire to Lincolnshire was a strategic decision focused on the long-term benefits for my children's future. Launching *For Sale Magazine* with Peter was driven by the awareness that newspapers were slowly dying off.

I was the first employee at Northcliffe to have a personal

computer, a feat that required considerable effort to convince the *Lincolnshire Echo* MD to let me have one built in 1984. Even then, it was clear to me that computers would inevitably improve performance in every aspect of business.

In Cornwall, I recognised that mobile communications, regardless of the cost, would significantly enhance my performance as a regional manager. The key was to resist their resistance, be bold, and take decisive steps into the future.

Introductions

It was my first day at work. Tony set up a meeting to introduce me to the senior advertising staff from all over Cornwall. There were about 16 managers and supervisors, and we were all seated around the boardroom table.

Then Charlotte walked in. The room went quiet, and everybody watched as she confidently took her seat. I tried to contain myself. I slowly closed my mouth and concentrated on keeping my composure and not looking at her.

She looked like a cross between Grace Jones and Madonna. She was very white skinned, like marble, with big blue eyes, blond hair, and a gorgeous face ashamedly adorned with red lipstick. She was statuesque, tall, and athletic; her short skirt ensured everybody could see her epic, long legs.

Tony asked me to stand up and introduce myself. He praised my abilities, expressing confidence in my role as his right-hand man, to execute his plans to consolidate the sales offices and the current publications and to launch new newspapers, and how together we would all build a new future.

As Tony and everyone filed out of the board room one-by-one into the corridors behind, Charlotte lingered by the door; she glanced over at me, her new boss. I walked towards her with my walking stick now visible to her for the first time. She looked at me like a cat looking at a fish.

"I look forward to working with you, Charlotte. Tony's told me wonderful things about you, and I'm sure we will soon have your newspaper dominating in your town of Falmouth," I spoke.

She smiled and said, "Oh, I know we will." I knew then that something was going to happen between us.

Accommodations

I had my one-bedroom bungalow in Lincoln. It was a new build. I bought it at an inflated price during the property boom, and I completed the purchase two weeks before Black Monday, 19 October, 1987, the devastating global stock market crash.

The world economy went into free fall, and property prices dropped daily. I was already in negative equity; the value had plummeted, and it was not a suitable time to sell. The procedure with NNG was to put me in a hotel while I found my new home. They would provide a bridging loan to cover the cost of buying a house until my bungalow in Lincoln was sold.

The company booked me into St Benet's Abbey, a Grade II listed property about three miles outside of Bodmin, dating back to 1411, originally built as part of an Abbey of Benedictine order, a historic building in 1.8 acres of gardens with the original chapel tower on the grounds.

It had just eight en-suite guest bedrooms. It was beautiful and believed to have ties to the Knights Templar; it was charming with its four-poster beds, coal fireplaces, and leaded light church-style stained glass windows. They told me to put all my meals on expenses. I ordered a case of Chateau Smith-Haut Lafitte Blanc to enjoy with my evening meals. It was all extremely luxurious, and I was enjoying life.

Initially, I based myself at the Bodmin office, *The Cornish Guardian*, as it was closest to the hotel, and gradually, I visited all our offices around Cornwall to learn my territory; that process helped me to choose where I wanted to live. Penzance office, *The Cornishman,* was lovely, but furthest away if I were to drive back to Lincoln at weekends.

Our company HQ was in Lemon Quay in Truro, *The West Briton* offices, so I wanted to be close to there; my favourite location was Falmouth. I found a lovely old cottage close to The Old Norway Inn in the tiny hamlet of Perranaworthal, on the A39 just six miles from

Truro and six miles from Falmouth; it was perfect for me, with two bedrooms, it was about 300 years old, full of character and in a beautiful part of the country.

CHAPTER 51
CHARLOTTE

Eventually, it was time for me to call on our Falmouth office, Charlotte's territory – the *Falmouth Leader* weekly newspaper. I was excited and nervous as I walked into reception. I was surprised to see Charlotte sitting at a desk, busy with a couple of her sales team members. She was highly focused and efficient at training her salespeople. My first impressions were particularly good. When she saw me, she invited me into her office, shutting the door behind her.

Despite her being married, Charlotte was very flirtatious; I was wary of getting involved with a staff member; I was still the new boy, and although single now, I was not looking for a girlfriend, least of all a married woman.

However, I found her so attractive; she was not simply good-looking but fun and exciting.

One Sunday, I was doing some shopping when my phone rang. It was Charlotte. She said, "Can I come and see you, please? I want to talk to you."

I was somewhat surprised and curious, so I said, "Okay, I'm at Tesco's now. Where do you want to meet? "

She said, "Just wait in Tesco's car park. I will come to you."

She parked her car next to mine and got out. Dressed in her riding gear – tight beige jodhpurs, knee-length black leather boots, a black jacket, and a riding cap – she looked rich and gorgeous. I could see she had been crying, and I said, "What is up?"

She replied, "I just needed someone to talk to. "

I said, "Have you been riding?"

She said, "No, I just told my husband I was going out riding." And she gave me a sneaky smile. I looked at her, a bit confused.

She said, "Can we go back to your place?"

We got on well, our conversation was easy and relaxed, and she began to confide in me about her unhappy marriage. She was convinced her husband was having an affair, as they were no longer having sexual encounters; she said she even tried walking around the house in the nude, and it did not stir his attention. I found that extremely hard to believe. I thought either the guy must be gay or, yes, he was preoccupied with another woman.

We spent the rest of the day together, and our relationship grew more intimate over the following weeks. Eventually, my will broke, and it did become an affair. However, after a couple of hot and steamy months, Charlotte felt guilty, and we both decided it was time to bring our fling to a halt.

A generous offer

It was Friday lunchtime when Tony approached me. "Are you going home to see your children this weekend?" he asked.

I looked at him with a hint of sadness and replied, "Unfortunately, I can't. My car is being serviced in the garage. I get it back on Monday."

Tony, always supportive, said, "Well, I won't need my car this weekend. You can take mine if you want to."

Tony's car was an impressive company vehicle, a brand-new top-of-the-range Vauxhall Senator. Surprised by his offer, I asked, "Are you sure, boss?"

"Yes, of course. You need to see your children," he replied with a reassuring smile.

The long journey

Monday morning, Tony walked into my office with a puzzled look on his face. "Where did you go over the weekend?" he asked.

I recounted my weekend exploits. "Like I told you, I went to pick up my kids and take them to my mum's house, the same as I do every time. Why?"

"You've put 1,050 miles on my new car in a single weekend?" he exclaimed, still in disbelief.

I explained my route to him. "Yes, Friday afternoon, I left Truro and drove to Lincoln, which is 350 miles. I picked up the kids and then drove from Lincoln to my mum's house in Maidenhead. On Sunday afternoon, I drove back to Lincoln and then straight back down here to Truro."

Tony shook his head, clearly astonished. "Bloody hell," he said, unable to hide his surprise.

3 June, 1989 – the man and the tanks

I remember the night of 3 June, 1989, with a haunting clarity. It was the night the world watched in horror as the Chinese Army launched a brutal military operation to crush the democratic protests in Beijing's Tiananmen Square. The news reported several hundred civilians shot dead, a stark and tragic contrast to the hopeful spirit that had filled the square just days before.

Tanks rumbled through the capital's streets, an ominous and terrifying sight. The Army advanced into the square from multiple directions, their presence punctuated by the random and ruthless shooting of unarmed protesters. The chaos and violence were unimaginable, marking a dark chapter in history. This event left an indelible mark on my memory, a reminder of the fragility of human rights and the price of seeking freedom.

CHAPTER 52
MEDITERRANEAN

One of the companies we worked with was a holiday cruise line that offered special reader deals in our newspapers. They reached out to me with news of their latest seven-day Mediterranean cruise and suggested I join them to experience the trip first-hand. They believed it would help me understand just how excellent their holiday package was before we promoted it to our readers.

At first, I was hesitant. Travelling alone still made me a bit apprehensive; having to use a walking stick and carrying bags was difficult, but Tony encouraged me to go and enjoy the break.

19 June, 1989
So, I booked a flight from Heathrow to Venice, where the cruise was set to embark. However, as a disabled traveller alone, my nightmare began. My flight was delayed, and the cruise ship had already left when I landed in Italy. Panic set in as I realised I was stranded with a return ticket dated seven days later. Thankfully, the travel company quickly arranged for me to fly to Athens, the ship's first stop; I'd miss the first day, but where I could board the second day.

The Mediterranean cruise was on a ship larger than any I had ever seen. It hosted thousands of people and featured shopping arcades, nightclubs, and a casino. I felt like James Bond.

As a VIP guest, the holiday company provided me with a guide named Antonia, a stunning woman from Florence in her early 20s. Her long brown hair and charming accent were captivating. We docked at a new destination each morning and set sail again in the evening. Our itinerary included Athens, Greece, the islands of Corfu, Crete, Rhodes, and Dubrovnik, in the former Yugoslavia, and finally, back to Venice. I explored the towns at each stop, lounged on the beaches, and soaked in the local beauty. Antonia and I developed a connection that went beyond professional courtesy, making the trip even more memorable.

One of my most vivid memories is sailing into Venice Harbour in the late evening. The band was playing in the background, the sky was getting dark, and the lights of the beautiful buildings twinkled and reflected on the water. I was in the ship's casino, recklessly gambling away all my Greek currency, knowing we were about to arrive in Italy. I put everything on red at the roulette wheel, and, of course, I won, doubling my money. Antonia laughed, and we celebrated by cracking open a bottle of champagne.

Lost in Venice

While in Venice, due to my slow walking and tiredness, I soon found myself lagging behind the tour group until I was utterly alone in a part of the beautiful city I did not recognise. Realising I was lost, I started to panic. I knew I needed to get back to the cruise ship and decided to take one of the exotic water taxis. However, I had run out of Italian currency and only had Greek money left from my earlier stop.

Standing at the taxi rank, very tired, leaning unsteadily on my walking stick and looking bewildered and anxious, a stunning older Italian lady approached me. Her impeccable style, elegant jewellery, and graceful demeanour immediately caught my attention. Her lovely accent added to her charm as she asked me something in Italian. I didn't understand her, and she realised I was English, and she repeated. "Are you okay?"

I explained my predicament to her, feeling a bit embarrassed. She took my free hand gently and said, "Come, I can pay your fare for you." Despite my protests, she insisted with a beautiful, reassuring smile. Thanks to her kindness, I made it back to the cruise ship just in time, grateful for the unexpected help from a kind stranger in such a magnificent city.

This adventure significantly boosted my confidence. It was not just a trip, but a transformative experience that broadened my horizons and deepened my appreciation for life's unexpected opportunities.

CHAPTER 53
PLYMOUTH

Once a year, each regional newspaper had to present its annual business plans to the Northcliffe Newspapers Group (NNG) Board of Directors for approval. This process resembled a roadshow, with the Chief Executive of Northcliffe and his Directors travelling around the UK to visit all the major newspapers in the company.

Each regional team, including ours, presented its business plans and budgets for review and approval. The board then made recommendations and adjustments and authorised the business plans for the forthcoming year. This rigorous process ensured that every regional newspaper aligned with the company's overall strategic goals and maintained a high-performance standard.

Plymouth v Cornwall

In 1989, the NNG Board decided to conduct the business plan presentations for both the Plymouth, Devon, office and Cornwall Weeklies within two days. This meant that our Cornwall executive team, including myself, had to travel to Plymouth and present our plans in their boardroom. The directors from London stayed in a comfortable hotel in Plymouth city centre, minimising their travel. This arrangement was unusual, and neither the Plymouth team nor we were particularly fond of the idea.

A few days before the meeting, Tony Wood had already mailed our business plan to the board for their preliminary review. However, the day before our presentation, Tony made some last-minute changes to our plan. He asked me to drop everything off and drive up to Plymouth that night so I could personally hand over a hard copy of the revised business plan directly to Gavin Simmonds. This man was the most intimidating person I had ever met, a quiet-spoken gentleman with half-round gold glasses and a pinstripe suit. He had an aura of power that made everyone around him nervous. Mr Gavin G. Simmonds was Chairman of the Government and Legal Affairs Committee, The Newspaper Society, Managing Director Northcliffe Newspapers Group Ltd., and Director Associated Newspapers Holding Plc.

This request from Tony added an unexpected layer of urgency and anxiety to the already tense preparations, underscoring the importance of our upcoming presentation.

An unexpected invitation

Plymouth had their meeting that day, and I arrived at the hotel shortly after it had finished. I walked into the reception area, my walking stick in my right hand and my overnight bag in my left. It was about 6:30 in the evening, and the lobby was bustling with Plymouth staff and London directors, all preparing to go to dinner. Their eyes were on me, curious about my unexpected presence.

Spotting Mr Simmonds, I approached him and said, "Excuse me, sir." He looked up and recognised me from his previous visits to the *Lincolnshire Echo* office. We had met two or three times before, and he had been particularly impressed with my work on the *Farming Echo,* given his interest as a keen clay pigeon shooter.

I handed Mr Simmonds the revised business plan. "Tony Wood asked me to bring you this, sir, so you have time to review it before our meeting tomorrow."

"Roger, thank you for that. Are you staying here this evening?" he asked.

"Yes, sir. Tony booked me a room," I replied.

"Well, in that case, you should join us for dinner," he said, much to my surprise.

I noticed some strange looks from the Plymouth management and the other directors. They seemed puzzled as to why Mr Simmonds would invite an executive from Cornwall to join the Plymouth *Western Morning News* team for their evening dinner.

As people began to leave for the restaurant a couple of streets away, I said, "It's okay, sir. There's no need for that. I need to take my bag to my room."

Mr Simmonds insisted, "That's okay. I'll wait here for you." Turning to the crowd, he added, "You chaps go on ahead. I'll wait here for Roger, and we'll follow on behind." The others looked a bit surprised and put out by this unexpected arrangement.

A rainy walk to dinner

The lift door opened, and I stepped out to find Mr Simmonds waiting for me. He took my free arm and asked, "Are you okay to walk? It's quite a way, about a quarter of a mile."

I thought to myself, "Oh dear, this is going to be tough. It's quite a long way for me." But I could not tell him that, not after he had waited for me. So, I replied with a laugh, "Yes, that will be fine as long as we can walk slowly."

We were about halfway to the restaurant when it started to rain. I felt awful – Mr Simmonds was in his Savile Row suit and Oxford leather brogues, getting drenched. "You go on ahead, sir," I said. "I'll catch up."

"Don't talk nonsense; I won't hear of it," he replied. "I'll help you. Come along now."

As I stepped down from the curb onto the cobblestone road, which was wet and slippery, I lost my footing and fell into a puddle. Mr Simmonds bent down, getting on one knee on the pavement, and struggled to help me get up. He was not a young man, nor was he particularly fit, and I felt incredibly embarrassed and awkward. But he was determined to help, and eventually, I managed to get back on my feet.

"I'm so sorry, sir," I repeated.

"Don't talk nonsense, boy. We are doing fine. We are nearly there. Come on," he said encouragingly.

We entered the restaurant, rather wet from the rain, and made our way to the table. Mr Simmonds, with a hint of mischief in his eyes, asked one of the executives to change seats, thus vacating the one next to his. He then told me to sit down. He clearly enjoyed the subtle disruption his actions caused, relishing his authority.

I, on the other hand, was incredibly nervous. Here I was, sitting with the board of directors from London and the senior executives from Plymouth. The tension was palpable, and I could feel the weight of every gaze, scrutinising the unexpected presence of an outsider in their midst.

The Liskeard debate

In our presentation, Cornish Weeklies planned to launch a new free newspaper in Liskeard, a small town in Cornwall about 13 miles east of Bodmin and 20 miles west of Plymouth. Plymouth also planned to launch a free newspaper in Liskeard.

The dinner conversation was filled with general banter as the food was served and drinks flowed. After the main course, Mr Simmonds shifted the discussion to the launch of the new Liskeard newspaper. The Plymouth executives across the table were justifying their objectives to Mr Simmonds when he suddenly turned to me and said, "So, Roger, tell me what you think. Should Plymouth launch a free newspaper in Liskeard, or should we let Cornish Weeklies do it?"

I was stunned to be included in this debate. Already feeling like an intruder, I was thrust into the spotlight. Despite being the youngest person at the table by a considerable margin, I tried to keep my composure and appear confident. I could feel all eyes on me, penetrating through the discomfort.

I turned to Mr Simmonds and said, "Really, sir, I don't think it's for me to say."

He slammed his fist down on the table hard enough to make everyone's plates and glasses bounce, then yelled, "If I ask you a fucking question, then yes, it is for you to say! Tell me what you think, Roger!"

The outburst shocked everyone at the table, and it hit me like a slap in the face. However, recalling the sense of theatre Mr Simmonds had displayed when we were lying in a puddle earlier, my confidence grew. I looked around the table, then back at Mr Simmonds, and said clearly, "I think it should be Cornish Weeklies, of course. Liskeard is in Cornwall, isn't it?"

Mr Simmonds pressed further, "So why does Plymouth want to launch a newspaper in Liskeard, Roger?"

"I think it's because they don't want us to do it, sir," I replied.

He leaned back in his chair, arms stretched forward with his palms flat on the table and laughed. "And there we have it! Exactly what I think, too," he said.

CHAPTER 54
PORTUGAL

One day, in late summer 1989, Dave called me with an enticing offer. He was heading to his parents' villa in Portugal for a week to do some handyman jobs before their visit and wondered if I would like to join him. Having never been to Portugal, though I had seen many of Dave's photographs, I was immediately drawn to the idea. The villa was perched on a hillside with a terrace and a swimming pool overlooking a picturesque valley. I quickly said "yes" and organised my flight from London to Faro.

Dave, who worked for an airline and got free tickets, arranged to meet me at the airport and join me on the same flight. However, at the last minute, I was informed that he would not be able to make it for three days.

He sent a message reassuring me that upon arrival, a lady would meet me, arrange for a taxi to take me to the villa and that the housekeeper would be there with a fully stocked fridge, allowing me to relax until he arrived.

Before leaving, I picked up a copy of Daniel Defoe's *Robinson Crusoe,* an original first print edition written in old English. I found reading it extremely challenging, but I decided to take it with me on this holiday.

When I arrived at the villa, its isolation became apparent. Once the housekeeper left, I was alone, with no one around and no mobile phones or email to rely on. Initially, the solitude was intimidating, but the luxurious surroundings and the incredible sun-drenched balcony overlooking the countryside soon soothed my nerves.

I quickly adapted to my circumstances and pulled out my *Robinson Crusoe* paperback. As I slowly began to understand the nuances of the olde English dialect, the story became enthralling.

Crusoe's transformation from a shipwrecked castaway to a resourceful survivor was both inspiring and thought-provoking.

My unplanned and unexpected solitude made me especially relate to Crusoe's loneliness during those three days. Wandering around the beautiful villa by myself, wearing next to no clothes under the scorching sun, was a profound experience of self-discovery. It was a time when I needed to understand my life as a single man, and this solitary interlude in Portugal provided the perfect backdrop for that reflection.

Three days later, Dave showed up, his usual lively, upbeat self, and got straight to work – painting doors, fixing cupboards and installing lights. As we were winding down that evening, he asked, "So, what have you been up to while you were here alone? Was everything okay?"

I reassured him that all was well and explained how I'd been engrossed in *Robinson Crusoe,* inspired by the lessons in his tenacious will to survive – how Crusoe learned to hunt mountain goats, catch fish, and find fresh water. It was a real lesson in determination and resourcefulness.

Dave chuckled and said, "Alright, mate, I will treat you tonight. I'm taking you up to a little café in the mountains. It's just a small, traditional spot, but they serve the best goat soup around. They've got that cheap wine, and there's always a bullfight on the telly. You'll love it."

We had four wonderful days together, lounging by the pool, sipping cold beers, and driving into the village to pick up groceries and a few choice bottles of port. It was yet another unforgettable experience with a dear friend I'll always cherish.

CHAPTER 55
RETFORD

As I was settling in Cornwall, it became clear that the good days were over. The rapid business growth we had been riding suddenly slowed considerably. Our optimistic business plans were quickly rendered obsolete, and we scrambled to rewrite strategies to manage a shrinking market. It was a stark reminder of how swiftly economic tides could turn, reshaping our expectations and forcing us to adapt to a new reality.

During 1987 and 1988, in the UK, we enjoyed robust growth of 5%-to-6% per annum, and our company business plans reflected that positive trend. However, in 1989, the economy took an unexpected downturn. Growth plummeted to 2%, and inflation surged from 3.4% in 1986 to 7.8%.

The fall of the Berlin Wall and economic shifts

The fall of the Berlin Wall on 9 November, 1989, was a momentous event that symbolised the first step toward German reunification. The air was thick with optimism as the world watched these historic transformations. Europe and the world were about to changc significantly.

Christmas of 1989 was once again spent joyfully with my children at my mother's house. By then, I was earning a good salary and could lavish some lovely Christmas presents on the family. Despite my efforts to see my children twice a month, it was not always possible due to the distance and demands of my job. When I did manage the 1,000-mile journey, it was a gruelling process.

I would start working from the Bodmin office on Friday morning, leaving Cornwall at lunchtime and heading for Lincoln, a 325-mile non-stop drive that took about 5.5 hours. I would arrive at their mother's house around 6:00pm. After picking up the kids, we would head straight down to Maidenhead, another 165 miles and four hours away. I would stop only for quick comfort breaks and eat in the car, finally reaching my mother's house around 10:30pm.

Saturday was dedicated to spending a full day with my kids and the rest of the family. Sunday morning allowed for a bit of rest before reversing the trip back to Lincoln and then continuing straight on to Falmouth, a total of 340 miles. It was an exhausting routine, and Tony was aware of how hard I was pushing myself.

Despite the toll, these trips were worth every effort. The joy of being with my children and family during the holidays made the long drives and sleepless nights seem insignificant in comparison. It was a testament to my dedication to keeping a close relationship with my kids, regardless of distance or the challenges.

In early 1990, after working in Cornwall for about 13 months, Tony called me into his office for a chat. He held the door open for me, and I walked in with my walking stick, leaned on his desk, and took a seat. After closing the door, Tony got straight to the point.

"Roger," he began, "obviously, we've had to consolidate a lot. Our planned work has been put on hold until better times. Now is not the time to launch new products. So, the job I envisioned for you here never really materialised, and now it's just a question of cutting costs wherever we can."

He paused momentarily, then continued, "An opportunity has arisen in North Nottinghamshire, about 20 miles from Lincoln and your kids. The *Retford, Gainsborough and Worksop Times* seeks a new Director and General Manager. It is a much smaller business, but it puts you in charge; you will be the senior executive in the company. You would report to the Managing Director of the Lincolnshire division and, ultimately, to the Head Office in London, but it would be your baby.

"The newspaper is haemorrhaging money now and desperately needs someone to go in, cut overheads, increase revenue, and stabilise the business to get it back into profit. Would you be interested in this? Especially knowing that it puts you back within a 20-minute drive of your children? You will stay on your current remuneration package and contract terms and keep your current car; they will also help you buy a new house in Retford.

The opportunity was unexpected, but it offered a chance to be closer to my children, a significant consideration given the exhausting commutes I had been enduring. It was a challenging role, but the proximity to my kids made it appealing.

I began my new role a couple of weeks before my 33rd birthday. Despite its small size, the *Retford Times* was significant in the NNG group. Established in 1869, its offices, built in 1928, were a piece of history. Supposedly, it was the newspaper where Lord Rothermere had worked as a young man, and he held it in remarkably close personal regard. This added a layer of importance to my task of getting the newspaper back on track.

Retford is a charming, wealthy market town on the River Idle, which flows into the River Trent nearby. It is a lovely place to live. Recognising the opportunity for a fresh start, I quickly bought a new-build three-bedroom detached house and furnished it, creating bedrooms for my children, who could now come every weekend.

The *Retford, Gainsborough and Workshop Times* was a traditional paid-for broadsheet newspaper published every Friday, and it was losing circulation. We also had a second newspaper, the *Gainsborough Target,* a free newspaper focused purely on the Gainsborough area. Both were losing money, especially the *Gainsborough Target.*

The challenge ahead was daunting, but my motivation to succeed was stronger than ever, fuelled by my proximity to my children and my desire to restore the *Retford Times* to its former glory.

CHAPTER 56
THAILAND

Dave had suggested we take a holiday to Portugal again, this time for a couple of weeks, to travel around, see the sights, and enjoy the villa with some friends. However, as 1990 rolled on, we struggled to synchronise our dates. Either he was available and I was not, or vice versa. By November, Dave suggested it would be too cold in Portugal anyway.

He then proposed a different destination: Reunion Island in the Indian Ocean, close to Mauritius, where he had a friend. However, upon contacting his friend, we found out they had booked a holiday in Thailand at that time. So, Dave suggested, “Why don’t we meet them in Bangkok instead? What do you think?”

To be honest, at that time, I had no idea where Bangkok was. I was not sure if it was in China or Taiwan. A quick bit of research revealed how fascinating and vibrant the city was. Intrigued by what I learned about Thailand, I said, “Yes, I’ll come with you.” Little did I know then that this incident of chance – this person had chosen Thailand for their holiday – would change my life forever.

Dave had been to Bangkok several times before. The luxury of working for an international airline meant he could travel the world for free. With four days off in between shifts, he would utilise a free ticket and fly to Thailand. In Bangkok, he bought cheap designer clothing and watches and sold them to his friends back in the UK for a profit. While away, he also indulged in the exotic nightlife of Bangkok and knew his way around the red-light district of Patpong.

We checked into the Royal Hotel in Bangkok, close to the Grand Palace. With Dave’s friend due to arrive the next day, he decided to introduce me to the city’s nightlife immediately. He took me directly to some beer bars in Patpong, where we watched sex shows. I was flabbergasted and amazed. I had been to Soho a few times, but this was completely different, vibrant, noisy, and exciting. The difference here was that it was all out in the open, proud, loud, not hidden and on the seedy side like Soho. The crowded streets, the aromas, the music, the beer, and the girls; it was all quite intoxicating.

The 1984 song that woke the world up to the delights of Bangkok had lyrics that hit the nail on the head. That night, I fell in love with one of those beautiful, golden silk-skinned angels. This unexpected adventure in Bangkok marked the beginning of a new chapter in my life, one that I could never have anticipated but that would forever change my perspective on the world.

'One night in Bangkok and the world's your oyster
The bars are temples, but the pearls ain't free
You'll find a God in every golden cloister
And if you're lucky then the God's a she
I can feel an angel sliding up to me
One night in Bangkok makes a hard man humble
Not much between despair and ecstasy
One night in Bangkok and the tough guys tumble
Can't be too careful with your company
I can feel the devil walking next to me'

We spent three days in Bangkok with Dave's friend, and the young Thai woman I met joined us on our visits to the Grand Palace. A Royal Palace, a stunning place, the location of the Emerald Buddha, and various Buddhist temples filled with intricate architecture and rich history that left me in awe.

The Grand Palace

In 1782, the then new King moved the capital city to the left bank of the Chao Phraya River for strategic purposes and used the canals to the west as defences for the new city. A palace was constructed, with grounds currently covering 218,000 square metres enclosed by crenellated walls measuring 19,000 metres. Like palaces in the former capitals of Sukhothai and Ayuthaya, this palace is also laid out with Halls of Residence and Throne Halls, administrative buildings, and a temple to serve as the Chapel Royal.

Dave, always eager for a bargain, wanted to go shopping and took us to Pratunam Market. It was a jam-packed maze of alleys lined with tiny market stalls selling t-shirts, jackets, dresses, jeans, shorts, shoes, and accessories.

This was where I enjoyed bartering for the first time, an exhilarating experience. Dave showed me how to negotiate prices and navigate the bustling market. This was also where he bought all his fake designer gear to sell back in the UK.

The energy of Pratunam Market was infectious, and I quickly got the hang of haggling. The sights, sounds, and smells were a sensory overload, but I found it exhilarating.

After hours of walking in the humid heat, exhaustion finally got the better of me, and I passed out. Dave and our Thai taxi driver managed to get me back to the hotel, where I crashed into bed to recover until evening, when the adventure began all over again. It was another unforgettable chapter in my Bangkok journey, adding to the ever-growing list of experiences that were shaping my perspective on the world.

With all his shopping orders fulfilled and his friend departed for Reunion Island in the Indian Ocean, I said goodbye to my new Thai lady friend, and it was time for Dave and me to move on to our next destination.

CHAPTER 57
PHUKET

We set off for Phuket; Dave eagerly showed me this beautiful tropical island. This was my first domestic short-haul flight, about an hour and 15 minutes, on a small aircraft, and I found it all extremely exciting.

We stayed in Patong Beach; we got a couple of rooms in Nordic Bungalows, located on the main drag down to the beach on Bangla Road. Stepping outside our car park, we were right next to the Hard Rock, which, in those days, was some concrete blocks with a rusty corrugated iron roof, an enticing Hard Rock banner, and lots of cold beer served by young Thai women with thunderous rock 'n' roll music booming out into the street.

A short walk further down the road, I was horrified to see a massive cage outside a discotheque. Inside the cage were a big bear and a chimpanzee. This was Thailand, and it was all hugely different.

Dave rented a motorbike from a local shop operated by a Scandinavian guy. It was a little dark red Honda Wave, perfect for zooming around the island in the hot sun with my walking stick. Getting on the back was a bit of a struggle, and Dave had to help me, but once I was on, I held on tight. We did not need to wear helmets in those days.

We explored different beaches around the island each day, and at night, we explored the bars.

In one bar, the Black Rhino, the Thai lady behind the bar, was intrigued by my story. She asked about my accident and recovery and suggested that she could help me. She insisted that Thai massage was a wonderful thing, and though I had heard similar offers before, I politely agreed when she offered to take me to see a special monk who could heal people like me.

The healing monk

The next morning, around 8 o'clock, there was a loud knock on the door. I opened it to find the lady from the bar, an old man, and a small Tuk Tuk, a Thai taxi. They had come to take me to a place called Chalong to see this extraordinary monk. Dave, groggy from the previous night's beers, was sceptical. "You're not getting in that Tuk Tuk with a couple of strangers. Are you mad?" he said. But I decided to go, and he reluctantly joined me, grabbing his shirt and bag.

The journey took hours. In those days, Phuket was mostly gravel and red dirt roads through lush jungle, not the concrete highways of today. Eventually, we arrived at a clearing in the trees where a bamboo hut on stilts stood; several Thai people were sitting outside. Inside, an old man, who must have been in his 80s, in white robes, was massaging another person. The lady instructed me to sit down and wait, explaining that the old man would not take payment, but I could donate in a silver bowl. After three hours, it was my turn.

The old monk used oils and balms with extraordinarily strong aromas. Underneath the hut, I noticed a pile of disused plaster casts and bandages that he had removed from patients who had previously received orthodox medical care from hospitals. He would remove these medical bandages, apply his ointments and potions, and then re-bandage using green leaves. It was all quite unbelievable.

As I waited and observed, I discussed with other patients and heard their incredible stories. A young boy who had been in a motorbike accident and was scheduled to have his leg amputated had his leg saved by the old monk. A young girl who had been left immobile in a hospital bed was now walking again, thanks to the old man – or so I was told. These stories made me both apprehensive and excited.

The monk's methods seemed unconventional, but his patients' testimonials were miraculous. This blend of scepticism and hope filled me as I underwent his treatment. I was eager to see if his ancient remedies and unorthodox techniques could improve my condition.

The old man asked many questions, which the lady translated for me. When I explained that I spent most days sitting in my office behind a computer or driving my car, he looked incredibly sad.

Through the lady, he told me that I must change my lifestyle and take responsibility for rebuilding my body. His fingers felt like steel, and his feet like wooden blocks as he walked up and down my back, squeezing my legs, arms, neck, and shoulders. The pain was excruciating, and I was crying on the bamboo floor.

After the session, the lady took me back to the hotel, saying the old man advised daily visits. Dave took me on the motorbike the next day, and we repeated the process for a week. To my astonishment, I suddenly found myself able to throw my leg over the back seat of the motorbike when mounting it, a clear sign of improvement. When it was time to leave, I promised the monk that I would return and stay longer for more treatment on my next trip to Thailand.

Dave's job at the airport involved a four-day shift of 12 hours on and 12 hours off. He could rotate shifts with his coworkers, allowing them to build up long breaks. However, one day, Dave got a call saying one of the guys covering his shift could not make it back, and Dave was needed at the airport within the next two days. He looked at me apologetically and said, "Sorry, mate. I have no choice, but I think you will be okay now. You know your way around, don't you?"

I reassured him, "Yes, of course. I understand the situation." Although nervous, I knew I would be perfectly okay navigating Thailand alone.

The bikc mix-up

We took the Honda Wave rental bike back to the Scandinavian rental shop. As we handed over the bike and keys, he looked at us and said, "That's not my bike."

We laughed, thinking he was joking. "Yes, of course it is. We rented it from you last week," we replied.

"You rented my bike from me last week," he said, "but this is not my bike."

Confused, we asked him what we should do about it. He suggested we take the bike to the police and tell them we found it, then return and find his motorbike.

Following his instructions, we went to the local police station, a small hut at the end of the beach. When we presented the bike to the police officer, he made a phone call. Within a few minutes, a young man arrived with a big grin on his face. He was a waiter at the big restaurant next to ours, and it turned out that we had accidentally taken his identical bike a few days ago. Freakishly, our key had worked on his bike, so we had no idea we were on the wrong one.

We went back to the hotel and found the Scandinavian bike right where we had parked it a week before.

We all laughed hysterically – even the Thai police officer understood the joke. We gave the young man 500 Baht for his trouble to make amends, and he seemed incredibly happy. Dave then jumped in a taxi and headed for Bangkok airport while I went back to my room to get ready for a night out in the beer bars.

CHAPTER 58

PHI PHI ISLANDS

The Phi Phi Islands (Thai: Mu Ko Phiphi) are an island group in Thailand, nestled between the large island of Phuket and the Straits of Malacca coast of Thailand. In 1990, the islands were still an unspoiled tropical jewel, covered in lush trees and fringed with golden beaches. The only way to land there was on a small wooden jetty by boat.

I booked a day tour not knowing what to expect. We cruised the beautiful Andaman Sea and eventually arrived at our destination. With the boat swaying gently from side to side, it was challenging enough for me to move around with my walking stick.

I noticed that most people were simply jumping off the boat into the water and wading up to the beach. The Thai crew, who resembled pirates with their nut-brown skin and gleaming smiles, noticed my discomfort. With a laugh and a smile, one of them bent over and suggested that I climb on his back piggyback style. I did so while another crew member took my stick and bag.

The squat, muscular sailor walked to the edge of the boat and, to my chagrin, jumped into the sea. The water came up to his chest, and he laughed and wobbled as he carried me to the shore. Other crew members helped me disembark from his back.

The cxperience was both a shock and a joy. I was experiencing absolute freedom here. People were compassionate, understanding, and unafraid to help me get where I needed to go. This was a defining characteristic of Thailand and its people that I would cherish throughout my life.

In 1990, the islands were thick jungles. There were no concrete structures; everything was built with wood and bamboo. It was a paradise of unimaginable beauty. The sunshine's colours, the clear turquoise water, the milky white sand, and the palm trees were mesmerising. One of the unique characteristics of these beaches was the absence of waves, allowing you to lay at the water's edge and soak up the sun.

Though there were very few people, walking on the sand with my walking stick was difficult, and getting up and down took quite some effort. I managed to reach the water's edge and lay down, staring at the sky with water up to my chest, in absolute bliss.

As I lay there, I heard a young woman's voice say, "Hello." I looked up, surprised to see an English girl. We chatted, and I soon deduced that she was on holiday with her father and her new stepmother. Despite the stunning scenery, she was not enjoying the holiday. She said it felt extremely uncomfortable, and she wished she had not come.

Her presence reminded me that, as captivating as the islands were, it's the people you meet and the connections you make that truly shape your experience. In 1990, we trekked through dense jungle to find a secluded beach, lying there with no soul in sight. No concrete, no noise, just wood and bamboo shelters tucked into nature's embrace.

As I sat drafting this in 2024, I could cry looking at photos of the islands. Concrete buildings, relentless commercialisation, and what was once paradise have been swallowed up. It's heartbreaking. But I feel a deep sense of gratitude that I could experience their untouched beauty before it all changed.

Oh, sweet Christina

Christina and I spent the next three days together, mostly lounging on the beach or drinking beer in bars. She stayed with me at my hotel, and we enjoyed each other's company as if there were no worries in the world; soon, we would both be going our separate ways.

Christina would become the last European girl I would ever make love to, marking the end of one chapter of my life and the beginning of another. I understood the people you meet and the connections you make can significantly shape your experience of life.

CHAPTER 59

CHIANG MAI

Christina returned to the UK, and I had enjoyed my time in Phuket, alone again. I was ready for my next adventure; I wanted to explore Koh Samui, another island I had heard so much about, much smaller and less developed. The airport there was new, having just opened a year earlier. I planned to fly the next day, 21 November, 1990.

The travel agent managed to book me a flight to Don Mueang, the domestic airport in Bangkok, but I could not secure a seat on the Samui flight, as all seats were booked.

Travelling alone and feeling nervous, I was unsure what to do next. The travel agent suggested Chiang Mai. "Have you ever been there?" she asked.

"No," I replied, "this is my first trip to Thailand."

"Oh, you'll love Chiang Mai," she assured me. "It's very different from Phuket but equally charming. It's Northern Thailand."

"Okay," I said, "book me on the Chiang Mai flight instead."

On 21 November, 1990, I landed safely in Chiang Mai, took a taxi to my hotel, and checked into my room. That evening, I was horrified to see the news: the flight I could not board, the one that was fully booked and the reason I was now in Chiang Mai, had crashed. Bangkok Airways Flight 125 had gone down on its approach to Koh Samui Airport, killing everyone on board.

The realisation hit me hard. Had there been an available seat, I might have been on that flight. The twist of fate that led me to Chiang Mai instead of Koh Samui was both sobering and surreal.

"Bangkok Airways Flight 125 from Don Mueang Airport to Koh Samui Airport. The small twin prop Dash 8-103 crashed on approach to Koh Samui Airport during severe weather, all 38 souls perished."

Subsequent investigation determined that the cause of the accident was the pilot's suffering from spatial disorientation, which led to a loss of control.

Exploring Northern Thailand

The young Thai taxi driver, Khun Art, whom I met at the airport and who took me to my hotel, offered to act as my local tour guide. For a fixed amount, he would drive me around for a full day. Energetic and happy, he seemed like a perfect companion for exploring the area, so I agreed.

This proved to be an excellent decision. Khun Art took me to many local beauty spots around the ancient fortress city. The next day, we embarked on a long drive into the northern mountains to visit the Kayan tribe, often called the "Karen long-neck people."

I was astonished by their extraordinary practice of wearing golden brass neck rings crafted by Burmese artisans, creating the illusion of elongated necks. This intriguing tradition, rooted in their belief that longer necks enhance a woman's beauty, has garnered both admiration and controversy. That evening, we stayed in an unbelievably cheap guesthouse in a small town and enjoyed a fantastic evening meal with music and beer.

The following day, we moved on to the Golden Triangle. Khun Art told me about the infamous drug lord, Khun Sa, who ruled the heroin trade in this region. We could see where the Mekong, Ruak, and Mekong-Loei rivers join from a mountaintop, creating a triangular sandbank in the middle of the water – hence the name Golden Triangle. The three sides of this sand triangle point to Myanmar, Laos, and Thailand.

It was an infamous territory dominated by Khun Sa, the Burmese warlord who reigned over this region and the global heroin trade. It was a place where it was kill or be killed, and the military had no influence. He reigned supreme from 1974 until he surrendered to Burmese authorities in 1996, and that led to dramatic declines in the cultivation of opium poppies in the Golden Triangle and foreshadowed the region's eclipse.

Amusingly, in 1997, my good friend and best-selling novelist Stephen Leather authored a book called *The Solitary Man*, and in it, he used my character and my name as the pilot of a DEA helicopter gunship who raided Khun Sa's camp and killed the infamous drug baron.

As it was time to head back to Bangkok, I arranged to meet my sister's old school friend, an English teacher at Chiang Mai University who also hosted a radio show on the city's local radio station. On my last evening, we met for drinks, and the next day, I left Chiang Mai.

On the radio, he played a song dedicated to me – *Country Roads Take Me Home* by Olivia Newton-John. It was a touching farewell to an unforgettable adventure in northern Thailand.

CHAPTER 60
BANGKOK AND HOME

When I arrived in Bangkok, my previous taxi driver, Khun Santi, picked me up at the airport and took me back to the Royal Hotel. I had just two nights left in Thailand, and I wanted to spend them with Chariya. I was indeed under her spell; it was magical, and I could not think of anything else except her.

She was an exotic dancer in a Bangkok club, and for her to miss work, I had to pay the bar fine, a small amount that I was more than willing to cover. She seemed genuinely happy to get away and spend time with me, and I was just as delighted to have her company.

When it was time for me to return to England, she travelled with me in the taxi to the airport. It was 5 December, the King of Thailand's birthday, and all the streets were adorned with gold decorations, flags, and portraits of the king. She laid her head on my shoulder as we filtered through the traffic. The streets were alive with celebration, but my heart felt heavy, knowing I had to leave.

At the airport, we waved goodbye, and I promised her I would return soon. The memory of her head on my shoulder, the golden decorations lining the streets, and the promise of return lingered with me as I boarded my flight back to England.

Realising I no longer wanted to be alone

One thing I learned from my holiday in Thailand was that I no longer wanted to live alone. Since my divorce, I have lived alone in my small bungalow in Lincoln, later in my beautiful cottage in Cornwall, and then in the new house in Retford. I have been to Ibiza alone, taken a Mediterranean cruise to Greece, Italy, and Yugoslavia alone, and even visited Portugal alone. Much of my time in Thailand was also spent alone.

Returning to a freezing cold and wet England and confronted with my dismal and soul-destroying task of making good, honest people redundant through no fault of their own, my world was really closing in on me.

I was so unhappy. I realised that three years of solitude was enough; I could not continue like this.

All I could think about was my love in Thailand and how much I wanted her. I ached inside, missing her presence and the connection we had shared. I knew I needed to be with her.

I never considered living in Thailand. My thoughts were solely focused on the idea that she could come and live with me in England if we were married. She wanted to.

She was 13 years younger than me and an exotic dancer, but I loved being with her. I genuinely believed she was sincere in her desire to escape that life. She was looking for a man who could provide her with happiness, security, and respect. Despite our differences in age, religion, culture, education, race, and experience, we complemented each other perfectly.

The longing for companionship and my deep connection with her made it clear that I was ready for a change. It was time to act.

I told my mother about the encounter and my new girlfriend, though I omitted the part about her being an exotic dancer. My mum quickly realised how captivated I was by this girl and how happy she made me. She understood that I needed an extraordinary woman, someone who could navigate life with my disability and tolerate the belligerent nature I had developed because of it. She encouraged me to pursue my dream, and I'll never forget her love and support during that time.

CHAPTER 61
BACK TO REALITY

The British economy continued to slow through 1990. In April 1990, Margaret Thatcher's Conservative government introduced the poll tax, which proved very unpopular. In 1992, the same government closed a third of Britain's deep coal mines, losing 31,000 jobs. Six of the eight mines in Nottinghamshire closed between 1989 and 1997. President of the Board of Trade, Michael Heseltine, was also closing down the coal-fuelled power stations.

The effect on North Nottinghamshire was devastating. Many of our readers and our neighbours lost their jobs in a matter of weeks. It was such a depressing time. During the 1990s, several power stations in the UK were closed as part of the transition in the energy sector and efforts to reduce carbon emissions.

Many surrounding counties, including Ferrybridge, closed in 1992, High Marnham Power Station in Nottinghamshire was closed in 1994, Iron Bridge was decommissioned in 1997, and Willington closed in 1995. Ince was shut down in 1997. Richborough Power Station in Kent, an oil-fired station, was closed in 1996.

These closures were part of a broader shift in the UK's energy policy, which included privatising the electricity industry and moving towards cleaner energy sources. The period also saw the rise of natural gas as a primary fuel for power generation, marking a significant transition from coal to oil.

Economic growth was not re-established until early 1993, with the recession's end officially declared on 26 April that year.

Rebuilding the *Retford Times*

During my years at the *Retford Times,* I spearheaded a significant transformation of the newspaper. We transitioned from a black and white broadsheet format on standard newsprint to a tabloid on wood-free white paper with a colour front cover. We modernised the masthead and updated the content, enhancing the classified section and creating a better property section.

Thanks to my control over the *Gainsborough Target,* I could offer package deals for local real estate agents, which was crucial in competing with the *Gainsborough Standard.* This newspaper had a near-monopoly on property advertising.

As the new boy in Retford and Gainsborough, coming from the south with my southern accent, I initially struggled to gain respect from the locals, especially regarding agriculture and property.

Around this time, the Halifax Building Society had branched out into real estate, opening hundreds of Halifax Property Shops around the country, including one in Gainsborough. This presented new competition for the local agents.

I discovered that the manager of the Halifax branch was another Southerner like me, facing similar prejudices. I arranged to meet him for lunch at a pub and discussed how we could change the market together.

The price for a full page of advertising in the *Gainsborough Standard* was quite expensive, and agents used it because they had no choice; it was the only place to find property listings. I proposed to give him four pages of advertising for the price of one if he committed to a 12-month contract. I planned to leverage this deal to attract other agents to our newspapers.

The strategy worked. The agents could not afford to ignore this offer, and within a few weeks, we secured most of the real estate advertising in the *Retford Times* and *Gainsborough Target.* This shift alone took us from making a loss to turning a profit.

I also upgraded our production system from hot metal to desktop publishing. This involved installing modems and training the typographers to use Apple Mac computers, we used FTP software to upload digital artwork files via phone lines for our printers in Leicester to download rather than creating hard copy paste-up work that had to be delivered by hand to Lincoln. This was a huge step forward and saved us a lot of time and money, although it unfortunately required some redundancies along the way, a part of the job I intensely hated.

These changes modernised the *Retford Times* and solidified its position in the local market, making it a more competitive and profitable publication.

Miss Retford Times competition

One innovative event that stood out during my time at the newspaper was the Miss Retford Times competition. For some reason, we had received an application to the Miss World competition, meaning that if we held a beauty contest and crowned a Miss Retford Times, she would be eligible to enter Miss United Kingdom and, potentially, Miss World.

Together with my editor and our fantastic staff, we organised an unforgettable event at the local social club. The night was sold out and lively, with guests paying at the door and enjoying a well-stocked bar. We had live music throughout the night and even set up a fashion show featuring work from a local designer and a wedding dress designer; I was incredibly proud as my eight-year-old daughter Stephanie was one of the models. She wore a bridesmaid gown. She looked so beautiful.

I served as one of the judges and invited several business contacts from around the town to join me on the judging panel. The competition was fierce, but in the end, a sweet local girl was crowned Miss Retford Times. The event was an enormous success, with a large crowd of enthusiastic locals celebrating her beauty and the festive atmosphere.

The Miss Retford Times competition not only increased our circulation but also brought the community together and showcased the talent and creativity within our town. It was a night of celebration, and I was proud to have been a part of it.

The misery of living alone

Two events compounded the misery of living alone. One morning, I came downstairs and noticed a tea towel draped over the back of one of my chairs; the back door was open. I assumed it was the lady I hired to do my laundry and clean my house. I called her name, thinking it was a bit early for her to arrive since she usually came while I was at work. Walking around the house, I noticed several missing things: my TV, the video player, an expensive leather jacket and more. Suddenly, I realised I had been robbed while I was asleep upstairs. It was a deeply disturbing feeling.

A couple of months later, another incident occurred. I was making toast when the bread got stuck in the toaster. Foolishly, I tried to free it using a knife. The electric shock not only melted the end off the knife but also sent me flying across the room, crashing into the wall. When I came around, the kitchen was on fire. I managed to get up and call the fire brigade, which arrived quickly to extinguish the flames, but not before the entire kitchen had been destroyed.

After these incidents, my mother insisted that I get married to Chariya as soon as possible. She was concerned about my safety and well-being, and these events highlighted the vulnerabilities of living alone in my condition. Chariya was on my mind, so I longed to see her; it was time to go back to Thailand, I thought.

Weekend relief with my children

Seeing my children on the weekends was my relief from the hard work, stress, and loneliness. I especially enjoyed taking my son Sam to his football matches. At about 10 years old, Sam was a superb footballer, playing for a local team in Lincoln. Their games took place all around the county, so we would drive to one town or another most Saturdays to watch him play.

Those days out and the matches were tremendous fun. Watching Sam on the field, full of energy and talent, filled me with pride and joy. It was a welcome break from my usual routine and an excellent way to bond with my son. These moments with my children Sam, Stephanie and little Harry were the highlights of my week and a cherished escape from the demands of everyday life.

CHAPTER 62
INDONESIA

My second trip to Thailand was in 1991. I convinced my sister and my good friend Glenn to come with me and travel around Southeast Asia. We arranged to spend a few days in Bangkok so they could see all the sights, and then we flew to Phuket. I planned to spend as much time as possible with the old monk while my sister and Glenn enjoyed their days around the beach.

This holiday allowed me to connect with Chariya and confirm if I was making the right decision to join her life. It is difficult to understand the dynamics of romance and a relationship in a holiday atmosphere, but I was sure I loved her. She seemed to love me too and wanted to get married and move to England to live with me and, as she would put it, "look after me".

After leaving Phuket, Chariya returned to Bangkok. Glenn, my sister, and I travelled by sleeper train a 20-hour trip from Bangkok to Butterworth in Malaysia, then across the 5.2-mile bridge to the nearby island of Penang. We spent a few days on the beaches there.

Penang was a spectacular island that was quite different from Thailand. The British colonial influence was noticeably evident, with some beautiful houses set back in extensive, shaded gardens; it reminded me of Surrey with palm trees and sunshine.

We discovered that 165 miles across the Malacca Straits, by hydrofoil, was Indonesia and the island of Sumatra. Looking at the travel information, we saw an idyllic place in the north of Sumatra called Lake Toba. It did not take much convincing for us to buy tickets to Medan.

Arriving in Medan, in Northern Indonesia, was extraordinary. I thought Bangkok was busy, noisy, and dirty, but Medan was much more so; it seemed years behind Bangkok. They had rats the size of spaniels. We stood at a local bus station to get our connecting ride to Lake Toba, surprised to see that the bus was a van that could seat about seven people, had no windows, and looked incredibly old. We all squeezed in. Other passengers included a lady with a chicken and a man with a television on his lap. It was very tight.

The 110-mile journey south to Parapat on the shores of Lake Toba seemed to last for hours. The roads were terrible; snaking through mountains was extremely dangerous, and the pace was languid. The driver only had one hand on the steering wheel, while his other hand was in a bag of pistachio nuts. It was terrifying.

Whenever he saw somebody walking on the side of the road, he would stop and encourage them to get on the bus. Even if they did not want to, he would argue with them; it slowed us down to the point where it became torturous.

Soaked in the darkness and terrified, we all looked at each other and started laughing.

Eventually, the journey ended, and we found ourselves at a hotel on the lakeside in Parapat. While it was the best hotel in the small town, it was ancient and seemed to have had no guests for a long time. To keep things economical, we rented a family suite on the top floor, which included a vast terrace overlooking the lake. It was gorgeous, especially at night. We had a television, and when we turned it on, we had a live satellite feed of Manchester United versus Spurs. Glenn and I celebrated with beers while my sister screamed in frustration at being in the middle of nowhere in Indonesia yet having a live feed to the Premier League.

The next day, we caught a ferry boat to Samosir, the large island in the middle of the lake. As we drew close, we could see wooden houses on stilts over the water, and naked young brown children raced, jumped and swam in the lake's cool water. There were no vehicles other than motorbikes, and the accommodation was just basic chalet-style bungalows. Prices were ridiculously cheap. To my surprise, many people in this part of Sumatra were Christians and had Christian and Indonesian names.

Several different ethnic tribes populate Sumatra, including the Batak, who live around the Lake Toba area. The Batak Toba houses are unique; they stand tall on stilts and are very recognisable, with their hornlike roofs reaching the sky. The Bataks practice a form of Buddhism, and local villages celebrate their culture and lifestyle – the last Batak king fought valiantly against Dutch imperialists until 1905.

Glenn rented a motorbike from a local shop that was nothing more than a bamboo hut covered with palm leaves. One of the staff there, named Thompson, asked if I would like to rent him together with his bike so that all four of us could travel around the island. Glenn would pilot one bike, and Thompson would take me and act as our guide. We jumped at the chance, and the cost was $5 a day.

On tour across the island, we were travelling down dirt roads. One of the unusual things we saw on the roadside in fields and on the mountainside looked like miniature church models with multiple little windows.

Thompson explained that a small church would belong to a family; when a family member died, their ashes were put inside the church, and the window would be covered. Those empty windows showed the person was alive and well, and this place was ready for them to rest.

What was interesting about this part of Sumatra was when the sun was out, and you were in the lower lands, it was remarkably similar to other tropical countries with palm trees and humidity. But take a short ride, and you would rise into a mountainous area more familiar with Switzerland, so to see an eagle was not unusual.

We were speeding down one of the red dirt lanes when we came upon a ravine crossed by a wooden bridge. The bridge was only wide enough for a motorbike. To my disbelief, Thompson opened the accelerator, bumped from the sand road to the wooden bridge, and sped across to the other side. I was horrified, and I could hear my sister screaming as Glenn put his head down and followed.

He took us to an incredibly remote spot where the cliffs dramatically tumbled to the lake, and stony shores stretched below. We began scrambling down the rugged rocks, Thompson searching for a large, dark cave that seemed to invite exploration. Armed with his torch, we ventured deep inside, only to be taken aback by what we found: four native women seated under the dim glow of an oil lamp, diligently weaving rush-type floor mats. They looked just as shocked to see us and appeared quite uncomfortable with our unexpected presence.

Respecting their unease, we quietly made our way back to the daylight. Thompson started explaining what we had witnessed, and we began the trek back up the cliff together. The ascent was far too steep for me to manage on my own, so Glenn offered me a piggyback ride to the top. He was wearing heavy boots, and I felt a knot of nervousness tighten in my stomach as I glanced down toward my sister below. Glenn was incredible; his strength and steady presence ensured we reached the summit safely.

We sat outside our bungalow on a pebble beach on the lakeside at night, drinking cold beers. As the moon came up and illuminated the jumping fish, it felt like something out of a fairytale.

Once again, Thompson felt that he knew a way to help me improve my physical well-being. He told me about hot springs in the mountains where locals, especially older men, would immerse themselves in the hot, steamy, sulphur-scented water. The minerals were said to improve muscles and circulation.

We drove miles down small tracks up into the mountains and eventually arrived at a place that looked like something from a Western movie – just a couple of shacks, a Coca-Cola sign, and the stinking smell of sulphur. The only things available were Coca-Cola, bottled water, tea, and hard-boiled eggs from the springs. They were delicious, and we once again enjoyed the novelty of this unusual destination.

Thompson encouraged us to climb some rocks to one of the hot springs. Someone had used red bricks within the stones to create a natural steaming pool. Glenn and I stripped down to our boxer shorts. My sister got in first; Glenn put his foot in and screamed in pain. "My God," he said, "it's absolutely boiling."

We sat on the brick wall and very slowly eased ourselves down into the seats below, up to our necks and shoulders. At first, the hot water was painful, but gradually, it disappeared until all we could feel was our heads and faces. It was like our bodies no longer existed. After a while, we got out, and the feeling was extraordinary. I felt like a rubber man – no aches, pains, or stiffness. I climbed back onto the motorbike feeling wonderful. Unfortunately, the effects wore off by the next day, and my aches and pains returned.

Another day, another adventure across the island. This time, Glenn's motorcycle got a puncture. Fortunately, we weren't far from the next village, so he pushed the bike while Lesley walked alongside him. Thompson and I trailed behind, taking in the scene as we entered the village. Domesticated pigs roamed freely everywhere, adding a rustic charm to the place.

We soon spotted a small wooden building that appeared to be the village police station. As we approached, we noticed a couple of officers lounging on chairs cleverly made from old car tyres. With his handsome features and long dreadlocks, Glenn bore a striking resemblance to Ruud Gullit, the Dutch footballer. The officers immediately took notice and started calling out, "Ruud! Ruud!"

A large man, bare-chested except for his trousers and shiny police boots, emerged from the station. It was clear he was the one in charge. As we got closer, hoping to get some help with our punctured tyre, we couldn't help but notice that he had his police badge tattooed right above his right nipple. We joked about his dedication to the job, and everyone shared a laugh. The officers even asked Glenn for his "autograph" to which he happily obliged. After that, they helped us fix the tyre, and we were back on our way, still chuckling over the unexpected encounter.

We came to know Thompson quite well. He was a lovely young man, about 20 years old. He was always dressed in a white shirt and looked smart no matter where he was going. His English was excellent. We discovered that he had wanted to go to a university in Jakarta. Still, because it was so far away and prohibitively expensive, he remained on the island working in the motorbike shop. He wanted to be an engineer, and when we quizzed him about the course, we discovered it was £200. Glenn and I decided it was a worthy course to invest in this lovely and promising young man, so we paid his entrance fee for him.

I am back in Bangkok, and for the last couple of days I went with Chariya to investigate the procedure for getting married. We agreed that I would return soon to visit the local registry office to perform the marriage ceremony.

Marriage

I returned to Thailand two months later, this time on my own. Chariya and I went to her local registry office, where we completed the marriage process and received our certificate. With this in hand, we applied for her British wife's visa. Unfortunately, Chariya could not get an interview with the British Embassy for six weeks, so I had to return to England alone, enduring an agonising wait for my wife to join me.

When Chariya finally arrived in November 1991, she found England very cold and shocking to her system. For a while, she wondered if she had made a mistake. I convinced her to hang in there and assured her she would soon adjust.

Celebrating our wedding

To celebrate Chariya's arrival in England, we hosted a wedding party at our local hotel. It was a beautiful event where we all dressed up, and friends and family from around the country came to celebrate with us. The atmosphere was filled with joy and warmth, marking the beginning of our new life together. The celebration was perfect for welcoming Chariya to her new home and sharing our happiness with those who meant the most to us.

I got her a place at Retford College to study English as a second language, and through my contacts, I got her a job as a waitress at the local hotel. She was pleased about this. Not only did she enjoy working, but she also earned a considerable salary compared to what she could earn in Thailand. She felt immensely proud to be able to send money to her mum and dad from England. She also signed up with the local karate instructor and started taking driving lessons. We soon settled down, and she became a stepmom to my kids, who absolutely loved her Thai cooking.

The travel company that had taken me on that memorable seven-day Mediterranean cruise reached out again, this time asking if I'd review a coach holiday to Amsterdam. I was thrilled and asked if I could bring my wife along. They agreed, so we went to London to sort out the necessary French visa and Dutch entry permits.

After standing in line in the French embassy for over two hours, we finally reached the desk, only to be told that the stamp on her passport was incorrect – it was dated 1991 instead of 1992, making it a year out of date. The clerk informed me that we'd need to go to British immigration to renew it. The taxi there alone would cost more than £130.

I didn't have the time or the inclination to pay that much, so I got creative. Using a ballpoint pen, I skilfully turned the "1" into a "2" and returned to the queue at a different desk. An hour later, we walked out with the French visa in hand.

The coach trip to Amsterdam was a blast. It was an excellent opportunity for Chariya and me to explore the city together. I held my walking stick in my right hand and Chariya's hand in my left, and we made our way slowly around.

One night, we went on a nightlife tour through the Red Light District, and it was an eye-opener, especially for my wife. She was shocked at how different it was from Bangkok – women sitting in windows like mannequins under bright lights and grubby men in coats hawking tickets. At one point, a man in a long leather coat grabbed her arm. Without missing a beat, she turned around and used her karate skills to deliver a swift kick to his knee. He stumbled back, and we carried on our way.

By the end of the four-day trip, we had enjoyed the beautiful city's sights, enjoyed the food, and explored the shops. It was an adventure we wouldn't soon forget.

CHAPTER 63
BUDDHA

"When watching after yourself, you watch after others.
When watching after others, you watch after yourself."
– The Buddha

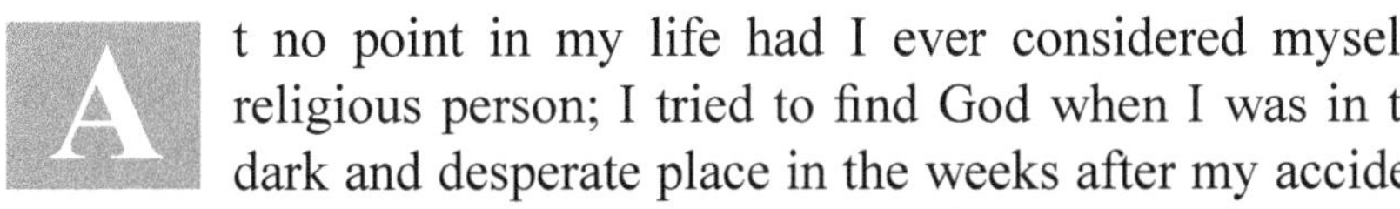
At no point in my life had I ever considered myself a religious person; I tried to find God when I was in that dark and desperate place in the weeks after my accident. I asked Jesus to help me search out the light, but I did not find anything other than a belief in myself, a realisation that it was me and only me that would get me out of that dark hell. I found my spirit in the love and support of my family and friends and my desire to live.

As I explained, we did not have a Bible when growing up in our house. However, the New Testament was necessary equipment at my secondary school. Morning assemblies included hymns and prayers. But it was not a belief to me or most of my friends and those around me; it was merely a compulsory routine we all had to endure. I never did feel that those teachers were trying to teach us that a belief in God and this Christian religion might genuinely save us.

There were many good reasons to fall in love with Thailand: the glorious sunshine, the beautiful tropical beaches and countryside, the amiable people, their live-and-let-live mindset, and, of course, the fantastic food. And, if you are a single man, of course, a beautiful woman.

What might surprise you, if you have never been, is that there is another attraction, a magnetism that pulls many to Thailand. I think if you ask many foreigners who settled to stay and live in Thailand, most will agree with me and tell you that the culture and religion are intoxicating.

I was certainly intrigued by the Buddhist religion and the country's dedication and love for their revered King Rama IX. It was not the dynasty, the traditional pomp, or the palaces, but the man himself who was deeply loved. This aspect of Thailand touched me, and my spirituality awakened there. I had first found 'myself' after my accident in 1973, my belief in my own 'sense of being'.

As I learnt about Buddha's teachings and their way of life, I realised a new respect for others, my own life, myself, and how I treat others – a connection I did not see or feel back home in the UK.

I was raised, lived, and worked around Maidenhead, the River Thames and Windsor Castle. I was familiar with our British Royal pageantry and the grandeur of our Royal heritage; I thought our monarch was a gracious human and should be respected. It was an inherent belief of our traditions, but I cannot say I admired the Queen in person.

I am not a Republican or a Federalist, and I have no desire to see the end of the monarchy; I believe it sets the UK apart and helps distinguish our country, but it is a cherished heirloom instead of a current need or solution. I grew up in the Church of England, and as the Christian religion, I had few choices. I never felt any affinity or obligation to it other than to respect it or keep others around me happy.

In Thailand, Buddhism is an entirely distinct experience. It is not a religion as such. There are no services to attend or hymns to sing; it is more about culture and way of life. The Buddha's teachings are profound guidelines to adhere to. It is all straightforward to understand.

It was January 1994, and I still lived in Nottinghamshire with my Thai wife, Chariya. We travelled to Thailand for a holiday. It was a chance for her to see her family and for us to spend some time together. At some of our favourite beaches and places we knew so well in Phuket. On 26 January, she took me to a small, ancient temple she wanted to show me. It was Wat Phra Thong, found in the island's central north. It was not on the tourist trail. There were other more spectacular-looking temples for that. This small temple is the oldest temple on the island, and it is famous for housing a half-buried golden Buddha statue called Luang Poh Phra Thong (Golden Buddha) on its grounds, also known as Wat Phra Phud, which means 'Temple of the protruding Buddha'.

There is a legend. Anyone through history who tried to dig the Buddha from the ground met a grizzly death. Some say that the Buddha was deliberately buried to hide it from the invading armies of Burma; others say it was buried in silt after a flood.

I could still walk quite briskly back then, but it wasn't easy. I was clumsy, my feet did drag on the ground, and I was rather stiff and ungainly. I could climb steps provided there was a railing for my left hand to steady me, and with my right hand, I could lean on my walking stick. I made my way around the beautiful gardens, looking at the buildings, taking in the history, the golden beauty, and the delicate artworks.

Chariya had been to Wat Phra Thong before. She felt it was vital for me to learn as much as possible about real Thai life and traditions, get away from the beaches and city centres, and indulge and learn, not just to explore as a tourist, soaking up the usual offerings for holidaymakers.

Hence, on this day, we were the only visitors to the temple. Chariya was familiar with the surroundings. She was less interested in exploring the place than I was; she made her prayers and went and sat beneath a mango tree in the gardens.

I was standing in front of the buried Buddha statue. It was beautiful, surrounded by an array of fragrant white, yellow, and orange flowers. It shone so vividly in the light. The figure from the breast to the top of the head was about seven feet tall. It was glittering and shiny gold, covered in thousands of small squares of natural gold leaf, tributes that visitors had made one piece at a time; the golden sheets were fluttering in the light breeze; it was astonishing.

I was soaking up the serene and peaceful atmosphere, enjoying myself, when a young monk approached me. He was smartly dressed in his fresh, bright orange robe, his shaven head shining in the sunlight, showing his unusually white skin. His voice was gentle and polite, his face handsome and kind. "Hello sir, how are you today?"

His English was excellent, and he spoke professionally.

"I'm very well, thank you," I replied, shocked that a monk had approached me for a conversation, which was not the norm.

"Excuse me, may I ask you a question?" I spoke.

"Yes, of course," he replied.

"How did this Buddha statue become buried up to his chest, in the ground? Was it cursed?"

He replied, "There are many legends, of the truth we are not certain; this statue has been here for more than one thousand years; the temple that stands over us now is not the first temple here; there would have been so many, they will have fallen, and many new temples would have been built here since then. But always, this Buddha remained in the same place; gradually, it became buried under a thousand years of ashes from candles and burning incense, from people's prayers."

"Amazing, it's wonderful," I replied.

"Excuse me, sir," he continued, "please follow me; my Abbot would like to speak to you".

I was curious and a bit nervous. I knew this was not normal and that something unusual was happening here as a guest in an exotic country like Thailand, especially when you are in a sacred place like a temple, and a monk asks you to do something, and you want to comply.

So, intrigued, I followed him slowly down the path to the back of the temple to a row of small, modest cottages. They were of basic construction, the simple accommodations of the monks. He took me to one of these tiny huts.

I tried to remove my shoes before going inside, as I knew that was the custom; he could see that I couldn't do it, standing up and leaning on my walking stick. I was wobbling, and he smiled and bought an old wooden chair. I sat down, and taking off my shoes took quite a bit of effort.

I stood up and went inside barefoot, where I saw an older man sitting cross-legged on a wooden bench; he was frail, the senior monk obviously; his robes were chestnut brown and as aged as him, he must have been in his late 80s, he wore round wire glasses.

He looked up and smiled. I knew it was polite and customary to bow down and wai to him (two hands together raised in front of your face, like praying). But I could not do it. I could not bend down significantly because of my weak back and legs, and so I could not wai, with a walking stick in one hand. I felt clumsy and embarrassed, but I did my best.

The Abbot grinned. I think he understood my predicament and signalled to the young monk to bring the wooden chair inside. I sat down on it, knowing it was rude for my head to be higher than his. I felt awkward and bent forward, putting my walking stick on the floor; I tried unsuccessfully to bow and wai from my seated position.

He acknowledged me, and I think he appreciated my understanding of cultural behaviour. I was incredibly excited. This was a mystical world about which I knew truly little; it felt extraordinarily solemn, and I felt privileged to be in this gracious company. The young monk was subservient and obedient in his service to the Abbot.

The young monk clearly understood my Western ways, and I guessed he had been to an international school in his youth. The young monk sat on the floor next to me and acted as the translator as the old Abbot continued talking to me.

The young monk looked at me and said, "My Abbot saw you were walking around the temple and looking at the Buddha. He wanted to meet you, and he wanted to know more about you."

I replied, "Please tell him I feel honoured and am very pleased to meet and talk with him."

The young monk translated my words, and the Abbot smiled at me. He continued talking to me in Thai, and the young monk translated once again. "Where have you come from? What country are you from? "

"I am from England. I am here on holiday with my wife, who is Thai."

Again, the young monk translated my words.

My wife had realised where I had gone; she visited the temple shop and bought the traditional orange plastic bucket filled with food and household items, a standard pre-packaged offering called 'alms' or 'sang khthan' as they say in Thai, which means to give necessities to monks as a way of making merit.

The bucket consisted of food items, cans, packets, tins, and other practical things useful to the monks' daily needs. She also had some sacred orange flowers. She was standing outside the monks' door, where she was visible for the Abbot to see. She told me to take these and to give them to the monk. Women are not allowed to hand things to a monk. They must leave any offerings on the floor for the monk to pick up.

I made a polite wai and presented these aims to the Abbot, he waied back to me and accepted my offerings, handing them to the young monk who took them to the small room at the back of the sparse hut and returned. My wife made a wai to both the Abbot and the monk, smiled and walked away back into the temple gardens.

The young monk continued: "My Abbot wants to know what happened to your body, what has broken you?"

I replied with my usual answer, which I had already spoken a thousand times. "When I was 15 years old, I had an accident playing rugby. I broke my neck. I was paralysed from the neck down for a long time. Because of that, I cannot run, walk or climb the way I used to. I can only walk short distances with the aid of my walking stick, and my hands and fingers do not work properly." I held out my hands to show him how I could not straighten them.

But, I added, "At least I can walk far enough to meet the Abbot."

The young monk translated, and another warm smile was on his face.

The room he occupied was very sparse. It consisted of the wooden bench on which he sat; it was his bed. Opposite the bed was an old ornate teak wood and brass grandfather clock – it was impressive, about six feet high. Next to that was an old, worn-out wooden cupboard, from which he took some very old-looking books.

He opened one book and reviewed its contents, which looked like an assortment of astrological charts. The young monk asked me, "Do you know what time of the day you were born? "

I told him.

"Do you know which day of the week you were born?"

I told him.

"And what were the date and the year that you were born?"

I told him. He did not ask me any other questions.

He gave the information to Abbot, who started to draw a chart with his ruler and pencils. I sat there for quite some time as he constructed this astrological map. After a long time, he completed this incredibly detailed chart. It looked beautiful, and he went ahead to explain to me the meaning he saw within it.

I did not realise it then, but I was about to hear the words that would change my life forever. It was one of those times in your life when you had to choose a path.

The Abbot began, and the young monk translated sentence by sentence.

"You're a good man, but troubled; events in your life have put you down, but you are strong, and you still have a light in your heart," he continued.

"You are trying hard to please all the people around you. You are facing too many directions at once, and this is pulling you apart. You are trying to be many people at one time; this is impossible; it is causing you great unhappiness and can only make other people who love you unhappy also."

Wow, I was not expecting this, and that is not how I thought I was.

He continued, "The only way to find peace is to find yourself. Watching after yourself is what you must do. This way, you are also taking care of those people who love you. They will also be happy when you are happy, and it is time to love yourself."

He continued, "The woman you call your wife is not the right woman; she is not suitable for you. You need a soft-hearted, strong woman from the north, not a 'jai lorn' (hot-heart) woman from the south. This will be better for you."

I thought this was strange, but then we argued a lot, and she was very hot-headed.

He continued, "You can be happy if you live in Thailand. If you open a shop or start a business here, people will come to you. You will have success. Maybe rent motorcycles or boats to tourists, but they will come to you, and you will be happy, successful, and fulfilled."

He continued, "You should have faith in your vision. You can cut the path for others to follow. Water is not your friend; beware when close to the ocean or on a river."

He added, "There are women in your life who love you deeply and want you to find happiness. There's an old lady who looks over you, who prays for you, and who will keep you safe.

"If you leave them to seek your path, you will meet them along that road, and they will see you happy, and they will be happy."

I immediately thought of my grandmother, who was over 90 years old then, and my adoring mother. My loving sister, who had travelled to Thailand with me the year before, and my young daughter, now living with her mother and her 'new' dad. They were all so dear to me. I realised he had not mentioned anything about my father, who had been dead for 14 years by this time.

As I pondered his comments, I understood what he was saying. My life was not fun. At this point, I had had a terrible time at work. Managing the business through a bad economic recession meant that I had to make some tough decisions. Making some staff redundant a year earlier was extremely hard. It was the most challenging thing I had done in business. My actions would change their lives forever. That wasn't easy to accept, but I had done it because it needed to be done.

Things were not much better at home. It was not home; I knew it was just a temporary base; eventually, my company would move me to another town. And I was only a weekend father desperately grabbing a few hours of my children's lives at weekends, bringing them to their second bedrooms at their second home.

My children's mother hated me with a passion. I was living with a younger woman. I was often overseas in hot, sunny places. She was rebuilding her life with her new husband, which did not appear to be going well; my children had to learn to live with her new man in his house. They were confused and unhappy with the situation. It was tearing us all apart.

My wife Chariya married me, believing we would build a life together. She had expectations of her own, but she found it difficult to see her future with me other than being a nanny to my three children at weekends in England, when deep down, naturally, she wanted a baby of her own; I was sceptical of palm readers and fortune tellers. It was all a bit of fun, not to be taken seriously. I had even swapped over the newspaper's 'Star Horoscopes' from one week to the following weeks, knowing readers would never tell the difference.

There is no doubt that on that day, in that situation, I felt unusually vulnerable with that man. The impact of his words penetrated me deeply. In those circumstances, I was prepared to believe anything. But I could not deny that the things that he talked about felt so real; it was me he was talking about; the Abbot was lifting me out of a deep pool of murky water; he was pulling back a curtain to show me my new future.

I felt my spirit breathe in, energised and, at the same time, overcome by his good grace. I do not consider this a religious experience, a calling from God. God was not involved; this was about my spirit and faith in myself. I felt touched and loved; this was about me and how I dealt with myself, how it was up to me to shape my life.

He gave me three small gifts. A small circular locket with a golden Buddha image for Thursday, the day I was born. The Buddha is seated and meditating in the yoga posture. The right leg is on top of the left; the right hand is on top of the left hand. Another gift was a piece of shiny black stone that was incredibly old, a standing Buddha, the carving so worn you could hardly tell what it was any more. The third gift was a stone amulet of Luang Phor Koon. He was a famous monk born in 1923 in the North of Thailand, and Thais revered him. It would bring me luck and good fortune, as this monk was famous for raising donations to build hospitals, schools, and temples many years ago.

I accepted my gifts, showed my gratitude, and asked the young monk if it would be all right for me to take a photo with the Abbot; he smiled and said yes, I am sure that would be OK, and continued talking to the monk in Thai.

The old Abbot got up from his bench and walked into the room at the back of the hut. The young monk told me he was changing and was extremely happy to be photographed with me. When he came out of the room, he wore a new bright orange robe and a different pair of glasses. He stood next to his grandfather clock, and I photographed him. Thank you so much for everything you have done for me today, and I left. I walked back up the path to the temple to meet Chariya, who was waiting for me.

I knew I would eventually leave England when the time was right, and I would try to make a go of it in Thailand with Chariya. She had an excellent job at the local hotel, attended English at college, and took her karate classes, but I knew she would prefer to go back to Thailand to live.

Chariya said, "Well, that was very special, darling. This monk is taking you to his room; you must have a good spirit, my love."

I answered, "So, how do you fancy coming back to live here in Thailand?"

Chariya flashed her beautiful smile; her eyes twinkled, and her teeth shone so big and white.

That was a special day in my life, and something changed in me. It was the day I decided life was not my pay packet, car, status, or relationships. Life was breathing, seeing, experiencing. I wanted to find my spiritual self and consume my life.

CHAPTER 64
NUMBERS

It was February 1994. A few weeks after meeting with the Abbot in Thailand, I met a South African fellow called Karl in a bar near Patong. He was a doctor and the editor of an English-language Thai medical magazine. I told him about my experience at the temple in Phuket, my meeting with the old Abbot, and how I plan to untangle my life in England, intending to relocate to Thailand by the end of the year.

I was still working in Nottinghamshire as the Director and General Manager of the *Redford, Gainsborough & Worksop Times* Company. The weekly paid-for broadsheet newspaper, the free weekly, and the *Gainsborough Target* were also under my control.

I was under the auspice of my ex-boss and now friend, Ted Stevens, the Managing Director of the nearby *Lincolnshire Echo,* a paid-for daily broadsheet and a weekly free *Lincoln Target.* My employer was Northcliffe Newspapers Group, based in central London, where they owned and ran more than 70 regional newspapers nationwide.

Employees like me were contracted out to work in the regional offices. My contract provided six months of notice, and I did not want to let them down, as I had nine incredibly happy and successful years with NNG.

Karl said, "You have all the skills and experience these guys need. You'll be surprised how easily you'll find employment with one of the big newspaper publishers in Bangkok."

"Do you think so?" I said, "What about the language? I do not understand Thai?"

He said, "You're a commercial manager; numbers are numbers wherever you are. Your job is to manage products and people, and besides, there are plenty of English language magazines and newspapers here, as well as *The Bangkok Post,* Thailand's leading daily newspaper."

He opened his Filofax and scribbled out a list of names and telephone numbers of some of the bosses and owners of the leading publishing companies in Thailand. I put it in my pocket and said thanks, and we drank some more beers.

By the time I had prepared my CV and drafted a compelling letter of introduction addressed to the half dozen names of CEOs of Bangkok publishing companies that Karl had given me, it was late March. I had explained in my letter that I had to provide six months' notice. Therefore, I was looking to take up a position around October.

I went into town and bought six sets of stamps; at that time, the Post Office had just issued a collection of stamps celebrating the 25th Anniversary of the investiture of HRH The Prince of Wales. The postage stamps consisted of five watercolour landscapes by Prince Charles.

My trick was putting all five stamps, the complete set, on the front of each envelope. I knew that this would stand out in the pile of mail and get the attention of each of the CEOs. I simultaneously despatched them and headed home, not thinking any more about it.

CHAPTER 65

IT'S JUST BUSINESS

It was early April, and I was taking a regular Monday morning management meeting in my office with my Editor, Nigel, my Production Manager, Mike, my Advertising Manager, Victoria, and my Secretary, Margaret. We discussed all the usual weekly schedules and made a few decisions.

At the end of the meeting, my Editor, Nigel, stepped back inside the office and closed the door behind him.

"Is it OK if I have a private word with you about something, please?" he said.

"Sure," I said, "what's on your mind, Nigel."

"I wanted to talk to you about one of the advertising sales reps, and I didn't want to do it in front of Victoria," he said.

"OK, why is that?"

"Because Victoria and Hannah happen to be close friends, and that is the problem. Victoria's not dealing with several issues in her department, and it is clear to everyone there that there is some favouritism towards Hannah. Everyone knows she is as useful as a chocolate fireguard when selling advertising. There is a lot of resentment building, as Victoria is protecting her," he said.

I replied, "OK, well, I knew they knew each other; how do you know they are so chummy? "

Nigel replied, "Apparently, Victoria's boyfriend and Hannah's boyfriend are close friends and have been for years. They all go out as a foursome, quite a lot, it seems."

I said, "OK, I see where you're coming from; what do you want me to do?"

"I think if you undertake some training which includes Hannah, you might be able to expose her weaknesses. Or go on some dual calls with her, and you can see exactly how uselessly she performs with your own eyes."

"Yeah, OK, I can do that; it's been a long time since I've done a dual call with any of the reps. I enjoy getting out of the office and meeting some customers, and hopefully, I'll be able to help the staff learn and grow. I'll arrange something," I said.

I left it for about half an hour. I did not want to draw attention following my meeting with Nigel.

"Victoria, do you think it would be a good idea if I did some dual calls with some of the sales team? I want to get a feel for how they're doing for themselves," I said.

"Yes, OK, why not if you think that's needed."

"Yes, I think it's needed; I should keep close to the action. I guess I'll begin with Hannah; can you ask her to come and see me, please?" I said.

A few minutes later, an extremely nervous 19-year-old Hannah entered my office. She was visibly unsettled, red-faced, and unsure of herself. Hannah had long blonde hair, a good figure, and was very pretty. She knew that, and she used it to her advantage, quite rightly, I thought. As a salesperson, she was hardly ever refused an appointment. People always seemed prepared to give her the time of day and listen to what she had to say.

"What calls do you have planned for this morning, Hannah?" I asked.

She hesitated, "I'm going to the garden centre next, at 11."

"OK, well, I am going to come with you. Please do not be nervous; it is OK. All I want is to watch you present the sale. I will not be involved; I will just observe. After your pitch, I will make my comments, and we can discuss how it went, OK?"

"Yes, OK, then," she said nervously.

We took my car, parked, and walked into the garden centre; she held the door open as I entered the head office, walking stick in one hand, Filofax in the other. Hannah introduced me to the owner. She explained I was the MD of the newspaper. I said "hello" and told the owner I was not here to sell; it was merely a training exercise for my staff today and an opportunity to meet him personally. I asked him if that was OK, and he said yes, no problem, let's carry on.

Hannah's pitch was nervously presented. She did not even know the client's current advertising schedule or where he was advertising. He was a regular advertiser in one of our main competitors' newspapers. I knew because I had made a point of looking, but Hannah was uninformed, which immediately put her in a weak position to offer advice. Then, as he asked for the costs, she got confused about the prices of ads of specific sizes, and things went from bad to even worse.

The client was polite but not impressed, saying OK, well, let me think about it, and I will get back to you. Hannah quickly took the opportunity to end the meeting, and we left the office, saying our goodbyes, and walked back to the car.

We sat in the car, and I said to her. "OK, Hannah, so how do you think that went?"

Immediately, she burst into tears, uncontrollably sobbing. I was shocked. It was terrible, but not that bad; it certainly did not call for this huge emotional outburst. I had already explained to her that I was there to help, I was not going to judge her, this was not a test, my goal was to analyse what was done well and what was not, to identify her weaknesses, and then work together on fixing them. I was there to help her improve and to become a better salesperson.

But she could not contain herself; she just cried and cried. I felt very awkward and uncomfortable; how would I handle this? I thought.

"What's the matter, Hannah?" I asked. "Surely, it's not that bad. We can sort all this out. There's no need to get so upset, is there?"

Through her sobbing, she squeaked, "I'm sorry, I'm so sorry."

I handed her some tissues, and she started to dampen her tears and blow her nose. Her face was bright red, and her hair was wet from crying.

I spoke: "Okay, look, settle yourself down. I'll drive us back to the office, and then we can chat later. We'll talk about things when you've settled down."

As I pulled out of the car park and headed back to Retford, she said, "I'm sorry. I know I'm useless at my job, but it's not just that."

By this time, I was feeling sorry for her. She was not acting; she was definitely distressed. I asked, "What else is it, then?"

She was breathing deeply, almost retching, almost coughing from the strain, her face still glowing red, her tissues soaked with tears. She continued, "My whole life is a mess at the moment. I finished with my boyfriend yesterday; he reacted angrily. He was horrible to me, and he said some wicked things about me."

She continued sobbing loudly, "Even my mother......" she didn't finish that sentence.

As we approached the office, I felt extremely uncomfortable with her state. Her reaction was far beyond a bad sales call, and I wondered what I had gotten myself dragged into here.

We were close to the office now. Hannah was very dishevelled and still distraught. I didn't think she would want to walk back into the office in that state.

I said, "Hannah, this is all incredibly stressful for you. Rather than going straight into the office like this, would you prefer to just come into the pub for a lunch break? I'll buy you an orange juice, and you can take your time and calm down, get yourself together, and then when you're ready, we can go back to the office, OK?"

She responded, "Yes, thank you very much, Roger. I'm so sorry. I shouldn't do this, but I can't help myself. It's all such a mess. I'm so upset with my life. Everything is going wrong!"

The pub

I told her to sit down in the corner, and I went to the bar and ordered two orange juices. Using my walking stick, I took them back to the table, one at a time.

"Okay, Hannah, you need to relax, dear. You're alright. Let me say that a pretty girl like you should not be getting so upset over a silly boy who does not deserve you. Look, you are only 19. You are young to be getting into such a state over a relationship. What did he do to upset you so much?"

She spoke, "We have been arguing quite a lot recently, and my mother does not like him at all. Yesterday evening, he asked me to wash his car. I thought he meant we'd do it together, but he was talking to his friend. When I stopped and walked away and told him I was not doing it, he got aggressive and insulting, and he called me some horrible names; it upset me!" She burst into tears again.

Once again, I felt highly uncomfortable having to listen to her woes. As a father to an 11-year-old little girl, I thought I would not want my daughter to end up with a nasty prick like this guy. I could not help feeling sorry for her. We sat side by side on a bench; I turned and put my arm around her shoulder, giving her a squeeze and a fatherly hug; her hair was wet and sticky and glued to her face, and I pulled it back over her shoulder.

I said, "Be strong, Hannah. You are a beautiful young woman who could get any guy you want. You do not need to be taking insults from a pig like him!"

She shuddered, coughed, and sobbed, grunting in agreement. "Yes, I know you are right. I am sorry I'm such a mess," she said.

After about 15 minutes, her fistful of tissues was soaked through, but she had finally composed herself. Her breathing was back to normal, and the redness in her face had begun to subside. A faint smile had returned.

I felt relieved that she had calmed down and had her emotions back under control. It was time to get her back to the office.

I said, "Are you ready to go back now? Do you feel up to it?"

"Yes, I'm OK now; thank you so much for being patient and understanding," she replied.

I said, 'If you are OK personally, we can resolve all these work issues, improve your sales techniques, and help you with all that. You just need to sort out your love life, and we should be OK.

Nick came to my office and asked, "So how did it go? What did you think of her?"

"She's an abso, Nick. What an ordeal." I explained to him in some detail what had happened.

He asked, "So what are you going to do? Are you going to keep her?"

I replied, "For the time being, I cannot let her go at the moment. That really would not feel correct in the current situation. Let us give it a couple of weeks and see how things progress."

"OK, well, it is your problem. I'm sure you'll sort it out, but I just wanted to ensure you were aware of things." And he walked back to his office.

My secretary Margaret walked into the room with a knowing grin across her face. She was much older than me, and we had an 'aunty'-type relationship.

"Hello Margaret, dear. Go on. What is it? Do you have something to tell? "I asked.

"So, how was your sales call with Hannah?" she asked, a smirk on her face.

"I think you know the answer to that, Margaret. It was a bloody disaster," I said.

"So, are you going to sack her at last?"

"No, not yet. I'm going to give her a couple of weeks to improve. I'll talk to Victoria about it and see if we can get Hannah back on track."

"Good luck with that!" said Margaret; she smirked again and walked out.

I spoke to Victoria and suggested she invest time in taking care of Hanna, helping her understand the required sales techniques, and meeting the standards we demanded. Otherwise, we would have to let her go in a couple of weeks. Victoria nodded in agreement and returned to her desk.

About a week later, I got a call from Ted, the Managing Director at the *Lincolnshire Echo,* my regional boss. "Hello, Roger, it's Ted. Can you come over this afternoon? We need to have a meeting," he said.

"Yeah, sure Ted, what's it about?" I asked.

"We can discuss it when you get here, OK? See you at 2 o'clock," he said, and he hung up the phone.

I drove the 20 miles to Lincoln; it was about 45 minutes to the *Lincolnshire Echo* when I parked and walked to his office. I sat in front of his desk, ready and waiting for 2 o'clock. He walked in. He had a glum look on his face. He shut the door behind him, making me feel uncertain about what was to come. He sat down and looked across his desk at me.

Then, looking down and unemotional, he spoke with some hesitation in his voice. "Roger, you have been accused of sexual harassment."

Stunned, I thought, was he talking about me or someone else? "What on earth are you saying, Ted?" I asked.

He put his papers back on the desk and ran his fingers through his hair. He was looking incredibly uncomfortable; he said, "Apparently, you sexually harassed a young salesgirl named Hannah?"

I gasped. "Are you serious?" I yelled in a raised voice. I could not contain myself. This was ridiculous. "What are you talking about? What is supposed to have happened?"

He replied, "In the complaint, it states that you took her to a pub one lunchtime, and while there, you made an inappropriate advance to her, touching her and talking in a lurid fashion about her looks and her love life."

I laughed, "This is outrageous, Ted, this is ridiculous; I never did any such thing."

"I believe you, of course, Roger, but this is above my head. The London office made this decision. The problem is when a complaint like this has been made against you, it must be investigated. I'm afraid I must suspend you from work while all this takes place."

He continued, "Christ Roger, I told you before, never even have a meeting in your office with a female unless the door is open, or you have a third person in the room. The law these days is so strict. All you need is for a vicious woman to make a complaint, and that is it. It must be investigated!"

I was flabbergasted. "Are you seriously telling me I'm being suspended from work?"

"Yes, I'm afraid so. That is the procedure. Just while we go through this process, the London office is dealing with this, not me. It will not take them long to decide on where we go from here."

"A decision, come on Ted, you know this is a bloody set-up, what the fuck is going on?' I said.

"Roger. I am on your side. They will get to the bottom of it and sort it out. In the meantime, please go home and not contact anybody at work, OK?"

"Calm down, are you kidding?" I stood up, grabbed my walking stick, thumped his desk, and said, "I'll go home, but this is fucking shite."

I got a phone call that night from my secretary Margaret. She had been working at the paper for 15 years. She was a Nottinghamshire lady in her late 50s, intelligent, organised, loyal, and hard-working; she loved the newspaper.

She was clearly shaken as she said. "They told us you had been suspended from work. I cannot believe it, and I know what happened."

She did even though she knew she was not supposed to contact me.

"Roger, there is something you need to know; do you remember you were asked to do an appraisal of Victoria by the London office regarding the vacancy and her potential promotion to Grimsby? You said in your recommendation that you did not think she was ready?"

"Yes, I reported honestly. She's not ready for a job with that many people; she can't manage the five she has here."

Margaret continued, "While you were on holiday in Thailand, I caught her going through your filing cabinet; she was shocked when she saw me come into the office; Victoria went red in the face; I knew she was up to no good. I asked what she was doing, and she said she was looking for an advertising contract. I told her to tell me which one and I would find it for her. She told me there was no need. When I checked, it was the folder with her recommendation that she had been looking at; I could tell she must have read it while in there, so she knows what you had reported back about her."

"The crafty cow," I said.

Margaret continued, "So, you know how angry she must have been with you. Well, that day, you went to the pub with Hannah, and soon after you both returned to the office, Hannah left again almost immediately with Victoria. I do not think this complaint had anything to do with Hannah. She is too young and naïve to think of making such a nasty complaint against you, especially under the circumstances. I know this was all Victoria's doing; it was her way to get back at you."

"Oh, for God's sake," I said. "I cannot believe this is happening, can you, Margaret? How can anyone think I'd do this? It just does not make sense; everyone knows I am a happily married man, I have a beautiful wife, and the last thing I need is to mess around with a 19-year-old girl from work; everybody knows what I am like. I do not go anywhere near the girls at work."

Margaret replied, "I know that, Roger, we all do. None of us believed her, so I had to call you and tell you what I know."

"Thanks, Margaret. It all makes sense now. Hopefully, I will get my chance to tell the facts when I go to London," I said.

Off to London

Two days later, I had to attend an interview with one of the Directors in London, a chat, he said, a guy I had never met before. It did not feel right. I knew several of the senior executives in London. None of whom were anywhere to be seen.

This new chap asked me what happened, and I told him exactly how it occurred. I explained my theory of what happened, about Victoria being the architect, to get back at me. He thanked me and opened the door to his office, and we said goodbye.

I drove back from London to Nottinghamshire, thinking everything must be OK. It is pretty evident that, in my position, I would not do that. I felt quite sure this guy would see it all for what it truly was.

The following evening, I was driving when I got a call from Ted. I pulled over to take the call.

"Roger, I have had a call from London HR. They have made a decision, but I am afraid it is grave news. You have been dismissed for gross misconduct because this is a sexual harassment complaint. I am sorry, but you cannot return to the office."

I went icy cold. Dumbfounded, I could not believe my ears.

He continued, "Because of the nature of the dismissal, your six-month notice period is void, and your dismissal is with immediate effect. That means you'll receive one month's pay."

He continued, "Of course, I told them this was unacceptable; that was entirely unfair. I insisted they pay you a three-month notice payment. They've agreed to that, but I'm afraid you're out today, and I need you to return the company car to the Lincoln office, please."

I felt gutted and fuming. I felt so let down. Where was the loyalty? Where is the justice? This is so unfair. It is just unbelievable. How can this be happening to me? I thought.

"Ted, I'm a disabled driver; the car is my legs; how am I supposed to get around without a car?" I was pleading by now, with no energy for a fight.

Ted said, "You can keep it for a week. I'll tell them I've got it, but you'll have to find something else by then. I'm sorry, there's nothing more I can do about this. The car belongs to London."

I was driving London's bloody car in a daze, not knowing what I was doing. I parked outside a warehouse on a quiet industrial estate; it was peaceful and deserted. Inside, I was on fire, screaming. I smashed the steering wheel with both hands over and over. Eventually, my emotions erupted, and I just burst uncontrollably crying. After a few minutes, I began to get control of my emotions again and try to think about what I should do.

I called my sister, Lesley, on my car phone and told her what had happened. I couldn't help myself. By now, the realisation had reached me. This was so seriously life changing. I was so lost. The deceit and dishonesty made everything vile, revolting, and difficult to swallow. It was a massive slap in the face. I asked her how I would ever get past this.

I told her, "I have been with that company for nine years. They promoted me four times, and I won three awards from the Newspaper Society. And they took the word of this silly young girl, who didn't even deserve her place in the company. She was only there because I was too soft to sack her. I had allowed her to stay."

Lesley said, "This is awful, and you can't let them get away with this. Do you have a lawyer."

"Yes, I do; the lady that did my divorce, I bet she'd love to get her teeth into this."

Lesley said, "Well, you must give her a call tomorrow, tell her you want to fight it, take them to court for wrongful dismissal, sue their arses."

I went home and told my wife, Chariya, what had happened; she was as shocked as me and knew I would not have misbehaved. She was upset at the thought of those people for disrespecting me.

Chariya said, "Roger, darling, it doesn't matter. These people are not good; they don't deserve you." She kissed and hugged me and smiled those big, bright white teeth at me.

She continued, "Don't think about it anymore. What will be, will be."

I looked at her and smiled. She was so calm and sure, and she had such faith.

I was far from cool. My future in the UK had been obliterated, my career in ruins after being dismissed from a public company on charges of sexual harassment. The humiliation was unbearable, knowing everyone in the industry would soon hear about it. It felt like I had slammed into a brick wall – my once-promising career had come to a screeching halt, crashing and burning instantly.

The anger I felt toward the corporate establishment consumed me. Years of arduous work meant nothing to them; they tossed me aside without a second thought. The betrayal stung deeply – their lack of trust, their cold indifference as they disposed of me like I was nothing.

Meanwhile, my family life was in shambles. I was already a depressed weekend dad, and my ex-wife, the mother of my three children, harboured nothing but hatred for me. She insisted that our kids call her new partner "dad " and even wanted to change their last name from Warner to his – Dickson.

My children confided in me that they did not want to call him "dad" and that it made them feel uncomfortable. I could not shake the belief that she was jealous of my happiness, bitter that I had remarried a beautiful young woman while her own life unravelled. Her partner, initially unwilling, had realised too late that he was caught in a trap – a quick affair with a married mother of three had left him trapped like a cunning fox.

Eventually, I came to terms with what had happened to me. The dream I once had of being a dad and husband in our Lincolnshire haven, growing old with my blossoming family, was dead. The catastrophic injustice I had suffered – the abrupt and unfair end to my publishing career – was the final straw. It was the sign I needed, the push that propelled me forward.

The only path left to me was a new life in Thailand with Chariya. It was time for a new challenge, a chance to escape the misery that had taken hold of me. Two or three years away to rebuild my career, to find some semblance of peace, and to start anew.

As the days passed, I took Lesley's advice and contacted Elaine, my former divorce lawyer. She was sympathetic and determined, ready to take on my wrongful dismissal case. With her help, I started gathering evidence and building my case, hoping to reclaim some dignity and financial compensation.

CHAPTER 66

ESCAPE PLAN

I wanted to get myself a replacement car as soon as possible. I did not want to use their bloody 'company' car. They can have it back, fuck them. So, the following day, I contacted one of my advertisers, Tony; he owned a second-hand car dealership and car repairs business, which he ran on the land he rented from me, next door to the *Retford Times* office.

The business was dire during the economic crisis in 1993. My main concern was finding ways to reduce overheads and find new alternative sources of income. When I converted the production department to desktop publishing, we had made a few staff redundant.

The *Retford Times* was based in the original old ornate red-brick Victorian building built in the 1820s, and there was also another building annexed, an iron frame structure, about 50 years old. Now, we had fewer staff, and I no longer needed so much space, so I divided the building into two by bricking up the adjoining wall and creating two separate buildings.

The steel frame building, together with our car park, created the perfect town centre space for Tony's motor business. It was an extensive workshop and space to park 50 cars. Tony took the lease, but he had a problem affording the deposit; I pulled a few strings to help him by allocating parking spaces for our staff cars. And so, the deal was done; he set up his Auto Center business there.

I phoned Tony, "Hi mate, you may have heard this news already, but I have parted company with the *Retford Times.* It did not end well. I do not want to go into details, but let us say we fell out big time. Now, I am in a bit of a spot. I must hand back my company car. Do you have a car you could sell me ridiculously cheap? I will need it for a few weeks."

Tony replied, "Yes, I can help you out. Come over to the yard, and I will sort something out for you."

I arrived at Tony's garage, and he walked me over to a white MG Montego. "Will this do you?" I looked at it. It was a clean, smart car.

I said, "How much do you want for this Tony?"

He answered, "You can borrow it for a few weeks, mate, as long as you bring it back in one piece," and laughed.

"Are you sure, Tony? That's very generous of you," I said.

"Roger, you helped me out when I needed something, so please take it. It's the least I can do," he said.

"You're a diamond, mate. I really appreciate this," I said.

That gesture wasn't just relief at a problem solved; the boost I got from having a serious businessman, a friend, and a colleague stepping in to help me so quickly and without hesitation felt really good. The next day, I took the company Mazda 626 back to the *Lincolnshire Echo*; Tony followed me in the MG. I parked the Mazda at the back of the *Echo*'s car park and left the keys in it. Tony drove us both back to Retford. I did not even bother to tell Ted I had returned it already; the London office wants their precious fucking car; well, now they have got it, let them work out where it is. Fuck them, fuck all of these lying, cheating, disloyal bastards, even Ted, what a wimp, he ducked out on me.

On reflection, I realised that this result was perfect for him and the business. I had already done the challenging work of halting the decline and righting the ship; the business was ticking along nicely.

But now, there was no more General Manager's salary to cover in the Retford office. They can sell my company house and recoup the bridging loan they provided when they moved me from the Cornwall office to Nottinghamshire.

The company car lease costs were also saved, and it was convenient; it was a good economic outcome for the company. Ultimately, I am sure that is how he saw it, especially during that harsh economic recession. I was still learning about the cut-throat world of business.

I spoke to my sister again, and I told her, "I have decided I will not go to the courts; fighting them is a waste of time and money; it will make it all public, and just the suggestion people assume you are guilty, the questions, the doubts and gossip. I do not need it."

I told her my decision to move to Thailand with Chariya and how I might give it two or three years there to see how it goes.

"Suppose I can find a new challenge and put some space between NNG and my ex-wife, Caroline. I don't want to hang around in this country at all, it won't be long, and we will be out of this shit hole and getting on with our new life."

I told my sister that leaving the kids was the most challenging part. But I would be back for a couple of weeks at Christmas. I would have them, and we would all be able to stay at my mum's house in Maidenhead, then I would fly them out for holidays to Thailand. I could come back again at Easter. I thought it would be great to have two solid weeks at a time with them, us being all together under my mum's roof, much better than how I had been snatching them every other weekend for a Saturday and Sunday morning.

"Yes," I thought, "accept what had happened, adapt to the new status, and act on a new plan by finding a new job in Thailand. It's simple, really."

Off to Birmingham

During my travels in Thailand, I met several English guys who worked as English teachers. They did not earn much money, but it seemed like a reasonable job; most were incredibly happy doing it. I had seen an advert in the newspaper, "Linguarama: Teaching English Abroad" it was a TESOL course teaching English to speakers of other languages. It was just a five-day full-time course in Birmingham; it was not too expensive and would give me an elementary certificate, allowing me to tutor children up to 14.

I applied, paid the fee, and started the course about a week later. I did not know Birmingham very well; I had been there several times for conferences and stayed in hotels. I had a friend, another customer, who had moved to Birmingham, and he used to live in Lincoln. He worked for a tractor dealership. I knew him when I was running the

Farming Echo. I called him. I told him what had happened and explained that I was leaving, going to Thailand to live, and needed to do this English course first. "Craig, any chance I could crash at yours for five nights?"

He said, "Yes, sure, no problem, mate. We have a spare room. You're welcome to use it. It will be nice to see you again."

I replied, "Thanks, Craig. This is a great help. I hope you've got time for some beers while I'm in town. It would be my pleasure to take you and your girlfriend out for dinner."

"Sounds good; I'm looking forward to it," he said.

The course was in Birmingham city centre. It was in a problematic location, pedestrianised, which meant quite a long walk for me. When I got there, I had to deal with a flight of stairs. Fortunately, I had my blue disabled parking badge so that I could park in the street not too far away on double yellow lines.

The course was challenging, considering I had missed my English 'O'-Level due to my stay in the hospital. The course leader was understanding and let me join anyway. If I failed the course, they still had their money.

It was an eclectic group of students, about 10 of us. A few were backpackers about to travel the world. A couple of the students were already teachers, but wanted to teach abroad, so this course was a valuable addition to any teacher's CV for working overseas.

One much older lady was the wife of a gentleman who held a senior position at the Inland Revenue. He had just landed a job in Bangkok, working for a business consultancy contracted to help the Thai government introduce a new computerised PAYE income tax system there. His wife was expecting to be in Thailand for at least three years; she realised she may get bored with her husband at work and her being at home alone in a foreign country, and so wisely, I thought, she wanted to get a job of her own there as a teacher.

I passed the TESOL exam and got my certification. I added that to my CV, and it was a comfort knowing that I had this qualification as a backup. If everything goes according to plan, I will get a decent job with one of the newspaper publishers, but if that does not happen for any reason, I can fall back on this English teacher idea.

CHAPTER 67

THE PHONE CALL

It was uncanny. The Saturday after I got home from the course, it was about 2:30pm. I was standing in my kitchen, Chariya was in the garden playing football with my kids, when the wall phone rang. I answered it and said, "Hello?"

A Thai voice came back at me, "Hello, is that Khun Roger Warner?"

I answered, "Yes, who is this, please?"

"My name is Sonthi," was the reply.

I knew Santi, a Thai limo driver. He worked at the Royal Hotel, near the Grand Palace, where I stayed on my first visit to Thailand in 1990 with my friend Dave Gray. We always hired him and his American car for a couple of weeks at a time.

I wondered why he was calling me, and I cheerfully replied, "Hello, Santi; how are you, my friend? "

I was expecting he would get to the point soon enough, and he was probably going to ask to borrow money for a new engine in his limo or something. Anyway, I thought, let's hear him out. I will soon learn the purpose of his call.

He continued, "Khun Roger, I got your letter and CV. They're excellent, but I was especially impressed with the idea of using the stamps. That was clever. You got my attention, and I want to let you know I have a job for you."

It took me a while to recalibrate. This is not my friend Santi, the Bangkok limo driver; this is Sondhi Limthongkul, the Thai media mogul. He is one of the guys I wrote to, and he is calling me personally. Wow, fantastic. Is this really happening?

Sondhi was a multi-millionaire Thai Chinese well-known for owning one of Thailand's largest publishing companies. He had a daily broadsheet, which was the equivalent of the UK's *Financial Times,* Thailand's biggest tabloid newspaper, the most prominent women's magazine, an English-language business magazine, and many more.

He continued, "I think you would fit perfectly with my plans. I have many businesses in Thailand and Hong Kong, so many newspapers, magazines, and radio stations, and we are about to launch our first website. I have Thailand's leading business magazine, *Manager,* which is in the English language, and I need a publisher with your experience. So, you should be a powerful addition to my team. You will be able to help us. When can you start?"

I replied, "Yes, that sounds perfect for me. It's really exciting. I have to organise my visas and vacate my home here. Can you give me a month to sort things out? I could be with you by June."

He answered, "OK, June it is. I'll have my SVP of HR contact you with all the details. She will take care of your visa and work permits. You can deal with her on everything. OK, nice to meet you, Roger." And he hung up.

I thought, "Wow, I'm back in the game."

At 37, my life had been a relentless roller coaster, full of dizzying highs and crushing lows. There were moments when the darkness felt overwhelming, and I came dangerously close to giving up. But I always found a way to pull myself back, reminding myself that my glass was still half full. I pushed through the hardships, believing that something exciting was just around the corner.

It was 1994, and I had my sights on the strawberry. My life was not over; it was just beginning. Bring it on, Bangkok. What do you have in store for me?

ACKNOWLEDGEMENTS

Writing this memoir has been an incredible journey, and I am deeply grateful to the many people who supported me along the way.

I want to thank my family for their unwavering love and encouragement. To my parents, Betty and Mick, long since passed, thank you for always believing in me and the values you instilled in me. The constant support of my sister, Lesley has meant the world to me.

Thanks also go to my children, who were victims in the mayhem of my life and, in recent years, to my wife for being my rock during the many hard times. Her belief in me kept me going when I needed it most.

I am also profoundly grateful to my friends, Deborah, Glenn, Dave, Martin and Howard, for their encouragement, feedback, and laughter and for listening to my stories over the years. Your insights and advice helped shape this book into what it is today.

I must express my appreciation to Mike Bridge, my friend and colleague. Thank you for your wisdom and for convincing me to tell my story. Your encouragement has been instrumental in helping me find my voice.

Lastly, I want to express my deepest gratitude to the readers. This book is for you. Thank you for taking the time to share in my journey. I hope you taste your strawberry, too.

With heartfelt appreciation,

Roger Warner